SHIFT H

MW00678274

Marcie,

It was a pleasure
meeting you tonight! Remember
when Shift Happens to
always feel and trust how
Amber Ray Cheal
13179

SHIFT HAPPENS

NIKKI WOODS

Copyright © 2016 Nikki Woods

ISBN-10: 0-9962513-4-0
ISBN-13: 978-0-9962513-4-1

Library of Congress Control Number: 2016915921

TABLE OF CONTENTS

Introduction 9

Preface 11

Fatherless to Freedom 13
    By Siobhan Howard Davenport

Purpose in the Pain 23
    By Precious Brown

Being King Flare 33
    By Ricky Ruff

Breaking Free—By Any Means Necessary 41
    By LaTanya Harris

Breathing With the Rhythm of God 53
    By Bricena "Cookie" Belle

Detours Still Get You There 67
    By Laurie A. Evans

Double Portions 77
    By Tammy Lewis

Dream Chaser 85
    By James 'Jazzy' Jordan

Finding Joy in Infertility 97
   By Mia A. Williams

Wipe Every Tear; Living With Depression 109
   By Ettie Jean Whitfield

With No Regrets 123
   By Keaira English

Forgive and Live; Letting Go Of The Pain 137
   By Christine Roebuck

From Fear to Faith 147
   By Lura Hobbs

God's Guided Moments 159
   By Deedra Jordan-Evans

Going from Good to Great! 167
   By Necole D. Tinsley

I Can Love, Am Lovable, and Loved 179
   By Audra R. Upchurch

Launched Into Destiny 191
   By Ella D. Carrol

Leaving Myself Alone 201
   By Stephanie Payne Williams

Live with Passion and Purpose 213
   Dr. Deborah Starczewski

Pride and Money 229
   By Shayla Boyd-Gill

Not on My Watch 239
   By Traci Henderson Smith

Purpose Fulfilled 253
    By Michelle Dawson

Battered But Not Broken 267
    By Denise Polote-Kelly

Show Up and Lead! 279
    By Natasha Gayden

Single and Satisfied 291
    By Sandra Jolla

Strong and Courageous, Not Afraid and Discouraged 303
    By Russell M. Williamson Sr.

The Courage to be Me 315
    By Leshawnda Larkin

The Long Journey Home—One Baby Boomer's
    Journey to her Entrepreneurial Dreams 327
    By Cheryl J. Ketchens

Tied to our Soul 339
    By Tina Tyus-Shaw

Weathering Life's Storms 349
    By Greta Smith

Why I Touch People 355
    By Tony Bethel

Rising From The Ashes 363
    By Kim Francis

Leap And The Net Will Appear 375
    By Valeta Sutton

Count the Miracles Along The Way 387
    By Nicole Johnson

INTRODUCTION

From Beyonce's nod to wife, power, and feminism with "Lemonade" via her record breaking "visual album" to the play "Hamilton" using rap to become one of the most celebrated Broadway musicals in years, it makes me smile to see so many different story-telling platforms being utilized these days.

Years ago when Bill Clinton was running for President, he and his staff would sometimes get off point and try to include a laundry list of issues to include in his platform. But since it was an era where unemployment was high and the middle class was finding it harder and harder to stretch a dollar, his campaign manager, James Carville, would often have to remind the President and his team not to forget the most important issue of all. Carville got so frustrated one day that he wrote in large letters on a board, "THE ECONOMY, STUPID!" That stuck in staff member's heads and would always bring them back around to the meat and potatoes of Clinton's campaign. Well, pardon my tough language but, "THE STORY, STUPID!"

We all have a story, and what I've learned from the two *Shift* collaborations that preceded this brand new one, no matter how similar the topics are—death, divorce, joblessness, homelessness, rehabilitation, ministry, autism, career changes, depression, low self-esteem, or following your dreams—no two stories are exactly the same.

The Shift Collaborative concept has taught me that the chapters birthed by these contributors was just as much for them as it was for the audiences that will read it. Even for those whose goal it was to only become a published author, they came away with so much more: a better, deeper, clearer understanding of who they were and more importantly, a better sense of what their truth is. We are the keepers of our truths and our truths are ours to share.

Whether you decide to publish your story by writing, singing it, speaking it, or painting it on a canvas, find a way to express it in your own way. Your joy, your pain, your trials and triumphs are life and light, energy and power. Release them!

The 33 *Shift* authors will inspire, encourage, and empower you on your journey toward moving on, moving through, moving out, or moving up. This is a "No Stagnation Zone."

I hope you enjoy it.

PREFACE

Just about the time I realized that helping people write and pub-
lish their stories was my true calling, my uncle asked me to help
him and my dad write a book. It would be about how being raised
by their father taught them to become strong men. They would
each write down their own memories about my grandfather and
I would put it all together when they were finished. I had heard
many of the stories they re-counted but there was a lot I didn't
know and reading about their lives from both perspectives was fas-
cinating. And even some of the similarities between their lives and
mine were striking.

My dad, Kennard, and Uncle Harold were raised by a hard-
working father who got up before dawn to go to his job. The two
boys would wake up, get dressed, get their own breakfast, and go to
school each morning. My sons were raised in a similar environment
and had to get themselves ready for school without me being there,
too. That's because I also have an early morning gig producing a
nationally syndicated morning radio show. Where I once felt guilty
about them starting their mornings in such a non-traditional fash-
ion, hearing about my daddy and Uncle Harold was validation that
strong, independent boys grow up to be strong, independent men.

In this edition of *Shift*, I'm also blessed to include chapters
written by my mom and my oldest nephew, Ricky. I've loved writ-
ing all my life but would never have expected for it to be the tie
that binds so many of my family members. Both my mom and

nephew's stories caused me to shed tears of sadness and joy. I know what it is like to dig deep and write about something personal. It is not easy, but it is freeing, and I'm so happy they trusted this process and me enough to participate. As they and the other *Shift* authors learned, there is power in telling their own story.

This year Bobby Brown wrote a tell-all book, "Every Little Step" that includes many unflattering stories about his late ex-wife, Whitney Houston, and their daughter, Bobbi Kristina, who both died tragically. Whitney's mother, Cissy Houston, wrote the following words regarding Bobby Brown's book and an interview he'd done with Good Morning America's Robin Roberts:

> *"Although the interview was supposed to promote HIS autobiography, he never spoke about his parents and siblings and any issues they might have or have had that impacted and may continue to impact on 'Every Little Step' he takes. Instead he chose to concentrate his comments primarily on Whitney. I can't help but wonder why. Whether I would have chosen Bobby for my daughter's husband is not important because the choice was not mine to make. She loved him and I believe him when he says he loved her. I only wish he had loved and respected her enough to make some of the negative statements about her and Krissi while Whitney was alive and able to respond from her perspective."*

If we don't tell our own stories we leave it up to other people to tell them for us. We give them our power to have the last word. I wish Whitney Houston had written an autobiography that addressed the questions we may have in her own words.

If you're ready to write your story, *Shift* is a collaborative platform that is available to people just like you.

What will people say about you when you are gone?

Take control of your legacy with what's true about you in your own words.

FATHERLESS TO FREEDOM

BY SIOBHAN HOWARD DAVENPORT

"It's one of the greatest gifts you can give yourself, to forgive. Forgive everybody."

–Maya Angelou

My thirteen-year silent grudge against my absentee father ended in April 2014, when I learned of his death. It's hard to fight with a ghost and frankly, I no longer had the energy to mount another battle against him. For 43 years I carried anger, resentment, and hurt for all he missed in my childhood. When he died, I felt abandoned all over again for what we couldn't have and what I most craved—a loving father/daughter relationship.

When you lose a cherished relative or friend, people will reassure you that memories will provide comfort. However, no one prepared me to positively deal with the bad memories or even the nonexistent ones. I don't have one single good memory to cling to on those days when I profoundly miss my father or have dreams of him.

Mama, who is my paternal grandmother, brought me home from the hospital to raise as her child. She effectively replaced my birth mother, who was more like an auntie to me. Mama and my parents agreed that two uneducated and unmarried teens couldn't raise a child. For the first six years of my life, we lived in Washington,

DC, with my parents drifting in and out of my life. I was 10 years old when I lost my birth mother in a tragic car accident. I cherish the few memories I have of her. I still loved her with the innocence of a child, who freely gives her love to those in her life. My birth mother is frozen in time as a 26-year old, who I believe loved me but just couldn't provide a good life for me. In contrast, my memories of my father are marred with the judgment that he had every opportunity to "parent" me and refused. During my formative years, the memories of my father are quite unclear because he appears as a shadow, hovering in the background, always elusive from my reach. I knew he was important to me but I didn't understand his role in my life.

At the end of kindergarten my great aunt relocated us to North Carolina because my grandmother had become ill. I didn't know it until years later but she almost died from an addiction to prescription narcotics. Mama was taken to our family home in Lumberton and took a year to fully recover. I was sent to Charlotte to live with my adult cousin, her husband, and their three children, who were around my age. Mama and I didn't have any physical contact during this time nor did we speak often, especially in the beginning. I deeply missed her and the bond we shared.

However, my cousin and her family helped me to acclimate to my new life as an honorary member of their traditional family. For the first time, I knew what it was like to experience the love of both a mother and a father, as well as having "two sisters and a brother." It was the simple things, like having a family meal with a father at the head of the table that meant so much to me. I cherished my time with them but I knew it was temporary. Although I was eager to reunite with Mama, I knew I would miss them deeply.

When I finished first grade, I happily reunited with my beloved grandmother, who promised God that if He delivered her from the brink of death she would re-dedicate her life to Him. We attended her childhood Catholic Church and became immersed in the church community. I went to Sunday School, participated in youth activities, and became an altar server, assisting the priest during mass. I clung to my faith and my church as the one place where I felt I belonged. It was hard to be a part of a family that didn't look like everyone else's. Although my church family embraced me as part of the tribe, I missed the year spent with my cousin's family. I longingly wished for a father to share tales from my day, applaud my dance performances, soothe my nightmares, and simply have as a source of love in my life.

My own father fell short at every comparison to the fathers I observed. Every time I looked forward to us spending time together, he managed to ruin it. My earliest memory of visiting my father was when I was nine-years old and Mama allowed me to take a plane trip alone from North Carolina to Washington, DC to visit him. As a non-flyer she was nervous for me, but I begged for the opportunity to spend time with my father. He was supposed to meet me at the gate but instead, he showed up hours later, never acknowledging my fear, nor apologizing, leaving me to wait in the back offices of the airport.

"You will not be punished for your anger, you will be punished by your anger."

–Buddha

Through her acts of kindness toward her family and community, my grandmother taught me the value of service. Although we lived off her meager disability pension, she used her own money to cook meals for the sick and drive the elderly to their doctor appointments. In addition to our strong spiritual life, my grandmother emphasized the importance of obtaining a good education. She instilled in me a belief that with hard work I could achieve any goal I set. Because of my insecurity, I became a people pleaser. My goal was to make Mama proud of me so I dedicated myself to being a good student.

School was the one area where I felt secure and didn't compare myself to others. For high school, I received a full academic scholarship to attend a prestigious all girls boarding school. The first and only time I saw my grandmother cry was the day I left for Virginia to embark on my educational journey. I knew then that although she may not have said it, Mama loved me.

While I was nearly 350 miles away in boarding school, my father's girlfriend threw him out of their apartment in Washington, DC and he promptly moved in with Mama. It felt as though she had replaced me. On my weekly collect calls home, Mama shared her frustration with his lack of motivation in finding and keeping a job, his refusal to help with household chores, and his disappearances with questionable friends for days at a time. I shared her anger and frustration, which was partly for her but mostly for me. By this time, my love and longing for him had slowly been replaced by deeply held anger and resentment.

I inhabited two worlds: my school, which had privileged young ladies from two parent households and my father's world of those who live on the fringe of society. I never felt completely comfortable in either world, especially since his world made me feel shame and embarrassment. His friends were people, like him, who remained perpetually trapped in adolescence, never taking responsibility for themselves nor those around them.

I learned to never talk about my father so no one would ask me simple questions, such as, "What does your father do?" I was friendly but guarded, which left me without fully experiencing the closeness of true friendship. Unknowingly, I continued to be guarded with everyone throughout adulthood. I often wondered how I could know so many people but have few to call if I really needed to be my true self. Simply, it was lonely on my island of one but I didn't know how to get off.

This guardedness also applied to men. I was leery of relationships and often remained single to the chagrin of those who knew me. They couldn't understand how I could have a good personality and be attractive, but yet be alone. I tried to read books about other fatherless daughters but they were a confession on all the statistics that most of us suffer—promiscuity, teen pregnancy, high school dropout, and drug or alcohol abuse. I was none of those so I couldn't find solace in other's tales.

I continued to seethe in anger, resenting my father's intrusion in my life, which had disrupted my once happy home with my grandmother. On my weekly Sunday calls from boarding school and college, my grandmother would update me on his latest transgression. My father quit another job and had to borrow money, he yelled at her or he simply disappeared with his friends for days at a time, leaving her to worry about his well-being. Since I was hundreds of miles away, I felt helpless that I couldn't protect the person I loved most in the world.

When I came home on the holidays or over summer vacation, I observed his sins and wanted to confront him. However, my grandmother would ask me not to say anything and let her handle him. This forced silence caused my anger to grow and contaminate my being. The day I finally exploded, which was the only way I could describe it, my father yelled at my grandmother when she asked him to run an errand for her. It was a small occurrence but it was my tipping point. I released 21 years of pent-up rage and frustration. As I called him every vile and ugly name I could think of, the rational part of my brain saw his look of utter shock and hurt. Although he remained silent, I think he saw for the first time the effects of his neglect. I felt powerful that I could hurt him as much as his absence had hurt me. Only Mama was able to quiet and calm me. I never apologized to him because I felt justified in my verbal attack. From that moment onward, our rare interactions were filled with caution from both of us but I arrogantly added a dose of thinly disguised contempt.

We continued this way until I called my father to inform him that Mama was dying. By this time, I was married. My husband and I had moved her from North Carolina to live in a facility for Alzheimer's patients near our home in Maryland. She lived there happily for nearly two years before becoming ill. After I explained Mama's dire circumstances, my father wanted to know if I was planning to sell her house so he could have his share of the proceeds. I hung up on him, justified that I could finally erase him from my life. I couldn't believe that even my father could be this heartless. Mama picked up the pieces that his self-centered lifestyle broke and discarded, including me. Now, when she needed him the most, he put his wants and needs first. I decided that he was dead to me. I was now free to live my life as the true orphan that I felt. Thus began my 13-year journey of silence and attempts to erase my father out of my life.

"Courageous people do not fear forgiving, for the sake of peace."
–Nelson Mandela

My reaction to my father's death was shocking to me. I always assumed I wouldn't have a reaction to it but calmly accept his death as the natural course of life. However, I deeply mourned him and how he passed. His friend told me that he was gravely ill with many health issues but it was kidney cancer that ultimately sped up his demise. While he refused treatment, he also asked his friend not to contact me. My father didn't want to be a burden to me and he was remorseful that he never was a father to me. I was saddened that he'd rather die alone than be rejected by me in his time of need. In my heart, I knew I would have been by his side. I not only mourned him but I mourned the end of creating a new possibility for us. We may not be able to have a strong father/daughter relationship but perhaps we could have something else that only we could define. However, his death ended all possibilities of that. What my father's death did was release me from my anger so I could begin a journey of forgiveness for him and honestly, for me. I desperately wanted a shift from anger to peace.

At the time of my father's death, I had a nine-year-old daughter and seven-year-old son. They had many questions about their absentee grandfather, which forced me to talk about him in ways I couldn't and wouldn't with others. I explained that he loved me but he was too young to take care of me, like their father and I take care of them. I partly believed this but still resented him and his life choices.

While I thought I forgave him, I made certain that his friends weren't invited to his grave side service in our family burial plot in

North Carolina. I reasoned that they were a bad influence and that I didn't want them near my children. So on an unusually cool day in June, my husband, children, my father's older brother, cousin, and I paid homage and buried him. I truly believed that in spite of my father's absence from my life, I was the dutiful daughter who took the high road and gave him a respectful burial. However, I didn't realize that I held on to my resentments and gave him a funeral devoid of friends because I believed that's all he deserved.

"To forgive is to set a prisoner free and discover the prisoner was you."

–Lewis B. Smedes

Like the Israelites, who wandered the wilderness for 40 years before entering the promised land of Canaan, I carried the weight of my absentee father's sins. I wandered, carrying in guilt, shame, and anger throughout my life. I lived in fear of being found out and judged by his actions. As a result, I never talked about him even to my closest friends so I could avoid the pain of sharing all he was and wasn't to me.

I smugly believed that I had taken the high road and forgiven him upon his death. However, it wasn't until I took a self-improvement course nearly two years after his death that I had to confront the hole in my heart that his absence inflicted. I was in the process of writing my memoir but reached a writer's block that I couldn't overcome. I thought the class could be instrumental in helping me resume my work. The instructor asked, "Who annoys you the most?" I thought that I didn't have anyone in my life who fit that description until a clear voice said to me, "Your father." As I chuckled, I thought no way, I've forgiven him. I even gave him a beautiful and respectful funeral and buried him next to my dear Mama. However, the more I thought about it, the more I realized that the voice was right. I hadn't truly forgiven him. I was still holding onto my "righteous anger" and it was preventing me from telling the story of my father and me. This was a story that I hoped to write in order to free someone from their prison of self-inflicted pain. But I couldn't help or free them when I was ensconced in my own prison.

"Righteous anger is still anger, pray to remove it from your heart."

–Siobhan Howard Davenport

In order to be at peace with my father, with all he was and all he wasn't, I had to admit that his absence hurt me deeply. Although I pretended otherwise, he influenced my every move, which led to fear of growing close with others. Because he chose to live on the fringe of society, I chose to walk on the "perfect" path of society. I was so fearful of messing up that I sometimes stayed frozen in place, unsure of what to do and where to go.

Out of college, I chose a safe career path of working in financial services when my heart clearly wasn't in helping wealthy people become wealthier. I stayed away from people who challenged me for fear that my lifelong belief of not being good enough would prove true. Although I made some bold moves in my life, I immediately followed them with the "safe and perfect" choice. I wasn't growing because it required too much risk of exposing myself.

I immediately turned to prayer to ask God for His mercy and guidance upon my life. I was tired of holding anger in my heart, while professing my virtues as my father's daughter. I also had to acknowledge that although my father's absence wasn't fair, I had many things to be thankful for him.

I was grateful that my father gave me life. I was grateful that my father entrusted me into his mother's care, knowing that she could and would provide a better life for me. And lastly, I was grateful to my father for giving me my purpose. I know that I want to share my story to help others reconcile with their estranged father. And if reconciliation isn't possible, then I want them to make peace within themselves over the hurt they endured because of the absence. Like me, who can't reunite with my father, I want to help others finally have freedom for a lifetime of shame, guilt, and anger over the absence of their father from their lives.

"It always seems impossible until it's done."

–Nelson Mandela

I marvel on how I could shift from a woman living in pain and fear, to a woman who is free to share her story with the world. This healing process wasn't easy but it is possible. I know my father loved me the only way he knew how to love me. Most importantly, I've decided that is enough.

During my shift, I learned the following:

- Be authentic and admit the pain that your father's absence caused. Be specific.
- Pray, pray, and pray. Ask God for guidance on how to show mercy to yourself and to your father.
- If possible, talk to your father. If not, then write a letter outlining the ways in which you needed him. But also include the ways in which you're grateful for him.
- Forgive yourself then forgive him. Free yourself.

To shift is never easy. It requires steadfast and diligent work that took me many years to overcome. But it's worth it. I'm no longer the angry and scared child who needs the approval from others that I never received from my father. I'm now a confident woman, who desires to help others by sharing my story. My hope is that my shift will help others to break the chain of pain and shift from fatherless to freedom.

PURPOSE IN THE PAIN

BY PRECIOUS BROWN

"In any situation you can choose to be bitter or better."
—Anonymous

Can you imagine going through life feeling less than a human being? You have the gnawing feeling in the pit of your belly that God created you to be something great but you do not feel worthy of it? Being ashamed of who you are, feeling rejected by every relationship, and no matter how hard you try, it seems to never be enough for anyone in your life. For the majority of my life, this is how I felt. I went from relationship to relationship trying to be enough of a woman to receive the love I desperately desired, just wanting someone to love me for who I am and not for what I could give them. It wasn't until I hit rock bottom that I finally got the revelation that I have always been enough for God!

At 19, I became a mother, stepmother, and then a wife. I had never addressed the emotional, physical, and sexual abuse issues of my childhood. I carried all my baggage into the marriage and so did my spouse. We were two broken kids now married with children and we struggled financially, emotionally, and spiritually. Regardless of what happened, I would not leave. The marriage was filled with many forms of abuse—alcohol, drugs, verbal, and emotional. But it was never physical until the final day.

It was the summer of 1992. I had been at our local teen hang-out as usual and as I was leaving, I heard, "Excuse me, can I go with you?" I turned around, smiled, and gave a side-eye glance before reluctantly responding, "Probably not!" He laughed and so did I. Little did I know we were going to the same destination, The Hammer Droppers, an after-hours club. There, he found me and struck up a conversation before we exchanged numbers. After that night, we talked on the phone for hours at a time. Almost instantly, our relationship became sexual in nature. He was hand-some, attentive, charming, and was in the street life—deep. My type of guy. All I could think of was, out of all the women he could have chosen, he chose me. I felt extremely special for the first time in my life. We dated off and on for two years prior to moving in together and creating a family with dynamics neither of us understood. Creating and continuing generational cycles of abuse, brokenness, and poverty.

Finally, I had the one thing I always wanted: someone to love me for me. He loved me, flaws and all. We shared all the secrets of our lives with each other, vowing to be together forever. I was his queen and he was my king. After five years and two more children, we decided it was time to become official; we got married. I was in fairytale heaven, refusing to believe my life was really a mess. Then it happened and I was devastated. One year after saying, "I do, forever," I realized he had been cheating. I had heard it for years but I just didn't see it or want to believe it. *He wouldn't do that to me*, I thought. We had grown together and no one could break our bond, or so I thought. But, oh to my surprise, I was about to get a rude awakening.

In December 2003, I was certain I wanted to know for myself if he was and had been cheating. I told myself on January 1, 2004 I would start my own investigation, so I purchased a purse calendar and started the tracking. Every move that he made I wrote in the calendar, whether good or bad days, I wrote them down. I wanted and needed to know. I had to track his every move. It was up to me to find out what was going on and if I had been a fool all this time.

Not only did I track his pattern, I started to research the phone bills. I knew something was going on but I just couldn't put my finger on it.

After eight months, I had the evidence that I needed. I had obtained the other woman's phone number from our phone bills. One day after work I decided to confront him, asking if he had his cell phone.

"Mine is dead," I said. "I need to use your phone really quick." He pulled out his phone and waited. "Dial this number." As I gave him the number, he stopped dialing midstream. He couldn't believe that I had the phone number. "Why did you stop? Dial the number," I told him.

He asked, "Why do you want me to call this number?"

I responded, "Why not? You call it all times of the day while you're at work. You call her more than you talk to me during the day." As we sat there, I contemplated what should happen next. He looked nervous, so I finally responded, "You know what? It doesn't even matter anymore." At that very moment I decided it was over.

From that hot day in August 2004 until May 2005 I was in a total depression. I'm not even sure how my children were cared for, got to school, or even ate. I checked out of life because I just could not believe that this had happened. During the depression, I had often thought of killing everyone in the home. I had even planned it so I knew exactly how I would do it. I would use our double barrel 12-gauge shotgun, killing the kids first, and then him, and finally myself. One day, life had become too much to bare. I sat in the car and cried and cried. I could not stop crying; it was uncontrollable. My friend stopped by my house and she saw me sitting in the car so she got in and asked me what was wrong. I wouldn't tell her. I continued to cry and she just sat there with me. After a while she began to pray. Then she started singing. She has a beautiful voice. We sat in the car for hours with me crying and her alternating between praying and singing. Finally, I started to open up and tell her my thoughts of killing everyone in our home so that my pain would stop. I rationalized that by killing the children, no one would have to worry about taking care of them. She began to tell me how God would not want that and it's the trick of the enemy because I had a calling on my life. I began to cry again and I remember saying, "I just can't take this anymore. I'm tired." She began to pray again. This time I felt different. I dried the tears on my face as she continued to give me scripture references and telling me how God had something for me to do. Although I couldn't see it, she knew it was there. I shared with her how I caught him cheating and she assured me that God would see me through. At that time, I was a believer but I wasn't saved nor was I trying to serve God.

By the grace of God and because of His obedient angel, I decided to give our lives one more chance. I began attending church with my friend and on October 5, 2005, I was saved. I started living my life for Christ but the call for drugs and alcohol was overwhelming and I backslid. I stayed with my ex-husband for three more years.

On August 8, 2008, I'd had enough. He had stayed out all night, again. I barricaded the doors so when he came home he could not get in. As the day went on, my sister convinced me to go with her to the State Fair. I had to get dressed so she took the children (mine and hers) to McDonald's, so I thought. As I was getting dressed, I heard someone come in the house. I thought it was my sister, but he kicked in our bedroom door and I could see death in this eyes. He started choking me, pinning me against the wall. I could feel myself getting light-headed, so I scanned the room for a weapon and noticed a steel bat behind the bedroom door. I had to get to it or I was going to die. I began to fight for my life. I got him off me and ran towards the door, grabbing the bat as I darted up the steps to get away. This was the first time he ever put his hands on me. I was in shock. For some reason, I didn't run out of the house. All I could think was, *I'm not going out without a fight.* He ran after me and when he got to the top of the steps, I hit him with the bat. By now, my sister had run into the house and saw me at the top of the stairs. She instantly grabbed a weapon.

After he realized I was going to fight, he went back downstairs and got his gun. The back door was still barricaded and I had to pass him to get out the front. As he came up the steps, he dropped the bullets to the gun. My heart was racing and my sister was screaming. It was like he didn't even see her. His jet black eyes were fixed on me. When he got to the last step I knew I was about to die. I grabbed his hand with the gun in it and we began to tussle. I could hear my sister yelling at the 911 dispatcher, "My brother-in-law is trying to kill my sister; he's going to shoot her, please help." Somehow, he twisted my hand with his and put the loaded gun to my chest before pulling the trigger. The gun jammed, and I remember thinking, *My kids can't find me like this*. That's when I felt the supernatural strength. I overpowered him, pouncing on top of him like a lion, with one knee in his throat and the other on his arm with the hand that held the gun. I screamed, "What is wrong with you? Why are you doing this?" It was like a light clicked on in his head. He jumped up, tossing me across the room, and ran out the front door. By the grace of God, I'm still here.

That very day, I left and never looked back. Once again, after seven years I was in a space I did not want to be. Alone and loveless. I didn't know what to do. This was the first time we had been apart since we were 19. I knew that I couldn't go back. And I needed to keep me and my children safe. But all of me longed to go back to my comfortable space. For the first time ever, I knew that I had a calling on my life but I didn't know how to get out of the mess I had created. I began to seek God regularly. By this time, I was off drugs completely but I was still drinking. I would go to work, come home, drink, and talk to God. For three years, He pruned me, taking me through all of my hurt and pain. He began to show me that the only way out was through Him. I began to lean on the Lord more than I had ever done before and my evolution was underway.

Although I was saved in 2005 I was not fully committed to God until January 1, 2012. In the midst of my contentment, something I never thought would happen again actually happened; I fell in love. This time I thought it was different. I believed he was Heaven sent and my second marriage would last forever. We dated for a few years prior to planning the wedding. He was everything I had asked for—loving, *honest*, romantic, independent, and he loved my children (who didn't meet him for the first two years), as well as treating me like a queen. We went to church together, prayed together, planned our every move together; we were best friends. We got married and it was supposed to be happily ever after. Almost instantly after exchanging vows, rings, and saying, "I Do," he changed. We didn't do anything together anymore. I was totally blindsided, having no idea it had all been an act. There was no more pampering, no more cooking, no more loving the Lord, nor sharing responsibilities. Everything stopped. I began to see that I married Dr. Jekyll and Mr. Hyde. A few months into the marriage, I discovered he divorced his ex-wife six months prior to us being married. Hindsight is 20/20, yet I am sure there were signs I missed or ignored but I just can't recall them because I was so happy.

During my prayer time, I said, "Lord, how could this happen again? I just knew that You sent him! I wanted this to last forever!" But God was silent. Because I didn't want to seem like a failure, I tried to stick it out. Once again I was crushed on the inside. I didn't understand it then but it is in the crushing that the anointing flows. It was during this time God gave me three interactive workbooks titled, *The Process of Change*. I did not know at the time that this was my second chance to a new beginning.

The books were only the start of everything. I had finally gotten the stories out of my system; I was free and able to begin to live. I could see clearly and was able to move forward. As I continued to struggle through the second failing marriage, I founded Power-N-You™, a personal development coaching enterprise. I poured myself into the business all day and night, learning all I could. I did everything possible to keep from coming to the realization that I was facing another divorce.

On November 16, 2014, I decided to call it quits. We had just had a heated discussion and he punched a hole into the door. Immediately, I recognized the signs. The violence. The flashback.

It was OVER! It had only been a short eight months that we were married before we went through the divorce and I just didn't understand. During my prayer time one day, I asked God, "Lord, did I hear you wrong? Did You tell me not to do this? Was I only supposed to be learning a lesson and I got confused? If so, please forgive me and let's move on." I accepted my truth. I hadn't waited on God nor did I seek Him before moving forward with the marriage. The glitter was there but there was no gold. Although I was crushed, I didn't fall into a depression and I knew God was still there. I was so excited. I passed my test! I learned two valuable lessons. Although I made a mistake, I didn't lose contact with God and I learned I could love again.

Through it all, I continued to go to church and worship God. But there became a pull that I just couldn't explain. So I began to pray and ask God, "What is it that I'm supposed to be doing?" and, "Why do I feel this way?" And He began to unfold the best parts of my new life right in front of my eyes. I shared a piece of my testimony at church one day and after service I was asked to speak at an event.

I was so nervous at my first speaking engagement that my knees were shaking, my voice was cracking, and I just could not believe that God had called such a mess to share with so many people. The room was packed and women were staring at me just to hear what I had to say. As I began to speak, I kept thinking, *Why me?* I was asking God, "How am I supposed to do this? They're going to think I'm crazy!" I started to tell my story and people began crying, people were praising God, and others were shouting. God showed me that day how my pain was turned into my purpose. It was all happening right in front of me. After I spoke, people were coming up to me saying, "I didn't know that you went through all that! You don't look like what you've been through," and, "Thank you for sharing your testimony because it helped me." I praised God like never before.

I had no idea that my life would never be the same. It was one engagement after another continually for months. God began to put people in my life that knew the speaking and coaching business. I was speaking more, had written the books, and now I was able to begin firmly establishing the coaching enterprise. Although I had been helping women through difficult relationship issues ever since my divorce, I had no idea coaching was something I could get paid to do. Almost immediately, I gained several clients and sold a couple hundred workbooks. I couldn't believe it. I was finally feeling fulfilled. I was being used by God and knew without a doubt He loved me, no matter what. I was finally on track. And I believed God was pleased.

Out of all the adversity I have overcome in my life, I would have never believed God would use me the way that He has. I am clear on what my purpose is and I walk confidently in my God given power. I am determined to help as many women (and men when the time calls for it) as God sees fit. With the programs that He has given me, I will be able to assist women with shifting their mindsets so that they too can accept their purpose and walk in their God given power!

This story is only a piece of the tip of my iceberg. Going through these situations allowed me to learn several things about God, myself, and others. I pray my lessons help you in this journey of life. It is important that you:

> Be honest with yourself, own your decisions, and do not easily dismiss the warning signs in relationships.
>
> Know that nothing you have been through will be wasted. It will all be used for the Glory of God. So I encourage you to stay the course.
>
> Seek God in all you do, stay focused on God no matter what it looks or feels like, and stay sober minded in the spirit and natural realms.

Going through the situations in my previous marriages demanded I grow emotionally, mentally, and spiritually. I would not have conceived this journey in my worst dream. But, without it, I would not be able to help those I am called to help. I thank God for every trial, tribulation, and setback because it not only showed me the POWER within but it also taught me I can truly trust God in all things and the POWER of His might. So, do not despise the pain you go through—there is **Purpose in your Pain.**

BEING KING FLARE

BY RICKY RUFF

"Poetry is the rhythmical creation of beauty in words."
                                                    –Edgar Allan Poe

I didn't start writing seriously and actually putting my work out until about 2013. I used to want to be a rapper with influences from such artists as Common, Chance The Rapper, NoName Gypsy, and Angel Haze. Aside from Common and maybe Chance The Rapper, I'm sure most people won't recognize the other artist I mentioned. That is because those artists are underground artists. My writing is heavily influenced by the rawness, absolute power, and the truth of underground hip hop. So when I started writing, a lot of my work had that sort of rhythm; that hip hop type feel to it. I started putting my work on Instagram first, allowing followers to provide feedback. The response was amazing. I had no idea so many people would enjoy my words. After that, I began to put a new piece out every week. My following grew as people started telling their followers about me; they in turn followed me, too. This kept up until February 10, 2014 when I left for the Army.

The whole plan for kids from the time they start pre-school is to graduate high school, go to college, and get a good job. Once you get to high school you're exposed to the military as an option if you don't go to college. There was not much exposure to any other field to explore outside of these traditional things. I didn't like school and thought going to the Army was a good thing, so I enlisted. While there, I fell into a depression of sorts. I'm sure not being able to write played a part in being depressed. I was mentally blocked and really couldn't sit down long enough to pen anything good so I gave up writing after a while. Before joining the military, writing was a release for me—a way to express any pent up emotions. I no longer had an outlet to express how I felt and it stopped me in my tracks. I wrote a few poems during my short time of enlistment, but nothing I feel was notable. During my depression period I developed some habits that got me in a lot of trouble and eventually got me put out of the Army with a General under Honorable Discharge. I regret the decisions I made but I am at peace with the idea that the Military was never for me.

Upon my arrival home from the military, I lied to friends and family telling them I sustained an injury as the reason I was discharged. The lie was filled with holes and I'm positive nobody believed me but it was left alone for a little while. I was still depressed and isolated myself from most of the people I would usually enjoy being around. When I went out, I put on a fake smile to entertain those around. Nobody really knew how I felt and I never told anyone. I struggled to find a place where I fit; a place where it was natural for me to express myself the way I wanted. I am the oldest of five kids with divorced parents and one of my biggest struggles was trying to distinguish myself from my siblings and gain acceptance from both parents. I wanted them to be proud of me and it seemed like I always fell short by a few miles.

Having a brother and a sister who are younger than me but doing better in life than me dealt heavy blows to my pride constantly. I tried being a video producer and literally walked around with a camera for half a year. I tried rapping, but wasn't very good at it. Rapping actually led to me writing more; I was a decent writer and once tried to write a book but was sidetracked. As I stumbled my way through, I discovered poetry, and it provided the outlet I needed to express my voice and unique perspective.

At the time I was dating a young woman; that was one of the happiest relationships I was ever in honestly. She had a close relationship with God, abstained from sex, and had a beautiful singing voice. When people looked at our relationship it was quite similar and oftentimes compared to *Beauty and the Beast*. I assume the label was earned from my old reputation, compared to how they viewed her. I was known for doing a lot of thing she probably would never have had any part of. Physically, she is a very beautiful woman; I looked beastly. She was a pure woman, and it was her that inspired me to start writing again. I was so in love with her talent and gifts it drove me to match her with my own. Even though we were in a relationship, I still kept to myself which naturally caused it to end—another deep regret of mine. But by the time our relationship was terminated, I was writing more, started telling stories through my poetry on trending and relatable topics such as Love, Sex, Hate, Racism, and Suicide. I found that I was able to write on topics I myself have never been through, with many pieces from a woman's point of view. My versatility is what caught people's attention.

I started going to college but like the military I felt college wasn't for me. It felt like my time was wasted in a classroom that was teaching nothing important. After a while I stopped going to class but still went to the school to use the Computer lab and the Veterans lounge. While there I wrote, edited, and published a book of poetry through Amazon titled *Mid-Mind Crisis*. I sold the book for $10 per copy and it did a lot better than expected for an unknown author. I was very proud of this achievement. After I wrote my book, I was approached by a young woman who was the president of our school's Black Student Union (BSU). She informed me how they had a meeting pertaining to the Black History Month showcase coming up in the next two months. She told me they wanted me to open the show by performing a Black History piece. At first I was reluctant to accept. I had never in my life performed before. After a week or so of mulling it over, I accepted and got to work on what would be my first ever live performance.

I practiced daily—at work, home, even while out with peers. I was excited. When the day arrived, I was nervous like I had never been before. The show started and they announced my name. When I walked on stage, I could feel every set of eyes and ears on me waiting to hear what I had to say. I had a young lady come on stage and sing a song with me to go with my piece. She started singing through her microphone. "One day, when the glory comes, it'll be ours, it'll be ours," a song by John Legend. I sat on a bench in the middle of the stage pretending to read a book as she sang, just as we rehearsed. When my cue came up I closed the book, shook my head in mock disgust, and stood up to look at the crowd. I had no mic, I didn't want one. Her song ended and I had a three second pause before I started to deliver. No backing out now. "Please!" I bellowed over the audience, "Make no mistake when I state facts about our current state and how we need to change!" I was in it. My movements suggested nervousness but my voice was clear and my message was strong. "Our textbooks cover the greats it sees as gr.... No, wait. Our textbooks cover the greats it wants us to see as greats!"

I felt powerful on stage sharing my ideology and points of view with an audience who seemed to love what I had to say. My movements became less nervous and more confident. I paced the stage as if I owned it; in my mind I did. "But next chance you get, look up some of my favorites like Chicago native Diane Nash, a Freedom Rider, or the escaped slave Frederick Douglass who broke chains to become a Freedom Writer, travel back to the 1950's and raise your voices with the Freedom Fighters...."

I was phenomenal. I had never felt like this before, ever. I was nearing the end of my piece and I had the audience by the ears. "They want to rest easy in their graves knowing they left their legacies in capable hands. Our capable hands as African American's best. Until.... The next generation has a chance to show us why they are African American's best."

I went back to my seat and sat down as the woman started to sing again but she was drowned out by the roar of applause. I could barely conceal my grin. After she was done we exited the stage; the applause was still going strong. I couldn't believe how successful my first performance had gone. It was amazing.

Once we stepped outside the auditorium, we shared a tight hug and separated to go find the people we arrived with. I was greeted by multiple people telling me how great of a job I did, and how much truth there was to what I had said. I was even approached by another artist, rapper, who asked me if I would work with him sometime.

After that I did not performed for a while. A few things happened and I ended up living with friends in a different city and found myself too busy to pursue a career in performing.

During that time I again fell into a depression. I rarely left my house unless it was for work. I gained weight quickly; a lot of things just tilted for me and it seemed I was unable to rectify them.

A few months after my first performance I was told about radio shows called Blog Talk Radio. These are spoken word networks. It was a Thursday when I decided to call for my first time. I called the number I was provided with and waited for my turn to recite a piece. When my number was called they asked for my name and location to which I replied, "KingFlare from Chicago." I was nervous again, being my first time on Blog Talk. I recited a piece out of my book called "I'm Ugly" and the hosts of the show seemed very pleased. After that I became a regular on Blog Talk. Just about every day I was calling in and reciting. I even had a poetry partner, Authentically Speaking, who called in with me sometimes and we would perform a collaboration poem.

In the midst of my constant calling in I caught the attention of one of the largest poetry groups on Blog Talk, WolfHours. I was contacted by a few of the members asking if I was interested in joining them. Previously I had been in two other poetry groups—Team L.O.V.E., which included myself and other artists such as Focus Outlaw, Poetically Cee Love, and Wordz. Team L.O.V.E. was the first poetry group I was ever a part of, and after a while, I became the leader. Another group I was a part of was called Poetyk Evolution which my poetry partner, Authentically Speaking, was a part of as well. Unfortunately both these groups disbanded and I was a bit reluctant to accept the invitation from WolfHours but in the end I did and I have not once regretted my decision.

Shortly after joining WolfHours I was invited to an event hosted by Word Warrior and AliEn, two artists from another radio station called DSR. When I got there the amount of raw talent in the room was overwhelming. I knew one person there and stuck close to her so she could tell me who everyone was. There were artists there that I've heard about but never saw in person like Hood Raised, Kenyatta, and Mz Conception. It was an honor to be in their presence and it was even more of an honor to hear them speak. Also at the event was a very well-known artist named Blaq Ice. I met him and gave him my business card not really expecting him to contact me but still humbled that he accepted it. When I was called up to the mic I performed a new piece called "Toast". I started off great and was doing very well until I said, "We kill each other for every which thing, but when it's black on black I don't hear a thing, so they must think that we think with primitive instinct and mean to see us extinct." The crowd loved that and asked me to rewind it. That threw me off and it took me a minute to recover. It was my first open mic and there were a lot of big name artists in attendance. I felt the pressure to do my best. And I don't believe I did my best in delivering an otherwise great content, so I was ashamed of the performance and deleted the videos my friend had recorded. As soon as I left I began practicing "Toast" in the car. A few days later, I received a call from Blaq Ice inviting me to join his group P.O.E.T. I instantly accepted the invite with excitement and met with Blaq Ice and other members later that month for a meeting. At this point I had decided to make poetry my career and my main focus. I started attending more open mics, even became a regular at some, such as Street Dreamers hosted by Dionysis, Smokin Word hosted by Skrypt, and Poetry On The Corner hosted by E. Dot. I was hosting my own open mic for a little while called Hot Shotz Open Mic.

I did my first paid feature February 9, 2016 at Poetry's Love Letter. This was also when I had made "Toast" my signature piece. Along with "Toast" I performed "I Like Her", "Reminiscent", and "Self Doubt". The crowd was small but they reacted with a lot of love. After my first paid feature I went on to perform at multiple shows and events, such as Speaking L.I.F.E., The Black Women's Expo, and just recently June 9th Black Poetry Festival which was held in Atlanta, Georgia. I am currently fighting to be nominated for New and Upcoming SpokenWord Artist/Poet of the Year award in the National Poetry Awards. I am more than positive I can win and have been striving daily to get more followers and supporters.

Looking at where I am now, I try to give advice to people who constantly have issues pursuing their ambitions. I always tell them the same things:

- Follow your heart and you will always be happy.
- Never settle for less than you earn.
- Your dreams are not limited to sleep. Chase them full heartedly.
- Don't conform to fit it. You may defy some people's expectations but as long as you're proud of you then you have succeeded.
- Stay positive. I am immensely proud of the progress I have made since I started writing to now. Poetry is my career and I take it as seriously as a doctor or a lawyer would take their careers. I look forward to being the great poet I am shaping myself to be.

"Where You Been At Bruh?"
I Just Been Coolin
"You Don't Know Nobody"
Man...
In my haste to be great I forgot the things that were most important to me
Few as they may be
I can never forget those who've always supported me
And my pipe dreams
Back when my only means of getting it was agreeing with Instagram memes
We've come a long way, haven't we
I say we cuz I can't just say me when explaining how I got here
Financially this is me
But Spiritually and Emotionally I used to be so weak
Discouraged when I realized my generation doesn't read
Seeking Validation from peers that surrounded me
But they just wanted to get cheap drinks and smoke weed
So I guess in my attempt to get new people to read
I lost my mind of a King and started to follow lead
I wasn't one to pray much
But some nights I was on my knees
Like
"Lord please,
I'm in love with poetry but you need to tell me if she isn't for me,
I can't take a heartbreak, stop me before I get too deep,
And if she's truly my mistress
And this romance was meant to be
Tellem I don't care if there's no money in poetry
I'll write while still finding ways to eat."
And that rings true when I said it to now as I live it
I won't make a clever metaphor for how I'm cooking the best in
        Ramsey's kitchen
Just understand for those who don't understand how I'm livin
I put my everything into my Poetry
So if you're not tryin to help me
Then There's NOTHING You Can Tell Me."

Haste To Be Great by KingFlare

BREAKING FREE—BY ANY MEANS NECESSARY

BY LATANYA HARRIS

"You may not control all the events that happen to you, but you can decide not to be reduced by them."

–Maya Angelou

I remember spending lots of time with my grandmother who we lovingly called Ma-Ma. She loved working in her garden where she planted fresh vegetables and herbs. She was an amazing cook and I loved eating all the different vegetables that she grew. Ma-Ma always tried to teach me gardening. I hated the bugs and worms in the dirt when planting the seeds but I loved to see everything growing. Ma-Ma had little sayings that made you think with hope and feel better about any situation you were going through. I talked and cried to her wondering if I would ever reach a point in life where I wasn't struggling, would I one day feel good enough, or be able to live the seemingly perfect life I saw others living. "Yes you will," Ma-Ma would say with such conviction. "I may not be here to see it, but you will make it. You will have all GOD promised and more. You have got to believe in yourself and have faith; He will see you through." My grandmother has been dead now for close to 19 years and the memory of her kindness, wisdom, love, and belief in me gets me through the darkest of days.

I've often wondered what causes some of us to see certain life situations with such hopelessness and despair that we begin to believe we are never good enough just as we are. For some of us, our mind tells us that the only way to escape the feelings from judgment, guilt, addiction, pain, loneliness, worthlessness, and fear is either living recklessly, broken, or not living at all. Why do some of us seek a false euphoria outside of ourselves by any means necessary?

One day I sat in my office reading an email sent to everyone in the organization from a colleague whom I will call Sandra. I was a Human Resources (HR) Manager and my phone was ringing off the hook with people calling to see if I saw the email and asking my thoughts about it. It was a goodbye note with a tone alluding to suicide. It spoke about escaping to hell as the only way out. As I contemplated what to do next, I prayed and decided to call 911. One of the Sr. VPs and a few others decided to go to her apartment to talk to her. Sandra had been with the company for 11 years. More and more people started texting me that they too, were going to Sandra's. The business unit was like a family and everyone was scared and hurting for her. When I called her emergency contact, her brother I will call Danny, and explained the situation, he shared that she had been depressed and also started using drugs (Crystal Meth). At the time, I had no idea what that terrible demon was until I read up on it later. However, she didn't miss any assignments at work and was a brilliant software analyst. Danny also mentioned that she had two 9mm guns at home and wasn't afraid to use them.

I decided to go to Sandra's, planning to convince everyone to go home where they were safe. I hoped to talk her into going into a drug rehab program. As I got close to her apartment, I could see that the police and SWAT team were there. I was allowed through and was directed to her apartment floor. It was a scene just like you see in the movies. I saw more firearms than I've ever seen in my life and guns with laser beams pointed. I could hear negotiation talks. Her door was cracked and barricaded by a dresser. They asked if I could talk to her and convince her to come out. I did get her to come to the door and look out. She never said anything but I could tell she was listening to me. As she moved away from the door, she said she was tired and going to lay down and would think about coming out. She asked if I could stay there with her. I agreed, told her I would be right there. As she moved away from the door we could see the guns, one in her hand and one in her waistband. I was never afraid. My only desire was to help Sandra and to save her from herself and all those guns the police had.

I went downstairs to the rental office where they allowed us to wait. I saw all the news stations outside and it hit me that I needed my faith in God more than ever to pull through this. Everyone seemed to be hoping I could say or do something to save her. I always had an answer or creative way to solve business problems but this was way out of my league. As I stared out of the window, out of the corner of my eye, I saw Sandra on the balcony ledge of one of the apartment units to the side of where we were. I got up to take a closer look and she was on the ledge with a gun in each hand, seemingly looking right at me. Our eyes locked for a quick minute. As I ran to the elevator to get to her apartment, I heard so many gunshots it seemed like fireworks. I heard police yelling. I ran back to the window, and saw Sandra lying on the ground. I sank to the floor and cried like never before. I felt helpless and like the biggest failure of my life. I realized I broke my promise to Sandra and left her. Although I only went downstairs, I still left the hallway outside of Sandra's door. I felt God didn't answer my prayers. I wasn't good enough to talk to God and have Him answer. *Why did I ever think I was?* I thought. I should have called some prayer warriors instead of me praying, were some of the thoughts running through my mind. The burden and pain I felt then, and several times since, caused me to wonder—how it would feel to live without pain and guilt of past mistakes, shame, a troubled heart, and restless mind. As I re-read Sandra's note I could feel her pain. I knew she tried to escape the lies her mind told her, by any means necessary.

I didn't have time to grieve. Her family needed me, the employees needed me and my family needed me. So, I did what we women do. I put on my Superwoman cape; my Goliath armor and I kept going. I cried silently but I pushed through the pain and guilt. Many things were slowly bubbling up on the inside. I just swept everything away. At that time, I didn't know anyone in my family who had gotten professional help for anything that wasn't medically related and I didn't want to be the first.

I wanted to prove my strength so I moved on autopilot. My mom said to me that I was changing and I wasn't my vibrant, full of laughter self. I realized that somehow I had lost my 'faking happy' skill that I had mastered for so long. Mom suggested I go talk to somebody. *Why, who, and no way,* were my thoughts. "I'm fine," was my answer, as always. It wasn't until I couldn't lie to myself anymore and most of my nights and part of my days were spent in tears, did I begin thinking that I needed to talk to somebody but I quickly brushed that thought off.

Through my journey to get through this tragedy and other pain, I did some inner work. However, I did my inner work the same way my kids cleaned their rooms; that surface-cleaning thing. You know, it looks perfect till you open the closet and everything falls out. Well, that's what I did in the form of lying to myself and avoiding the truth. I hid stuff in other places in my mind and never dealt with my feelings. I felt I knew all about therapy. I was in HR, for crying out loud, and we are therapists every day, right? I ignored many warning signs and decided I could brave this alone, and I did.

It had been 13 years since that dark time in my life. The times when I loved people who didn't love me back in the same way. The times when I used to make other people's happiness a priority, while they made mine an option. The times when I let what other people thought of me rule and ruin what I thought of myself, and how I lived my life. The times when I felt guilty for not being able to save Sandra. I figured that freedom had come at last. For years, I secretly put myself in a mental and emotional cage, while playing the "I got it all together" game to the outside world and even my inner circle.

Even my loving husband couldn't help me to see the door was always open in my self-made cage. All I had to do was trust God and step through it.

I have yet to face another tragedy like Sandra's and have come to terms with the fact that saving Sandra wasn't my divine assignment. However, the feelings of not being enough, and being held captive by what other people thought of me, which I buried and told myself I had healed from, reappeared when we moved to Dallas to begin a new life.

I accepted a new position in Dallas and everyone was excited, including me. The kids were doing well in school and sports. I was a part of the "sports mom club" and life was good. My parents still lived in Cleveland, Ohio and had been divorced for many years but remained great friends.

My mom moved in with us shortly after we arrived in Dallas. She is the strongest woman I know besides my grandmother. I often pray to have the courage, forgiving heart, and selflessness that my mom does. She has overcome some major things in her life and I am so proud of her. Mom decided to give up Cleveland and come live with us to help with our two amazing children while we climbed the corporate ladders.

My husband traveled the majority of the time. He was known as a road warrior. I learned how to balance being a wife, mother, and having a demanding career most of the time alone. We learned to love and grow together while apart which wasn't easy.

Somehow my husband and I made this long distance life work for us. I found the greatest peace and comfort with my husband. I used to think if I had a great marriage and six-figure career life would be perfect. I later found out I was wrong. I had stuff on the inside of me that all his love, support, or my salary couldn't fix.

I became the queen of looking great on the outside, while crumbling on the inside. There was an old saying my grandmother used to me tell me: "A bird can fly so high, but it always has to come down to the ground for its food."

My dad was still in Cleveland and had survived a major stroke with little to no visible change. He taught me so much about life. He was always there when I needed him and was a perfect example of a great father. Dad had a minor stroke and total body breakdown while visiting for my daughter's high school graduation. He was in and out of the hospital and physical rehab facilities and then stayed with us along with my mom, for over a year. I realized he didn't need to be alone. Dad had agreed to permanently move to Texas. He could afford a beautiful assisted living place. I made all the negotiations and paid the deposit. I was comforted knowing I could look after him and he would not be alone. However, shortly after things were confirmed he changed his mind. He became angry and fought the move to Texas. He was fighting to hold on to his independence and I was fighting to keep him close. I believed taking care of Dad was my assignment as his oldest daughter but how I'd do it, was what I had to let go of.

My health started to decline. I have chronic pulmonary Sarcoidosis, which is an autoimmune condition similar to lupus. It's the growth of abnormal masses or nodules (granulomas) consisting of inflamed tissues in my lungs. I was having more flare ups which consisted of shortness of breath, persistent coughing, and fluid in my lungs with stress being one of my triggers. You don't hear much about this dreaded disease. The treatment my doctors used was Prednisone, which is a corticosteroid. There were times when I had been on high dosages, which had many side effects.

Some of the side effects I experienced were severe mood swings, extreme tiredness and insomnia. Prednisone also causes weight gain and a round moon looking face. My weight went up well over 200 pounds. During this time of what seemed like a downward spiral with my sarcoidosis and Dad's health up and down and him pushing more to go home, I also found out I had an early stage cancerous tumor on my colon. It was ultimately removed and we agreed that with my already compromised immune system, I would be monitored and not do anything further unless there were more findings. I was blessed not to have to endure chemo or radiation therapy; thank you Jesus once again. I just pulled out one of those Superwoman capes and kept moving.

My mom's health also started to decline and she had a couple of surgeries with slow recoveries. There was a time when both parents were in the hospital or a medical facility at the same time. The pain of seeing your parent's health decline is beyond hard. Being their sole caregiver caused me to fall on my knees daily for guidance and strength from God.

Depression and anxiety found their way back into my life and brought despair and helplessness with them. I experienced some leadership changes at work and my dream job became a nightmare. The quick rise to the top of the corporate ladder and a fast and harder fall to the bottom of it pushed me over the edge. I felt like I was falling short in every area of my life—wife, mother, daughter, and leader. I shared with my mom and husband that things would be better if my time to be with God came now. The other side, with no hurting heart or brokenness, would be better. I sat alone many late nights, the negative replays of the day racing through my mind.

One night in particular, I was holding a pill bottle with tears flowing thinking about dumping them in my mouth and drifting into an eternal sleep. God broke through my thoughts saying, "What if you believed in Me and all I've promised you? What if you turned it all over to Me? What if you studied My word and I taught you how to let Me love you? What if you finally believed that I think you're more than worthy?" I heard God's final whispers for that night saying, "I have an assignment for you on earth and I won't let you leave just yet."

I didn't know what to do because I felt so trapped in a yoke of bondage. Trapped in my toxic mind and body, trapped that I couldn't heal my parents and make my dad happy, trapped that I had a traveling spouse and that I believed I wasn't good enough for the career I loved or anything good, really. Broken. Unfinished. Thoughts of my husband, children, parents, and grandmother flashed through my mind. I knew then, I needed to get rid of those pills and break free from those negative thoughts that kept me in captivity. I cried out to God to please save me and set me free. I decided I had to let God break those strongholds and find the divine strength to live by any means necessary.

At that moment, I realized how broken I was. While I was focusing on pleasing and caring for other people—I missed seeing my own despair. I was knee deep in it before I realized it. While I was praying for God to fix other folks, He was actually revealing to me what was true and real in the situations and within myself, causing me the most pain. John 8:32 says, *"Then you will know the truth, and the truth will set you free"* and Galatians 5:1 says, *"It is for freedom that Christ has set us free. Stand firm, then, and do not let yourselves be burdened again by a yoke of slavery."* Both scriptures came to my mind.

As I progressed through personal healing and spiritual growth, I also began the journey of forgiveness. I forgave myself. It centered around forgiveness for allowing myself to be held captive by thoughts, events, and people that hindered the abundant and effective spirit-filled life God planned for me. After this burden was lifted, my inner shift happened in ways I never imagined.

My prayer life strengthened and my understanding of God's word grew. I'd come to remember that I have had prayers answered. I've gotten blessings. There were moments I felt God had finally thought I was worthy enough for some good things to happen to me. God showed me that I didn't want to die with an unlived life. I started to accept that God wanted to do something in me and with me—yes, me of all people. I committed to breaking free and courageously re-invent myself in the strength of God.

I stopped allowing my primary focus to be on someone else instead of God.

I stopped believing the lies my mind whispered.

I stopped playing the victim.

I stopped allowing my life to be molded and shaped by others.

I stopped living in a downward spiral full of what I didn't want.

I stopped being this so-called superwoman I had been for decades.

I was able to do this by surrendering to God-in every way. The following 10 principles helped me take action:

- Drawing closer to God. I began seeking, listening, and trusting His guidance through one-on-one time in His word. I got up early each day to ensure I had uninterrupted time to pray and learn via bible studies. I listened to worship music and utilized workbooks and downloaded video lessons taught by Beth Moore or Priscilla Shirer.

- I accepted counseling and the help of my family. I retired the superwoman capes.

- I surrounded myself with a select few as my prayer circle that could help me in this season of my life bring my issues into perspective. I find that cutting yourself off from others when you have something you don't feel you can share will only intensify your pain. If you don't have a prayer circle, find at least two people who believe in the power of prayer and ask them to pray with you weekly.

- I finally let go of the guilt of my mistakes and the things I had no control over. I released the responsibility from others who had not been supportive of me and realized that when God wants you to accomplish something, He will enable you to do it.

- I decided I wasn't going to let all I went through be for nothing. I was going to recycle it, let God redeem it, and turn it into a glory story to help someone else. I was made stronger and I gave God the glory.

- I remembered that my trials were not forever. If I remained faithful, they would accomplish what God had intended.

- I exercised every day and ate more alkaline foods. This helped to rid my body of acidic toxins and live a healthier lifestyle.

- Before I went to sleep, I read scriptures that spoke truth to my circumstances.

- I read a new book every two weeks about iconic women—starting with the biblical story of Esther—business and entrepreneurs who've made positive impacts on the world which allowed me to grow by providing wisdom, inspiration, and knowledge.

- I created a war room for prayer, praying as if my life depended on it and it did. God showed me every day how to have peace in my soul. I read Philippians 4:6-7 which says: *"Do not be anxious about anything, but in every situation, by prayer and petition, with thanksgiving, present your requests to God. And the peace of God, which transcends all understanding, will guard your hearts and your minds in Christ Jesus."*

God brought new sister friends into my life and opened my eyes and heart to see my true passion and talent for professional development coaching, public speaking, and writing. God aligned people to help me maximize the gifts He gave me.

I found freedom through the transforming power of Christ. I learned to accept that God's deliverance comes only when He's ready. I've grown to truly love the most important aspect of my life; how I feel about myself on the inside. Our job is to believe; God's job is to do the impossible. We don't get to choose what pieces of us God decides to use. His strength is made perfect when we give Him our weaknesses. God led you to me at this moment for a specific purpose. I'm sharing my story of trials to triumphs, fears to freedom, depression to deliverance to remind each of you, that detours do not cancel our destinations. This is written for the late night whispers haunting us and telling us that life here on earth isn't worth living. The broken and missing pieces create a wonderful kaleidoscope of your beauty within. You're not alone. We are not alone. We must learn to embrace every part of us, the truth of who we are, or we will spend our lifetime wasting our always-present grace surrounding us every day.

I still have hard days but I know I'm surrounded by joy and I'm worthy of the love of the King of Kings and so are you. I don't know if you are flying high right now or if this is the time God has brought you down to the ground for your food. No matter what has happened to you or what you're going through now, don't ever forget that you have the power within to change your future. There is glory in your story, you just have to make a list of "good" things in your life right now to see it. God is capable of making you better. He can take every moment or circumstance you've been through and the life you thought was wasted and use it as a backdrop to create a beautiful story that helps someone else to believe and have hope. God is not expecting perfection. You have to learn to trust Him with your pain. While we think we are waiting on Him, He's actually waiting on us.

I wanted to present this Superwoman who was perfect and worth His love so that He could use me to do His will on earth. He wanted me, just as I was. God's plan is always much better than our own. Don't let your past talk you out of your future, your destined treasures God has for you. I feel so grateful that sharing my story may help others. I was worthy all along and so are you. God reminds us that He has much more for us than what we see from where we've fallen.

My grandmother wanted me to learn that good food can grow from a tiny seed planted in the ground with the right amount of care given to it. Now, I understand that we all should learn at least the fundamentals of gardening. We need to turnover the soil of the past and dig up those weeds, the lies, and ugly circumstances in our life and pull them out by the root. God will renew our soul and plant new seeds of HIS truth to reap a bigger and better harvest. We have to keep watering our inner garden with His words. Even when the worst happens, it will get better even when we can't imagine how. We will be happy again. I'm living proof of that. We've got to stop the unhealthy cycles of striving and truly learn to love who we are and recognize the gifts and grace we've been given. I've been so close to hell, I still smell like smoke but I made it through the detours of life. I found freedom, strength, love, and light in the arms of Christ Jesus. I've built more spiritual and emotional muscle than I've ever imagined. Please don't ever give up. There is a way to the other side of living life, feeling, and being enough.

I know what my grandmother's saying really means now and I'm in alignment. "A bird can fly so high but it always has to come down to the ground for its food." Spiritual food for the soul allows us to soar to unimaginable heights. I still give more than I receive, love hard, but most of the time, I laugh more than I cry. God has dealt with my insecurities and brought me to the other side, to freedom. I see things so differently now. The world of truth outside of my cage of lies. I know I'm unfinished and finally love it. I pray you will stand in agreement with me, that we ALL are unfinished and will be while here on earth. GOD says that's just fine. We are worthy and deserving of God's unfailing love and He will use any means necessary to show us.

"Though the mountains be shaken and the hills be removed, yet my unfailing love for you will not be shaken nor my covenant of peace be removed," says the Lord, who has compassion on you. Isaiah 54:10

BREATHING WITH THE RHYTHM OF GOD

BY BRICENA "COOKIE" BELLE

"Those who put everything in God's hand, will soon see God's hand in everything."

–Unknown

I learned to breathe when my mother died. When that covering was removed I grew up. I was no longer Fat's oldest child living up to her approval. I became a full-fledged woman searching for my identity and my life's purpose. I realized that many answers could be found by examining my relationship with my mother.

I was born the Saturday before Mother's Day and she called me her First Mother's Day present. She was 19 years old, had dropped out of high school, and married a year earlier; more for provision than love. She told me of her family's financial struggles and how she was embarrassed when her shoes fell apart at school. She could not afford to replace them or buy clothes. Her mother told her my father was a good man, and he was.

Because of her limited education, my mother took great pride in the accomplishments of her children. She worked in a school cafeteria and was an award winning baker. Job titles were important to her. For instance, she preferred to tell everyone that I was the Marketing Director for a mortgage company. At the same time, her being home for me made it important for me to be home for my children. One of my favorite memories is her being at home when we returned from school. "Hi, Angel. How was your day?" she would say to each of us as she smiled and hugged us. I felt warm, protected, and that she would always be there for me. My mother had her timetable and plan for my life. She'd say, "By the time I was your age I was married with three children." My mother spent her entire 73 years living on one street. She and my father started out in a small house given to them by my grandfather. For years my father tried in vain to persuade her to move to another area. He eventually built her dream house at the end of the same street. She was not interested in moving outside of her familiar environment. She was content to stay a respected member of the community with "the biggest house" in the neighborhood.

I am a product of her molding and shaping—both good and bad. As I grow older I look more like her. I am told I have her mannerisms. Sometimes I catch myself mimicking her actions and saying her words.

Chasing Perfection

What should I eat, more importantly not eat? How much weight should I gain for a healthy baby but not too much to lose afterward? Where are the manuals? Oh, there are parents and baby magazines. I'll subscribe to three: *American Baby, Parents,* and *Modern Family.* The obsession began the day I found out I was pregnant. The mission was clear—to be the *best* mother and bring out the *best* in my children. Always doing what was *best* for them, at all cost. I was the self-appointed Managing Director of their lives with a self-imposed mandate from God. They defined me. My personal success or failure as a mother was measured by their appearance and behavior; and later as they grew older, the choices they made. All the baggage within me shaped my parental skills. They were *my* children and *I* knew what was best for them.

Ending my banking career to become a stay-at-home mom and my husband's steady climb up the corporate ladder created the perfect environment for me to build *my* family structure *my* way. Balancing that perfect structure was always a struggle.

My son was selected to participate in a program for high achieving students when he was in fourth grade. I attended a presentation for the parents and the first thing the presenter said was, "Children who are perfectionist usually have parents who are perfectionist." So there it was, out in the open. I could no longer deny my concerns about my son's perfectionist tendencies or the same behavior in me. Public failure embarrassed him. I constantly pushed my son to move beyond his fears and try new things. Given a choice of options he would be paralyzed with indecision and agonized over making the 'perfect' choices. When he could not choose, or took too long to choose, I chose for him.

When my daughter was in 5th grade she brought home a C on a math test and I flipped out. She did not like math and was not interested in the extra help the teacher offered before school. "Mom, it's just a C." It's not like it's the end of the world," she said. It was not the end of the world but it was totally unacceptable to me. I started driving her to school early to get help from the math teacher. I knew she felt the pressure and there was a lot of stress and tension between us, so we discussed our issues in writing.

When she became a senior in high school, my daughter wrote to me, *I know you wanted another perfect child...*

I wrote back, *No I do not want another perfect child. We would be a very boring family without your energy, creativity and sense of adventure... I never compared you guys.*

She wrote back, *You didn't have to. He was always there in his perfectness.*

That broke my heart and confirmed my concern that she felt the weight of her brother's shadow. They had the same 5th grade teacher and she came home one day furious that the teacher called her by her brother's name. "And I'm not even a boy!" she'd shouted.

I decided to stay at home when my daughter was born. My son was 4 ½ years old and all of my limited energy was focused on training, educating, and developing my children. They were my job and I took pride in my work but it was totally out of balance. After graduating college I complained about my lack of energy but found no help from the doctor. I adjusted to my new energy level but it had become an issue again. I often felt drained and was constantly looking for energy supplements. With the limited energy I felt forced to choose what to do first—dinner, clean house, play with the kids, play with Daddy. I was often frustrated and disappointed because I felt I made the wrong energy investment. I promised things I could not deliver and my husband usually got what was left over. One day when the kids were ages five and one and my husband came home from work, the house was a mess, the kids and I were still in our pajamas, and there was no dinner cooked. He did not say a word as he looked around and took in the scene. He did not have to speak. From the look in his eyes I heard him loud and clear. "What have you been doing all day?" That day, like many others, I could not get in gear. I sat on the sofa, looked around, saw what needed to be done, but had no energy to get up and do it.

Reality Check

Finally, I had insight into my energy issue. In January of 2008, I was diagnosed with Scleroderma an autoimmune disease similar to Lupus. An autoimmune disease is one in which the immune system turns against one's own body. The immune system creates excess collagen as it works to repair an injury that does not exist. It can also cause inflammation and pain in the muscles and joints. People with Diffuse Scleroderma often are tired, lose their appetite and weight. Initially my symptoms were limited to Raynaud's disease where my hands and feet turned white in response to cold temperatures. If I did not start warming my feet immediately, they no longer supported my weight and I'd fall. When my hands would turn totally white picking up items was painfully impossible.

Grocery shopping was an adventure, especially the frozen food section. Once my body started to cool, I knew it was time to wrap up the shopping and leave the store. I adjusted by wearing gloves, using hand warmer packets in my gloves and shoes, and always having a sweater, jacket, or blanket to keep warm. I took two Prilosec tablets every day and slept with my head elevated to prevent acid reflux. I read everything I could about this disease and learned that while symptoms varied from patient to patient, there was no cure. My doctor was one of the leading experts on the disease in the country and her vast knowledge and calm demeanor gave me comfort.

In January 2010, I became anemic. The doctor gave me iron supplements but they were not working. I lost my appetite and energy level and was literally living and sleeping on the sofa for months. Each day I sank further into a hole of which I could not get out. My husband and daughter, who was a senior in high school, were living life around me but I was not plugged in. One day she came home from school and stared at me. I am not sure what caught her attention. Was it the fact that I was in the exact same spot when she left that morning or was she seeing me for the first time? "Mom, you've lost a lot of weight!"

Her big, beautiful eyes were larger than normal and I saw the fear and shock on her face. I thought, *Lord, let me get up off this sofa. This girl thinks I am dying!* And when I did get up, I saw myself: frail, dry skin, thinning hair, and 30 pounds lighter. I went from a size 8/10 to 0/2. I was only getting dressed for church on Sundays so I had not paid attention to the weight loss. I just thought a particular outfit did not fit any more. I tried on everything in my closet and nothing fit. Everything I did not want to be, I had become.

I willed myself back into action for my son's graduation from college in May 2010 and my daughter's from high school in June 2010. Later that summer I was in South Carolina with my son and daughter and my anemia was at its worst. I did not want to bother anyone by asking them to get up and do something for me. So I waited until they were up and made my request.

My son exploded, "Every time I get up you want me to do something."

I said, "Yes, I wait because I don't want to bother you and ask you to make a special trip."

He said, "Well, it is aggravating and I have lost every ounce of empathy I had for you!" He left the room where we were watching television together. I felt like he had taken a dagger and stabbed me in the heart.

At home I did not ask for help because his father made me feel that I was interrupting him or 'playing the victim' card. Unless someone has personally experienced Scleroderma, they cannot relate to the lack of energy. They feel you are trying to manipulate or control them with requests to do things for you. I vowed at that moment that I would do what I could and learn to live without the rest.

I thought back to my mother's last months. She wanted to leave the nursing facility and come home. She entered under a rehab plan but did not fully cooperate so that window was closed. In a family meeting, the nurse explained to us that she would need a special bed and 24 hour care if we brought her home. The care-taker would have to go through three separate training sessions before being qualified. After the meeting we realized that was not an option for us but all that my mother heard was she needed a special bed to come home.

My mother told her girlfriend, "I took care of people all my life now it is time for someone to take care of me." She did not consider the fact that her children were in their 50s with serious medical issues of their own. I was called in to the dialysis center where the social worker explained to me that my mother was demanding more attention than their staff could provide. Under these circumstances they usually asked a family member to come in during the four hour treatment period. My sister worked a full-time job, my brother and his wife owned a print shop, and I lived out of state. I could not commit to providing family assistance. It was stressful and I went to my mother and told her, "I hope I never put my children through what you are putting us through."

That experience made me realize that if I wanted to be a part of my children's lives as I grew older I would have to remain mobile and self-sufficient. After my mother's passing my daughter told me,

"I hope you know that when you are old you cannot come live with me." I assured her that she was not my plan for compassionate refuge. Her father and I would have other arrangements.

Redemption

In October of 2012 God gave me a deeper understanding of His Power, and His design for my marriage. I was in South Carolina dealing with my Mom's recent fall and resulting medical issues. My husband was in Illinois working with his new company. After one week my blood pressure escalated due to the Scleroderma. I called my primary doctor and rheumatologist in Texas because nothing was working. I ended up in the emergency room and scheduling an emergency trip back to Texas to see the Scleroderma Specialist. Unbeknownst to me, my husband scheduled a trip back to Texas the same weekend. So instead of returning to an empty house I was picking him up from the airport. I had never been so happy to see him. In that one weekend God gave me more insight into the strength of our union. I realized I needed Marty—the very essence of him. His presence calmed my fears, regulated my thoughts, and assured me that everything was going to be okay. God was rebuilding our foundation.

Relapse

After coordinating the sale and move of our home in November 2012, the death of my mother in July 2013, double graduations again in May 2014, I found myself again void of energy and on the sofa. I had not fully recovered or regained the weight from 2010 and was fearful as the memories of my last episode came flooding back. I knew that if I stayed on the sofa this time, I would die. My illness had become the focal point of my life. Every movement, every thought was limited by my illness. I had allowed my physical limitations to rule my mind. I saw my life through the prism of Scleroderma and not through the eyes of God. I struggled to walk in my healing, struggled to make the right choices expending my limited energy, struggled to jump over the hurdle of depression, struggled to accept my changed body. I wondered what healing looked like and if I would recognize it in me.

I decided to focus on the spiritual aspects of what was going on in my life. I cried out to God, "What am I supposed to learn from this? Let me get the point and move on!" I was demanding an answer and He was preparing me for a journey.

Final Surrender

My daughter was returning to Texas for graduate school and I needed to help her find an apartment. I was tired, disappointed, and frustrated. My doctor tried to comfort me. She did not tell me not to go but we both knew the reality. I could not physically walk through the airport. Not to mention negotiating the August Texas heat. My presence would have been a hindrance to my daughter. She needed to get a lot accomplished and not have to worry about me keeping up. I knew the reality but that did not keep me from wanting to be there with her. My children could always depend on me. I was only a cell phone call or text away. There to solve any problem, ease any pain, move any obstacle.

My daughter was old enough to handle her own business, and she did. So, why was I so upset? Did she need me, or did I need her? Was I concerned about letting her down or letting her go? What does a reformed 'Helicopter Mom' do when her children are grown and gone? No longer able to hover over their every move, I felt I was losing control and my sense of purpose.

God had dealt with me before. When my son was away at school sick, all I wanted to do was go to North Carolina, check into a hotel with him, and take care of him. I could not because I had another child at home still in high school. I was restless, uneasy, and torn. God impressed upon me, "What can you do that I cannot?" I knew God could take care of him (better than I could) but I felt I needed to do something. When was prayer not action enough? Does it not move the hand of God? Yes, we know what God can do. But where is our faith to trust and believe? If we truly believe that He can, why do we feel the need 'to do' something? I had to come clean and surrender. It was time to let go. Either God was in control or I was. Not both!

Restoration

"For God hath not given us the spirit of fear; but of power, and of love, and a sound mind."

2 Timothy 1:7 (KJV)

I decided to let go of the reins and journey through *the will of God concerning me.* I listened to His rhythm, and for the first time, looked beyond my physical challenges to see what He was showing me. My recovery accelerated in January 2015. I received a colonoscopy and immediately my energy was restored. I could now mentally focus. I firmly believe that nothing happens in my life without God's permission. I was determined to understand why I was on this journey, what God wanted me to learn from it, and how it was preparing me for my purpose.

It had been two and a half years since my mother's death. It was time to open Pandora's Box and review my relationship with my mother. Time to fully mourn my loss and discover who I really was and why. My mother inherited Polycystic Kidney disease from her mother. Thankfully it was not passed on to her children or grandchildren. She spent 33 ½ years on dialysis, the same amount of time Jesus spent on earth. She was near death when she started dialysis. I prayed a selfish prayer, "God please don't let my mama die. I want her to be at my wedding and I want her to see my children." Three years after that prayer I met my husband. My children were ages 25 and 21 when she passed.

After she died several people told us of her generosity. She was a giver; giving any and every thing to anybody, but I felt some people took advantage of her generosity. I also felt she gave many times because of low self-esteem. She took food to the staff of her various doctor's offices and delighted in their praise. Was she feeling that we took her for granted and no longer valued or appreciated her or her cooking? One day I heard her pastor preach about the 'Gift of Giving.' Then I understood. It was not about self-esteem or the need to feel appreciated. It was the sheer joy she felt touching someone's life and making their day better. My brother, sister, and I feel we are reaping the benefits of the seeds she planted. She raised three adults who understand from example, *it is more blessed to give than to receive.*

Children in the South learn their place. They are to be seen and not heard. Until her death I was always her child. I never wanted to do anything to hurt or embarrass my mother. All of my hard decisions were made with underlying thoughts of the impact on her. "The first time you have sex you are going to get pregnant" kept me a virgin in high school and college. "You've gained weight since the last time I saw you" kept me conscious of my weight.

I thought I was finally independent when I graduated college. A grown woman making her own decisions. But my mother always found a way to make her opinion known. She used her passive aggressive technique to make sure I knew how much something meant to her and how disappointed she would be. Like her insistence that I name my daughter (Martie) after my husband Marty. I was named after my father Brice, thus the use of the nickname Cookie. Before my mother passed I wanted to reconcile and clear the air on some things. She did not want to take that journey with me. Fortunately, God has a big eraser. I cannot remember what was so pressing that I wanted to work out with her. He has given me *peace that surpasses all understanding.*

Since we were not able to talk things out, I had to review her actions to learn a few life lessons. I remember her struggling for relevance in her last two years. Without the ability to cook and have others sing her praise, she was restless and lost. That was her purpose, her gift, her calling, and she took pride in it. She did not enjoy being alone, reading, knitting, or crafting. Cooking was her hobby and her life.

Yes, I was the perfect child who grew up to be a perfectionist control freak. Like my mother, I was a people pleaser who cared about image and what others thought. I was horrified of failure and any public display of imperfection. I tried to control everything. I felt justified in my controlling actions because surely God had given me these children and they were my assignment. I was so busy taxiing them to their scheduled activities—soccer, basketball, baseball, tae kwon do, dance, swim lessons, golf, girl scouts—that we never had time to develop an intimate emotional relationship. I did not create an environment where they felt they could come to me to talk, and know that I would listen.

As they grew older, I never gave enough consideration to their feelings or thoughts of what they wanted. I felt I knew best what they should do. We were building a resume to get them to college. I expected them to live up to their full potential at all times. Looking back, I realize I expected them to work as hard to please me as I had worked to please my mother. I was emulating my mother's behavior on a higher level.

Lessons Learned

"Faith sees the invisible, believes the unbelievable, and receives the impossible."

–Corrie ten Boom

Looking back, I realize that I was living life on a hamster wheel. Constantly running to catch up. Never ahead or winning the race. Never really in control. Faith does not demand control. Faith is not afraid to let go and trust.

"And be not conformed to this world: but be ye transformed by the renewing of your mind, that ye may prove what is that good, and acceptable, and perfect, will of God."

Romans 12:2 (KJV)

As a former athlete, I knew there was a reservoir of energy to tap into if you pushed beyond the wall. Your mind had the ability to take you places your body did not think it could go.

"…He is not far from each one of us. For in Him we live and move and exist…"

Acts 17:27-28 (NLT)

I have come to know that God Is My Everything. It was not until I was totally void of energy that I realized how much I need God. I remember watching people walk, afraid I would forget the mechanics of coordinating my arms and legs. I took nothing for granted and was grateful for every movement I was able to make by the grace of God!

"The truth is, the rhythm and depth of your breath directly affects the state of your mind and the health of your body."

–Nadya Andreeva

I have learned the importance of deep breathing and its many health benefits. With Scleroderma I take an annual pulmonary test to measure my lung capacity. I recently joined a gentle yoga class for increased flexibility. The instructors emphasize the importance of deep breathing. I realized that I was going through life with shallow breathing. The only time I breathed deeply was when the doctor said, "Take a deep breath." In order to breathe properly you need to breathe deeply into your abdomen not just your chest.

The Rhythm of God

"In everything give thanks: for this is the will of God in Christ Jesus concerning you."

1 Thessalonians 5:18 (KJV)

If you let God direct your path and set the rhythm, you will live a life of peace, tranquility, organization, energy, impact, motivation, expectation, and renewed love!

"Trust in the LORD with all your heart and lean not on your own understanding in all your ways submit to him, and he will direct your paths."

Proverbs 3:5-6 (NIV)

Looking back, I can see that God has been there, setting the drumbeat. I was not always obedient or stayed on path but I had a heart toward God. Every time I felt I could not go on He reached out to me. On one of my doctor visits to Houston, He formed my profile in the clouds as I looked out of the taxi window. Upon arrival at the medical center, I was a broken mess and in need of God's touch. God's Angel driver hugged me, prayed for me, and told me everything was going to be all right.

I have gained a second chance and a pathway to the 'Soul Mate' relationship I want with Marty. I love him more today than I did on our wedding day 31 years ago. He has proven himself to be the man I thought he would be. I appreciate his tolerance in the early years when I was so out of balance. Now that it is just the two of us, we are taking the time to improve our communication. I am no longer concerned about burdening him with details of my symptoms. He is no longer concerned that I am playing the victim. As I strive to live life to the fullest I feel his support and appreciate his assistance. I value and appreciate the 'special gift' God has given me.

I respect my children as adults. I apologize for not listening more when they were younger. I now realize they have their own lives and their own God-given purpose and destiny. I am no longer pushing them to be what I want them to be. I want them to be everything God created them to be. Learning to mind my own business has not been easy but it has been rewarding. They seek my advice and sometimes text just to share. I feel I am now the mother they need.

My life is not perfect but I am no longer striving for perfection. I am living my purpose one day at a time, building my family structure God's way. I see my purpose unfolding and I am learning to walk in it.

The Shift

I am so grateful and blessed. I have come to know that a life of balance is not a destiny but a journey—living each day according to God's plan. Be flexible enough to change direction on a moment's notice as directed by God, and sensitive enough to meet the needs of those who God placed in your path. I found my balance in God. My "To Do" list is now a guide not a mandate. I find myself asking God to guide me during the day and help me make adjustments as needed. I am more relaxed and less stressed. I am learning to live in the moment.

Breathe Deeply My Friend!

DETOURS STILL GET YOU THERE

BY LAURIE A. EVANS

"If you can find a path with no obstacles, it probably doesn't lead anywhere."

–Frank A. Clark

I sat in my counselor's office with a wide smile on my face. I felt butterflies brought on by my uncertainty of how my parents would receive the news of me qualifying for early graduation. At the dinner table with my whole family that night, I announced the great news. My parents were elated but equally concerned about what I would do from then until I left for college. I assured them I would find a job, work, and save money to help with the expenses freshman year in college would require. It took a bit of persuading, but before the dinner dishes were washed and put away my parents gave their consent with one caveat: I had two weeks to secure a job or I would be back in high school.

As promised, I interviewed for a position as a teller at a large bank and received an employment offer. I was seventeen years old, working in an industry which required a very strict "business attire" dress code. Every day I wore a beautiful dress or suit with my flesh toned hosiery and high heeled shoes. My male co-workers were sharp as tacks, donning suits with starched shirts and ties. In my mind, this appearance personified unparalleled success. No one could tell me that I was not a grown, successful, adult making a lot of money! Trust me, my pockets were far from "deep." In reality, they were extremely shallow. Yet, at seventeen I was convinced I had arrived. It wasn't long before my misguided impressions led me to decide I would not further my education. I had a new, more tangible plan; I would climb the ladder within the bank two rungs at a time and become a manager, then work diligently toward earning a promotion to officer. When I shared my decision with my parents they were devastated.

That swift ascent up the bank ladder was more like a slow crawl up Mt. Everest. I grew tired of waiting for a promotion and concluded that I needed to find another source of employment. Accepting my next employment opportunity would bring about another detour in my life. My new Manager, Patricia "Pat" Russo, was an amazing woman and instantly took me under her wing. She taught me everything I needed to know to eventually take on the position of Assistant Manager. After much success within the organization a conversation with Pat changed my life. As I sat in her office, with a straight face, that still shone with the affection and respect she always gave me, she said, "You are worth your weight in gold but you will never have my position." I was confused and instantly became angry. I mean, exactly who did she think she was to tell me what I could or could not do? She continued telling me the truth about the world of business and how, as a woman, I would absolutely need a degree in something in order to move on and reach the full potential she saw within me.

I began to witness that God will allow us to wander off of His map for our life, yet He will put us right back on the route He has planned for us. I left Pat's office ready to follow God wherever He led me. I thought I was ready but I allowed the dream killer called Doubt to enter into my mind and cause me to question if going to college was the right thing to do at this point in my life. I talked to the one person I knew would help me confirm this was the right decision—my dad. I recall saying, "Daddy, I think I am too old to go to college." He gave me a look of understanding that

I witnessed from him many times before and replied, "Let me ask you this, how old will you be in four years after college?" I quickly responded twenty-seven. Just saying it out loud made me cringe with embarrassment. He shook his head in agreement and continued with another question: "And how old will you be in four years if you don't go to college?" In that moment, it was like a 200 watt light bulb illuminated in my brain. No further words were exchanged, just a big hug that said, "Thank you and I love you!"

My choice of schools changed for several reasons, but my desire to excel never wavered. The first day I walked onto the campus of Shaw University and saw all the beautiful faces in every shade of brown, just like mine, I knew my choice to attend an HBCU (Historically Black College and University) would be the best years of my life. And there were many good times, accomplishments, challenges, and heart wrenching losses during my four years at Shaw. My best friend, supporter of my dreams, and first man to love me—my dad, passed away on Mother's Day evening, my freshman year, just one day after I arrived home for summer break. My heart broke that day forever. I felt an emptiness in a special part of my heart that I knew would never be fulfilled. To this day, I feel guilty. Had I gone straight to college after graduating from high school he would have been able to witness me receiving my degree instead of merely hearing me earnestly promise that I would finish college while he lie passing away on a gurney in a cold emergency room. He was there in spirit on the day my name was called and I walked across the stage, and he continues to be present during the special occasions in my life. I wish he would not have witnessed me going through pain while he was battling with his own pain related to years of heart disease. But that was not my Creator's plan; that was not the way He wanted it to be.

Instead it went like this…

One fall morning during my first semester of college I woke up with relentless pain. It felt as though red hot needles were being jabbed through several of my fingertips. My fingers had changed to a bluish purple color. My eyes filled with tears, while my heart pounded with fear. I knew that something was terribly wrong. For weeks I had been extremely tired. I just attributed it to getting accustomed to my rigorous college life. After talking to my sister, a senior living down the hall, and calling my parents, it was unanimously decided that I needed to come home to visit my doctor. The next afternoon I stood in LaGuardia airport waiting for my brother to chauffer me home to Connecticut. The following morning my mom and I waited for my doctor to enter the exam room where I sat on a hard exam table, shivering cold, wrapped in a paper gown loosely tied at the waist. When he finished with all his routine questions, poking and prodding, he left the room while I dressed.

In the middle of a silent prayer, asking God over and over to please let me be okay, I heard a faint knock at the door. It was time to hear the diagnosis. I heard the word "sclero" something. *Excuse me?* Once again, I heard only part of this word that he was telling me was the reason for my recent symptoms. The second time I caught the ending of the word, "derma." Being a child who had grown up with eczema I was familiar with the word derma. I breathed a sigh of relief thinking that this condition would be treated and relieved like the dry patches of skin that covered my wrists. Eczema was a nuisance, but certainly something easily managed. The third time I heard him clearly. "You have an autoimmune disease, Scleroderma." (*Systemic Sclerosis*) My moment of relief was vehemently shattered. Life, as I knew it, would NEVER be the same. This word, which I couldn't even pronounce, would alter me spiritually, physically, and emotionally. It would transform my outlook on life.

Over the months and years following the diagnosis, my body would become a violent and ruthless stranger. I fought to stay well and deny this heinous disease entrance into my life. Yet, Scleroderma began to take control and proving without a doubt it would now dictate *the* what, when, and where in my life. Shortly after my diagnosis, being able to rise in the morning and put my feet on the floor without feeling like a Mack truck driven by an enemy that relentlessly rolled over and over me, became only a memory.

Having the ability to wash my hands, brush my teeth, or comb my hair without experiencing excruciating pain no longer was a possibility. The dramatic changes in my health made me cognizant that I had taken so much for granted.

"Treasure the small things and take nothing for granted because you'll miss it all one day when it's gone."
—Nishan Panwar

I developed open sores on my fingers and toes, called *ulcers*, which required months, sometimes up to a year to heal. Sometimes they didn't heal at all and became infected down to the bone which resulted in immediate amputation to avoid me from becoming septic and possibly dying. To date, I have had to face the decision that amputation was necessary four times. I have had to endure agonizing burning pain, the equivalent of torturing yourself with harsh concoctions of rubbing alcohol and Epsom salt poured onto open sores. Pain that would take my breath away; pain that reduced me to curling up on the cold floor screaming for mercy and reminding God that He promised not to put more on me than I could bear. I wanted to know why He hadn't given me cancer instead. With cancer I felt there would be an end to my fight—I would go into remission or eventually die. I cursed Him and pleaded with Him to see that I was bearing all that I could and sincerely unable to bear any more.

I had no idea that it was possible to be so angry. This war caused me to disown my Lord and Savior and question all I was raised to believe. I felt like He had abandoned me and I no longer wanted to have anything to do with Him.

I was shaken to my core the day I woke up in the same ER my father had passed away in with black charcoal all around my mouth and in-between my teeth. My mother, aunts, and cousin Etta were standing by my bedside with red, tear filled eyes. I felt lucky that my stomach didn't need to be pumped and immensely grateful that Etta listened to the whisper of God telling her to check on me, even though months had passed since we'd spoken, the result of a petty argument. When in unrelenting pain I know just how easy it is to over medicate and find yourself on the borderline of death by accidental overdose. It is not some rare occurrence that only affects celebrities, superstar musicians, or the rich and famous. The devil continued to have his hands all in my business and helped me to move farther away from the blood of Jesus that once comforted and protected me. I allowed that no good chief of evil—*Satan* and Scleroderma to pulverize the solid rock of Christ I once stood upon. My faith had become smaller than a mustard seed; it was non-existent. Without my faith the course of my life was surely going to bring about many dark and lonely times.

> *"Trust in the LORD forever, for the LORD GOD is an ever-lasting rock."*
>
> Isaiah 26:4

A number of my friends wandered away. I scrambled to protect myself from emotional turmoil following each departure. My college boyfriend, who was my best friend, confidant, and cheerleader from day one of my diagnosis, unexpectedly left me after six years of dating with these words: "You and your disease are becoming a roadblock on my road to success." For years those words haunted me and engulfed me in the fear that no one would ever want me. It had me question if I had lost all value in light of this affliction. My soul cried. One day it amazed me when he apologetically reached out to me, after over fifteen years, to say he was battling his own inescapable affliction and wanted to apologize. I won't lie, there was a small part of me that wanted to say, "See, you left me without a compassionate thought for all we shared and Karma, being the bitch she is, got you back for me!" But because I was making a shift in my life to begin finding my way back to God I forgave him and for a few years we remained in contact.

> *"The weak can never forgive. Forgiveness is the attribute of the strong."*
>
> –Mahatma Gandhi

72

I was complacent about the mediocre care that I was receiving for my illness, particularly while residing in Delaware for much too long. One night while lying in a hospital bed in Newark, DE for yet another excruciating, non-healing, infected, ulcer that required hospitalization to control the pain with a patient-controlled analgesia pump, my outlook on my life shifted. While lying there, I acknowledged that I had permitted Scleroderma to dwarf my happiness and cause me to simply exist. I decided that it was time to take back what rightfully belonged to me because God had perfectly planned and gave it to me... My LIFE. I was ready to be the heavyweight fighter I had always been inside and take control of my life and find a better way to knock out this monster. I had reached a point where I refused to allow "IT" to also continue affecting the lives of my blessings; my husband (*now ex*) and our two beautiful pre-school children. The three of them had become collateral damage in my war against Scleroderma. It was time for my husband to just be a father and not both parents because I was suffering endlessly. My children deserved to have a mother that could show them what it meant to be resilient and be able to get up and take them to the park to play. I had to put my armor, that I wore during my Shaw U days, back on and be a determined and fierce advocate for my health.

It is imperative to be the head coach on your healthcare team and not a spectator standing on the sideline. Remember that God is the Owner of you and all the players on your team and He has the ultimate say in what will be. If a doctor tells you no and you believe that doctor is wrong, listen to the "Owner" and move on for a second opinion. If your questions are not being answered, do not be afraid to let your doctor know directly that you need more clarification. You are the coach—stand up for yourself. You and God are the only two who know YOU. There are no books that a doctor can read, there is no website that a doctor can peruse that will give him more knowledge about you than you have. You know you better than anyone else ever will!

When you begin to advocate for yourself be prepared for God to continue pulling out the crabgrass and weeds from your garden of life that He knows will strangle your flowers growth and prevent you from having a lush green lawn.

This includes doctors, too. I can now chuckle about a "Dear John" letter I received from my Rheumatologist after I asked him about a medication he was prescribing. I still cannot believe he broke up with me via United States Postal Service mail. He immediately was regarded, in my mind, as less than a man who had to hide behind a letter instead of being the professional he took an oath to be.

After a long, tedious task of trying to gather contact information I located and met, by phone, my living angel named Rosalind "Roz" that I affectionately call Ms. Roz. During that hospital stay, I recalled reading an article written by Roz in *The Member* Magazine of The Scleroderma Foundation, "Scleroderma Voice." The article shared her story about her great success with a new treatment using the medicine Flolan (*Intravenous vasodilator*). I spent a great deal of time on the phone with a 411 Directory Assistance operator pleading for her to give me the private telephone number belonging to Roz. God moved things for me that night, as He continued to do, even though I turned my back on Him. Roz and I spoke for at least an hour that evening. A week later, I was on an airplane headed to Austin, TX where my mother-in-law, "Mommie" ironically had recently moved to. It was like the universe (God) had aligned everything with exact precision to lead me to the treatment which would give me back so much of my life by alleviating the constant, debilitating ulcers on my fingers.

Me and my new I-35 "Road Dog", Felicia a.k.a. The Best "Sister" in-Law in the World would make the trip to Memorial Hermann Hospital in Houston, Texas to meet with the renowned Scleroderma Specialist, Dr. Maureen Hayes three times for my treatments that were very successful, before I had to make an extremely difficult, unwanted move to Seattle to support my husband's career. Fortunately, I was able to continue my treatment with a similar drug. That 3,000 mile move ripped me away from my family and life long, true friends. I was dragged kicking and screaming to this miserable, rainy, grey state of Washington. From the very moment that I was told the move was inevitable I began to experience nightmares which showed me this transition would lead to the demise of my marriage. Although I was not born with a "veil over my face", as old folks would say, clairvoyant, nor in the psychic profession with Miss Cleo those fears came true. This new place which I still do not call home, is where the man who vowed to love me until death parted us, engaged in countless unforgivable infidelities. His reckless pursuits defiled our union, nearly destroying me from the inside out. Suffocated by horrific life depleting depression I became imprisoned to my bed. Living on the other side of the country, away from loved ones, the decline of my mental, emotional, and physical health were easily disguised. I should have won an Oscar for my stellar acting, portraying that I was living a glorious, fairy-tale lifestyle, like a cast member of the fictitious "Housewives of Seattle" during my phone conversations with family and friends. God held me through all of this turmoil. He continuously bestows His blessings upon me, restoring my physical and mental well-being. I have built an amazing team of health care providers with a wealth of Scleroderma knowledge. My Rheumatologists, Dr. Jerry Molitor and Dr. Jeffrey Carlin, have done an incredible job keeping me healthy and ensuring that I am not faced with the need for additional amputations. Together we will continue to search and try new treatments to improve my chronic fatigue that leaves me EXHAUSTED during the day requiring multiple naps and my other Scleroderma related issues. My love and faith in the Lord has been abundantly restored. I am so grateful that I have a loving and forgiving God who never turns His back on us even when we turn away from Him. I encourage anyone faced with an illness to keep your faith and know that the blessing of a cure may come any day. I am not cured of Scleroderma but have been blessed to receive relief from many of my debilitating symptoms. I remain hopeful that one day there will be a cure for Scleroderma and the other over 80 different autoimmune diseases that affects approximately 50 million Americans. My dear Sclero Sisters and Brothers, you are always a part of my prayers as I feverishly pray for our strength and perseverance as we work toward a cure. Together we are SCLERO-DERMA STRONG!

DOUBLE PORTIONS

BY TAMMY LEWIS

"Instead of shame and dishonor, you will enjoy a double share of honor. You will possess a double portion of prosperity in your land, and everlasting joy will be yours."

Isaiah 61:7

The year 2009 was going very well for me. My oldest son graduated high school and was accepted into a university, I had just received my acceptance letter for the Registered Nurse (RN) program, and my business was thriving. I will admit once I went back to nursing school, I felt maybe I'd bit off more than I could chew. Half-way through the program I started to second guess myself, because the business was so demanding. One of my friends, who also was a nurse, propositioned me about buying into the business and becoming an equal partner. I thought about it for a while and agreed to the terms. Shortly afterwards her spouse lost his job and she was unable to buy into the company. After careful consideration, I decided to move forward anyway and borrow the money from my credit union as a buy-in and use it for marketing for the business. Just before graduation we sealed the deal. We were both so excited. I must say the excitement was short lived. I was doing most of the work because she was working full-time at the hospital. I tried my best to be okay with it, because we'd been working on two large contracts. One contract would bring in $2.4 million annually and the other would be $3.6 million. After we land these contracts neither of us would have to work as hard.

The day finally came when we got the call. And not only did we land one contract, but we landed both and at the same time! We were so excited that we didn't know what to do. I remember us driving down the street together in her van screaming from excitement. This was a major accomplishment. It took almost a year to get there but we finally made it. All of those late nights that I was up, for all of the clients that I had to service—because there was no one else—and for all of the days that I worked alone—the payoff was finally here. We signed the contracts and sent them back to the companies and now all we had to do was wait.

That night, I received a call from my business partner and friend asking if I could meet her at the office the following morning so that we could talk and I happily agreed. The next morning when I arrived at the office, she was already there. I turned to her with a smile and said, "Good morning."

"Good morning," she responded.

"So, what'd you wanna talk about?" I asked.

"I just wanted to let you know that I have hired someone to replace you. You can still continue to do the marketing, because you are great at that, but someone else will be taking your place."

Okay, so at this time I was looking around the room waiting for someone to jump out with the cameras, but by the look on her face and the tone of her voice, I knew that she meant what had just come from her mouth.

"Ummm, what do you mean by you've hired someone to replace me?" I asked with a slight change in attitude. Her response was that she thought that it was a good business decision. She'd already hired a full staff. Needless to say that conversation did not go over very well and this story doesn't end on a happy note because "Greed" has a mind of its own.

We both had to hire attorneys because there is no reasoning with greed. We went back and forth, speeding unnecessary money.

I had depleted all of our savings. I had no income coming in and our home went into foreclosure. I started borrowing money from my mom and step-dad who graciously gave it. After a while, I decided to just give up and start over. The healthcare industry is not very big and the word was getting around. The clientele was starting to suffer and I didn't want to do that to them and didn't want that reputation for myself either. I told my attorney that I just wanted my phone and fax numbers and my office space and she could take all of the clientele. She agreed. At that point she now had all of my computers, all of my office furniture, all of my clients, and what felt like all of my dreams.

I went to the State of North Carolina to apply for a new licensure only to be told that they were no longer giving licenses in that state. Can you image what was going through my mind? I tried to plead my case, but it was not debatable. I told the person which whom I was speaking that I wanted to submit my application with my fee of $560 anyway. She told me that it would be a loss but would accept it. For the next two weeks I called almost every day trying to get some-one to listen to my story. I got the same response every time. I did the only thing that I knew how to do—I got in bed and cried. I cried for weeks. I didn't have the strength to even shower and dress myself. I called one of the elders in church and talked to her and she prayed with me and told me that I needed to come back to church. The fol-lowing Sunday, I decided I would go to the first service. I walked in with a heart of coal. I didn't want to be there. I was mad. I was hurt. I think I was more upset about the friendship than anything else. As I was driving to church that morning, I reflected back on the whole ordeal. As I thought back over that year, I remember something my mom said to me that first time she met this friend prior to my going into business with her. She said, "Tammy, I don't think that I like that girl. Maybe you shouldn't do it."

I argued saying, "Momma, she's cool. You just have to get to know her." I probably should have taken both mine and my mom's advice. I should have gotten to know her and I should not have allowed her into my business as an equal partner.

During the church service that Sunday our Pastor just happened to be speaking on forgiveness. He talked about how in order for God to forgive us, we must first forgive others who have wronged us. We must pray for those who have wronged us. He said that God could not get things to us if we were harboring unforgiveness in our hearts. This is what got my attention. He even said, "The enemy comes to kill, steal, and destroy. He tries to steal our families, our children, our businesses." Wait. Is he talking to me? I couldn't believe it. It's amazing how God works because at that moment I knew what I had to do.

From that day forward I started praying for her and her family. Trust me when I say that I didn't want to do it. At first I did it grudgingly, but after a while it got easier. I was still kind of confined to my bed. One day, my husband told me that I should get up. That day I went to the mailbox only to find a letter from her attorney wanting me to sign a non-compete. This would mean that I could no longer work in the industry. The anger just came rushing back. I immediately went in the house to call the State again, but before I did, I asked God to give me favor. When I called I got the same lady again and her story did not change. "I'm sorry, Mrs. Lewis, but as I have explained before, we are no longer granting licenses for the State of North Carolina." I then told her my story again and explained that I had received a letter from her attorney and they wanted me to sign a non-compete.

"What? You got to be kidding me! Don't you sign anything. Just hold on one minute. I'll be right back."

She then placed me on hold for what seemed like five minutes before returning. When she got back on the line she asked if I could come in next Wednesday for a survey and I replied with, "Yes ma'am." She told me to bring my policies and she would see me then. I cried so hard because I knew that this was the breakthrough that I needed.

The following Wednesday, I went in for my survey and she found that I was missing ten pieces of pertinent information. She said to me that she is not supposed to give me a license, but she trusted that I would get the information needed in my policies and licensed me effective immediately. "Thank you, Jesus!" No one will ever know the feelings that came to me that day because I've never been able to put them into words. All I know is that God was all in that situation. It's funny to me that the moment I started praying for the person who betrayed me, God started to bless me in ways I could not image. I know that you are probably thinking, *Oh that was awesome! Look at God!* But wait, there's more.

Exactly one year after I was licensed, business was really starting to pick up again. Since word had gotten out about what happened, many didn't want to do business with her. Also, I was the one doing a lot of the behind the scenes work that she was unfamiliar with. So here we are a year later and I hear she has sold the company. Here I went again with those feelings that I tried to control but were getting away from me. I was sitting at my desk at work and thinking that she stole my dream only to sell it. I was furious, but had to reflect back on that sermon that initially caused me to pray for her. I found out a week later that she was working as a nurse for one of the companies that we were going to enter into contract. It took everything I had not to be mad.

Shortly after I'd heard about her selling, the owner of the company called me. I was so mad that I hung up on him. He continuously called me and I hung up every time. One day he called from a different number and asked if I would just meet him at his office for a brief visit and he would never bother me again. I agreed. When I got there he went on and on about all of these companies that he had which angered me, because I needed him to get to the point. As I looked around and saw everything that belonged to me, it brought back some bad memories. Finally, he said to me that he'd heard about what went on with my partner and me and that's when he decided to purchase the company. He then asked what I was driving. I told him that I was driving a van and asked why and he said that he wanted to give me my company back. I looked at him and said, "I'm not giving you a dime. She had taken all that she is going to get from me."

He looked at me and said, "This is why I first told you about my other companies. I don't need your money. Pull your van around so that I can help you load up all of these things." That day my business was restored times two. God had given me a "Double Portion." I could not believe it. I was happy to get my clients back. God was behind the scenes working the whole time.

Two months after that I received an email I thought was spam, but it kept populating in my inbox, so finally I called that number associated with the email only to find out that I had been nominated and was to receive an award. The award was "Top 50 Entrepreneurs of the Triangle." I could not believe it. Exactly two months later I received another email from *Business Leader* magazine stating that I was nominated and was to receive an award for "Top 300 Small Businesses of the South." This just blessed me. I was so grateful to God. Everything was starting to turn around. I had just received notice that I had been awarded a large contract with the federal government and I was well on my way. It's funny because I never thought that I would have been there again. I was back in business and happier than ever.

Two months after my last award I attended and award ceremony where I had been invited and surprisingly I was a recipient of another award. God was in full effect. The award received was for "Outstanding Healthcare Career Development." I received this award for creating jobs and working with the unemployment commission. I can't tell you the thoughts that were going through my head and this was only the beginning. Shortly after that I received and call from a show called *Health Briefs with Terry Bradshaw*. They wanted to interview me for their show. This is when I took a serious look over my life and what had transpired over such a short period of time. People will come in and out of your life, but the one thing that remains true is that God will always be true to His word. My business may have been stolen from me, but the vision was always in me. Anyone at any time can try and steal and replicate something that you have created, but only you can carry out the vision. The vision is and always will be yours. No one can take that from you, especially if God has given it to you.

While business was continually growing, so was my heart. Believe it or not I continued to pray for my ex-business partner and her family and I was actually beginning to do it was a softened heart. I realized that she could no longer hold me back; only I could do that.

Later that year, I received another unexpected phone call. This time is was from *Forbes* magazine. They wanted to interview me and feature me in their magazine. I must say that was a defining moment for me. That was the day that I stood up and said, "I made it."

I love to share this story with people because it is one that each time I tell it I feel that same emotions every time. The reason is because it's when I learned to trust "me" for the first time in my life. Being a nurse had always been my dream. I knew that I wanted my own business right out of high school. I knew what kind of business by the time I was twenty-one. What I didn't know was that I would accomplish it.

I was a teen mom right out of high school. I was told that I would never amount to anything. I was told by someone that I loved that because I lived in low income housing, I was exactly where he thought that I would be and would become exactly what they were. I took what everyone said about me to heart. I chose to believe them instead of listening to what God had to say about me. I tried to take my own life and almost succeeded. According to society, I'm not supposed to be here. According to God, I'm right where I'm supposed to be. I shared my story because I want people to know that no matter where you are and no matter what it looks like, God is always in the background putting in work.

Today, I am a home care and business consultant. I am still doing what I love but in another capacity. I now help others do what they love. I spend my time speaking at local colleges, churches, and half-way houses. I volunteer working with young ladies who were just like me. I want them to know that they matter and that their stories matter. My goal is to help them to do what others say they can't do. I want to teach them how to mute out and rule out the unqualified voices. At the end of the day the only opinion that matters is yours.

Even though things worked out for good, this was something that could have been avoided. So, I say to you, if you are looking to partner with someone for a business venture:

- First, stop and think if this is something you really need to do. You may just need to employ someone to oversee certain areas of your business. Had I done that, I would have had those large contracts initially and grown my business to where I could have had all of the key people in place and franchised that I had originally planned.

- Also, make sure that you know who the person really is. Pay attention to everything, even the people in their circle, because they could be the unqualified voices that are whispering to them.

- And the final thing that I would ask you to do is to pray and wait to hear from God. If you don't hear from Him, that may be your answer.

No matter the events and how they transpired, it was a very good learning experience and it opened up many more doors.

DREAM CHASER

BY JAMES 'JAZZY' JORDAN

"Success is knowing your purpose in life, growing to reach your maximum potential, and sowing seeds that benefit others."
    –John C. Maxwell

I don't have any Al Jolson music in my collection, but I do feel a strong connection to the Aretha Franklin version of *I'm Sitting On Top of the World*, the song Mr. Jolson originally made famous back in 1926. "I'm sitting on top of the world, just rolling along, just rolling along."

On top of the world in my penthouse apartment, in Building One at Galaxy Towers, I spent evenings looking across the Hudson River from high on the Palisades at the millions of glittery lights up and down Manhattan. Most often with fascinating guests—sometimes in big, lively groups, other times as one-half of an extremely and joyously intimate twosome. On the Fourth of July, when Macy's put on their fireworks show for all of New York City, it was right out my window. If I sold tickets, I would make some lovely money. All year round, the parties on that top-floor apartment were so intense that if my walls could talk, I would have had to pay out hush money in the millions.

For work, I reported to a corner office in the Sony Building at 55th and Madison Avenue, in the heart of New York facing down

Madison Ave with an 11ᵗʰ floor view that was like a web-slinging scene in a Spiderman movie. All around me, there was nothing but the best of the city—from the Trump Towers to Apple's biggest store to Central Park. I could jump on the E-train and get all over town in no time, or have a driver take me to parties and wait for me until I was ready to be driven back to the office or the penthouse. I was indeed on top of the world. But it wasn't always glitz and glamour.

I am the youngest member of a twelve-member family; there was my father, mother, six brothers, and three sisters. When I was four years old, my mom escaped her womanizing and physically abusive husband, whom I never got to know, and moved her family piecemeal to New Haven, Connecticut from South Carolina, where she single-handedly took on all child-rearing duties. It was tough growing up. The family's poverty was severe and humiliating. To keep the family together, everyone needed to pull together. My mother did her best, and you will never hear me complain because of what my mother had to do to keep food on the table and clothes on our backs. She worked day and night as a domestic and doing any other task she could find; holding two or three jobs at a time. I helped by scrubbing pots for a Jewish bakery through my high school years and brought home free day-old pastries and bread for both my family and neighbors.

After turning eighteen and graduating from high school, I was my own man and wanted to get away from New Haven to see the world. I told my mother, "Mom, I'm going to the Air Force in three weeks."

She responded, "How can you be going in the Air Force in three weeks? I didn't sign any papers or anything like that. How can that be?"

"Mom, I'm 18 years old. I went down, took all the tests, and did what I had to do. I'm going into the Air Force in three weeks." That was the extent of the conversation.

Joining the Air Force turned out to be one of the best decisions I'd ever made. I lost my Afro but gained confidence and determination.

I was stationed at Lackland Air Force Base, San Antonio, Texas for basic training and from there to Kadena Air Force Base, Okinawa, Japan. I had a break before leaving for Okinawa so I decided to go home for two weeks to catch up with family and see what was going on in my 'hood. It was awesome to be home again and see my brothers and sisters. They even had a welcome home party for me with all my friends, and it was a blast.

The next day I sat with my mother on the front porch and told her that I needed money to get back to the base. She looked at me and said, "I know you're lying. You would have never come home if you didn't have money to get back." She was right. She knew her son. I did not know it then, but that would be the last time I saw my mother alive. She died six months into my 18-month stay in Okinawa. I was devastated and felt alone in the world. No father and now no mother. I felt, with six billion people on the planet, I had nobody to love me, yet I was fortunate because the Air Force helped me become a man and prepared me for a life without my mother.

After my stint in the Air Force, I returned home to New Haven and started my first journey into the adventure of being self-employed. I became a Disc Jockey, spinning tunes at house parties, weddings, and any social event where people wanted music and momentum. I tagged myself James "Jazzy" Jordan. It was a self-appointed nickname, but one I'd come by honestly. One warm night during my Air Force service an elegant, soft-cheeked young woman slow danced with me and whispered in my ear, "I'm almost sorry I came here with him," she told me. "You're jazzy." She was already spoken for by one of my best friends and roommate, making her untouchable.

Jazzy can mean all sorts of things, like sexy and adventurous, free-flowing, and spontaneous. That was me, or at least that was a certain side of me. Another side, the "James" aspect of my personality, was careful and conscientious, respectful, and always focused on maintaining a strong position. Jazzy loved a good time. James intended to be ready whenever opportunity might show its beautiful face.

Now, when I got into the DJ booth, James and Jazzy were united, and both headed in the same direction. The two were a solid team, offense and defense in a single, seamless package, working the room with flair and taking care of business at the same time. I had access to my full potential and not only did I control my destiny, I controlled the pulse and flow of superb parties all over town. It meant being the ultimate music maestro, conducting the beats, tempo, melody, mood, and movement. It felt awesome. I was the supreme commander of fun and made people feel entertained. Soon I was one of the top street disc jockeys in town.

Working as a party starter was fun, and so were the various toys and beautiful clothing I was able to acquire with my suddenly healthier-than-ever cash flow. But it wasn't enough. I had no intention of abandoning my climb, and I wanted everyone to know I was the number one DJ in town. That required me setting out to win the 1979 annual competition for street disc jockeys in New Haven. I wanted to win badly so I entered, prepared, and practiced for the battle like I was Muhammad Ali. Among street disc jockeys, the turntables were the principal tools of our trade and were called the Wheels of Steel. My wheels had all the momentum. I was going to ride them to the top.

After a marathon exhibition, I was one of the six contestants still standing. The showdown had reached the penultimate phase— go hard, go long, or go home. One aspect of the competition I could not have prepared for was going without sleep. I was good on limited doses of sleep, but I knew my body. Six hours was my minimum, and it had always been that way. I've never been the guy who wanted to party all night. I'd rather go to bed on schedule, whenever possible, with sweet and agreeable company. Most of my opponents used chemical enhancements to stay awake and also to keep their edge. My strength didn't come from a pill. It came from an innate ability to thrill the audience. I was going to win by dealing from strength. I was not about to use drugs for this competition. I hadn't yet become a vegan or even a vegetarian, but I had plenty of respect for my body. I knew that I had to keep my edge and my alertness by exercising sheer will.

My drug for the evening was an incredibly beautiful woman, a redhead with African roots, whose green eyes and vibrant smile were brilliant enough to pull my eyes away, from time to time, from her gorgeous frame. But she wasn't mine. She danced up to the front of the stage whenever one of my sets began. All I had to do to keep up my energy and my edge was to focus on pleasing her. The rest of the crowd could follow along on our personal and highly hormone-inflected dance. And they did, happily. However, in the closing moments of each set, she would vanish. My dream that night was to sweep up the trophy, and then the redhead, in close succession. That imagery eclipsed all fatigue as the hours flew by, like a potion that inspired my natural best, not a drug that hijacked my mind and spirit.

The last stage was a true endurance run. It ran for eight hours, divided into four segments of two hours each. During those 120-minute segments, each competitor had to kick out a 20-minute set. It's hard to describe the energy, the desperation, the intensity, and the sweat that flowed over those eight hours, but every guy was determined to bust through like a running back using every ounce of strength and finesse to punch through a defensive line. The crowd was tough, too. If you didn't impress them, they would let you know in a heartbeat.

It came down to a close battle between Henry P., Leo The Lion, and me. I smoked them. For every turn at the mic, I put on a brand-new outfit that was even more vivid and eye-grabbing than the one before. I played music with an energy level you would not believe. The turntables were on fire, the speakers were steaming, and the crowd danced itself crazy to my beats. I looked around for my muse, hoping to take her home. But by then she had vanished for good. I had won, though, and from then on I had the right to tell everyone in New Haven, "I'm the DJ of the year."

DJ of the Year was a small dream in the bigger scheme of things, but I wanted it and I fought to make it come true. I planned, I worked both hard and smart, and the plan unfolded like magic. I was determined to win, not because there was a big trophy to take home at the end of the battle, or a big purse; I wanted people to know what I could do. And that was all I got but it meant the world to me. Everybody should experience the way I felt that day. But I had help from above.

The next target in my sight was radio. New Haven is the home of Yale University, which owned and operated their college radio station WYBC, a volunteer-run commercial radio station. I applied for a job there as an on-air DJ, a job without pay. Most of my air-time came between 11:00 A.M. and 3:00 P.M. on Saturdays and Sundays. I loved every unpaid minute of the radio gig. It gave me visibility that translated into a few DJ gigs in the evenings. In my mind, I scored myself a scholarship, a tuition-free ride at a professional radio school. At the same time, I was busily compiling tons of real-life, hands-on experience.

My time on the air attracted lots of new listeners for WYBC; thanks to synergy with the local following I'd built up from DJ-for-hire work. Even though I sometimes struggled financially, I was living sweet and large. I was 28, on my own, with a great gig on the air. I drove cool cars and had all the trappings a person my age could want. My only income, though, was from spinning at events. Sometimes I was flush with cash, sometimes not. But I was carving a path toward bigger goals.

At that time I was living on the second floor of a multifamily dwelling. My oldest sister, Laura, not only lived below me, but she also owned the house. Even though the landlady was family, I had to pay my way. Sometimes I barely kept the lights on. But I did not care. I was learning a lot, and I loved the work, living on the radio at WYBC hurt so good, and the itch got stronger every day. I was determined to keep scratching that itch. When you chase your dreams, pay attention to how you feel every day. If you feel good most of the time, chances are you're going in the right direction. One way to know if you're on the path to success is if people around you can see that you're intense, but they sometimes can't tell whether you're working or playing, that shows you must be on the right road.

I volunteered at the station as much as I could, beyond just weekends. It didn't even feel like work for me, more like structured playtime. I loved to paint pictures with my voice and to know I was entertaining my audience. I patterned my style after that of the guy I praised as the master DJ of all time—Frankie Crocker of WBLS in New York City. New Haven sits about 75 miles outside New York City, so I had almost daily opportunities to study the master's methods and madness. In addition to the great Frankie Crocker, WBLS was home to a host of other black superstar announcers. And on the other side of town, there was KISS FM, another great soul resource. Whenever I wasn't on the air myself, I was plugged into either one or the other of those dynamic NYC stations. I said to myself, "This is it! I've got to be on the radio!"

By stepping straight into the radio scene, by indulging and even encouraging my natural fascination with the artistry of the great New York jocks, I began to understand how they made their magic happen. Then gradually, I learned how to make my kind of magic. My dream was to do what my boy Frankie Crocker did. He was on air 4:00 P.M. to 8:00 P.M. during the afternoon drive time, that popular slice of the clock when people head home from work. Afternoon drive time was key to my radio business master plan. My next stop was a low-rated independent commercial New Haven station, WNHC AM. Management there had decided nothing else was working so they flipped the format to urban contemporary and it gave me the courage to take them my demo tape and resume.

Much to my surprise and dismay, they hired somebody else for the slot; someone they decided had more going on. They didn't care for me or my style but they had other slots to fill so with a bit of reluctance they signed me up for their graveyard shift. That hurt. Even if you were fantastic, energetically, and stylistically knocking it out of the park night after night, it could be forever before anyone noticed. No one was awake during those hours except for cops, pimps, ladies of the evening, and a few all-night truckers passing through.

At that time I wasn't the smoothest radio guy in the world. In fact, I was plenty rough around the edges and had not worked out some of the nuances of being a professional announcer. What WNHC management didn't understand right away was I already developed a significant New Haven audience. Between the volunteer station and playing in clubs, I had a built-in following. Everybody knew me in the black community, and I mean everybody. From midnight to 6:00 A.M. looked like my destiny, and I was going to embrace it. At least, that's the agreement I made with myself the day I was hired. But in fact, I never actually did that show. Not one single night of it.

I went to WNHC super early on my first day to put in some unpaid hours before my shift. I wanted to get totally comfortable with the layout and the equipment so I could hit the ground running at the stroke of midnight. As the time grew closer to 4:00 P.M. management became nervous. Their golden boy scheduled for the afternoon drive had not shown up. Then four o'clock arrived, but Golden Boy never did. With their backs against the wall, management had no choice. On a one-night basis they handed me the keys to afternoon drive. I felt poorly prepared, slightly nervous, and mistakenly gave the wrong number for listeners to call in. Instead of having them call the dedicated hot line number, I read the number for the station's main phone line. Imediately the switchboard went crazy. Secretaries ran into the control room, pleading "What are you doing? Everybody's calling the station!"

My first thought was that I put myself in deep trouble. "No," they said, "it's all right. But we don't understand what's going on. Nobody ever calls. It's always dead." Within minutes of my opening the mic, there was so much excitement that the phones lit up like the Rockefeller Center Christmas tree. The 4 to 8 P.M. show, afternoon drive, became my inevitable shift. I may have been an emergency substitution but from day one I earned it. From day one forward, I owned it. By the time my first shift was winding down, management had decided to double down their bet on James "Jazzy" Jordan. They said, "Why don't you be the music director, too." I agreed instantly. Going from overnights to afternoon drive and music director was just another part of my evolution.

I wanted this job more than any other job in my life. It fulfilled so many of the dreams that Frankie Crocker inspired in me. Being on the radio, talking to people, creating some happiness for listeners—that was what I wanted to do. It was a good start for Day One, and I knew there was more on the horizon for me.

There were exceptional people in my life who, though made of human flesh and blood, were angels I needed to embrace and then ultimately release when their transformative roles were completed. Looking back on the people that came to inspire me can best be described as my angels.

There's a major difference between a dream chaser and a daydreamer, and this is what *makes a dream chaser.*

- **Desire**

  Dream chasers affirm their greatest desires, believing that nothing is impossible. Desire is the starting point of all achievements. Dream chasers don't make excuses, and they finish what they start. They have an open mind and are not swayed by other people who try to bring them down.

- **Faith**

  Know your core purpose is fundamental for chasing down those dreams. Dream chasers set clear intentions to steer themselves in the direction they want to be, meaning they're equipped to make tough decisions and can easily turn down things not aligned with their core purpose. Rather than spending precious energy doubting their chosen path, dream chasers focus on being the very best version of themselves.

- **Surround yourself with other Dream Chasers**

  Good vibes are contagious, so dream chasers make sure they surround themselves with people who lift them up and believe in their dreams no matter how crazy they may seem. You become like the five people you spend the most time with; choose these people wisely.

- **Get out of your comfort zone—on a regular basis**

  As humans, we crave a level of certainty and often stay where we feel comfortable. Out of fear of the unknown, it is easy to stick to the familiar. The danger is missing out on all those amazing opportunities that are only possible if we take the risk and make the leap. When contemplating a bold move, ask yourself: What is the worst thing that could happen? What is the best thing that could happen?

- **Organize, plan, and run your race**

  Dream chasers don't concern themselves with what other people are doing; knowing full well that everyone is on their unique journey. Dream chasers have their own drum beat, not trying to align with the world. The world falls in line with dream chasers, not the other way around. A word of warning: it can be a lonely life, the life of a dream chaser.

- **Persistence/Never give up**

  If a Dream chaser finds themselves staring in the face of failure, dream chasers will choose to pick themselves up and keep going when things go wrong. If achieving your wildest dreams was easy, everyone would be doing

> it and the world would be a different place. Good things come to those who work their butts off and never give up.
>
> - **Make decisions**
>
>   Dream chasers don't procrastinate. They just do it. Fear, doubt, indecision are the biggest blockers working against us. They are the main three enemies of a dream chaser. Ask yourself this: What am I afraid of? Success?
>
>   Why are you procrastinating?
>
>   Do you truthfully believe in yourself?
>
>   Let me help you: It is hard, and you could fail but you will not if you are determined to succeed.

Frequently throughout my life I've had connections delivering beautifully-targeted, sometimes life-saving guidance. What others might call hunches or insights, I experienced directly-spoken messages of essential advice as positive proof of heavenly favor. Guidance is accessible to all willing to accept and embrace the divine mysteries of the universe. At the end of the day, success is about you and what you bring to this world, not what you take from it. That belief earns you a permanent perch sitting on top of the world.

So now let's talk about the dream chasing journey. I live by this—1 Corinthians 2:9, says, *"But as it is written, eye has not seen, nor ear heard, neither have entered into the heart of man, the things which God has prepared for them that love him."* Your destiny is waiting for you, so what is stopping you? Here is what I know: quitters never win, and winners never quit.

FINDING JOY IN INFERTILITY

BY MIA A. WILLIAMS

"For this child I have prayed..."

1 Samuel 1:27

Every woman is capable of becoming a mother. Like a fingerprint, the road to motherhood is unique, and each story contains its own message of hope, promises, surprises, expectancy, and sometimes even uncertainty, confusion, and doubt. Every woman's story is different: some experience the miracle of pregnancy after having prayed and fasted; some use in vitro fertilization (IFV); there is surrogacy, artificial insemination, step-parenting, or adoption; and then there's just good old-fashioned naturally occurring pregnancies. Some women raise their nieces and nephews as their own. Some women become community mothers by nurturing, feeding, caring for, and loving on the neighborhood children. Some women are spiritual mothers, praying for and with us, and offering Godly wisdom to help guide us through this crazy, beautiful thing called life. Some women are mothers to four-legged, furry friends or friends who chirp, slither, scamper, or swim. No matter how it's achieved, our stories illustrate and reinforce that motherhood is beautiful, sacred... divine.

For many women, being a mom is one of the most important roles they will ever take on. It is a role that is fulfilling, gives us great meaning, and teaches us to be selfless, to sacrifice, and to love unconditionally. I've heard women describe motherhood as the most intense love that they've ever experienced. But for all the joys of motherhood, the journey leading to motherhood is sometimes heartbreaking.

My own journey to motherhood is a complex hybrid of "am" and "want." I "am" a mother to an amazing son through marriage, and I "want" to have biological children. After three years of trying, what my heart desires most eludes me. This is my journey to find joy in infertility.

My original plan was not to have children. I was the oldest of three children and therefore bore the brunt of the responsibility for my younger siblings. My mother taught me early on about being responsible, and I had my fair share of whoopings and punishments for trouble my siblings got into while under my care. In my mother's mind, it simply boiled down to, "You're the oldest. You should have been watching them."

My mother wanted a life for me that was better than hers and her parents before her, so she demanded excellence. As the oldest, I had to set the example for my siblings and younger cousins. Perhaps this shaped my views that I would excel in life by going to college, becoming the first person in my family to earn a Bachelor's degree, and have a fabulous career traveling the world. I envisioned that this future would somehow be hindered if I had to drag around diaper bags and baby formula. I had a plan for my life, and that plan simply did not include having children.

Not that I didn't value family—I cannot imagine a family more close-knit than mine—but somewhere along the lines, I equated success and excellence with awards and achievements. In my immaturity and youth, I thought that you had to sacrifice one to have the other. Not to mention the fact that I absolutely *love* children; in addition to my siblings, I babysat nearly every one of my fifteen younger cousins. As a teenager, I earned money over the summer and on weekends babysitting, and as a young adult, fresh out of college, I worked at a daycare facility. It was one of the best jobs I've ever had. I love kids and they love me. I am the person who will arrive to a birthday party solo and leave with a car full of kids headed to my place for a sleepover.

The exact moment when God shifted my heart occurred the night I gave my final presentation and completed the capstone course in my Masters program. I was only supposed to take one year off between undergrad and grad school, but as life would have it, one year turned into six, so when I finally completed my Masters, I was ecstatic to have finally achieved this goal I set so many years ago. Not to mention the countless hours of sacrifice, studying, writing, tutoring, and completing projects and presentations were over.

I arrived home after my final presentation and grabbed my laptop, bag, and books from the back seat—for the last time—and walked to my apartment door. I could have jumped in the air and clicked my heels together I was so happy. I opened the door and clicked the light switch, instantly flooded with the familiar… and the foreign. My couch was where it had always been with my favorite painting perched above it; my desk sat in disarray, scattered with pens, highlighters, and printed drafts from frantic last minute changes to my final presentation; my bookshelf sat against the wall, its orderly array of books, candles, and photos the antithesis of my desk. But instead of the warmth I typically felt when returning home, I only felt the vast emptiness of the space.

A harsh reality hit me: while my classmates had gone home to their respective spouses, children, and loved ones, I came home to beautiful *things*. There was no one there to embrace me and tell me how proud they were of me; no one to pat me on the back for a job well done; no one to celebrate with. The Kate Spade bag on my arm could not propose a toast in my honor. Macy's was not going to throw me a parade. Dooney & Burke did not show up with a cake and balloons. I was alone.

I once heard Oprah say that life speaks first in whispers, then nudges, then eventually a full-blown disaster. Well, I had turned a blind eye to all of life's whispers and nudges and I was standing in the center of a self-created disaster. Somewhere along the line, I had forgotten what mattered most after God: family. I was immediately humbled and reminded that in my stubbornness and determinedness to be independent, career focused, and driven, I had become alone.

God used that moment to show me what a gift family is and to remind me of how valuable and precious it is to have people in your corner rooting for you, praying for you, and pushing you when you don't have the strength to push yourself. He showed me how I had substituted store bought items for true happiness and meaningful relationships. Like I had been given the correct prescription lens after years of seeing just shadows, I had new vision for my future, and I knew God's will for my life included a family. Eight months after this shift, God blessed me with a husband and a step-son.

It's now three years later and despite our best efforts we have not been able to conceive. It pains me to accept that I am one of 1.5 million women in the U.S. between the age of fifteen and forty-four experiencing infertility. The Center for Disease Control and Prevention (CDC) defines infertility as the inability to get pregnant after twelve consecutive months of unprotected sex. Infertility is broken down into two types:

- Primary Infertility refers to couples who have not become pregnant after at least one year of having sex without using birth control methods.

- Secondary infertility refers to couples who have been able to get pregnant at least once, but now are unable.

There are many myths and misconceptions surrounding infertility. One of the biggest is that all infertility is the same; it is not. There are many different stories, reasons, and contributing factors why people have difficulty conceiving including age, smoking habits, endometriosis, thyroid problems, ovulation disorders, Polycystic Ovarian Syndrome (PCOS), low testosterone in the male, exposure to Sexually Transmitted Diseases (STDs), cysts, fibroids, exposure to environmental toxins and lead, medical exposure such as chemotherapy and radiation, and just the general category of "unknown."

In my case, tests have not revealed anything wrong. I am healthy—I could stand to lose a few pounds, but I'm healthy nonetheless. I take vitamins. Drink water. Avoid soda. Don't smoke. Cut back on coffee. And yet… nothing. All the tests so far have not revealed any underlying issues contributing to my condition, and honestly, this doesn't make it any easier to cope with. Perhaps if I knew exactly what the issue was I could *do* something about it. On the other hand, if I knew the exact reason, would it cause me to lose hope?

My husband and I are praying our way through our infertility struggle. We are praying for a miracle, leaning on one another and learning to trust in God's timing. The best way I can illustrate my day-to-day struggles with infertility is to share my most intimate moments as told through my journal. The following is a compilation of my journal entries, reflections, prayers, and silent cries to God in my journey to find joy in infertility.

Seeking Answers Where There Are None

People bombard my personal space with their heartless, thoughtless questions—*"Why don't you have children?" "When are you going to start having babies?" "No babies yet?" "What are you two waiting on?" "Why aren't you pregnant yet?"*

To all of those questions the answers are, "I don't know." If I could pinpoint a cause, perhaps I would be able to fix it or take some corrective action. Perhaps it would be easier to say, "I don't have children yet because I have (fill in the blank)." Would it be better if I could hand them a pamphlet with my issue, its symptoms, and causes and say, "See? This is not my fault!"? Would people be more understanding if I had a better excuse than, "We're waiting on God."?

I need to be fair; sometimes our loved ones don't realize that even the simplest questions can inflict unintentional pain. They don't realize how simply watching TV can bring about an outburst of hysterical crying, and that every baby shower and birthday invitation is a potentially painful trigger. On my end, I have to realize these questions are normal and should be expected. I need to remove my emotions and be able to respond with grace. "Yes, we want more children. Yes, we are trying. As far as we know, everything is okay. Please, just pray for us."

I have suffered in silence. I have felt alone. I am constantly afraid. I have dealt with feeling guilt and shame for not being able to do something my body should be able to do, something that for other women is so normal. I don't know why we are not pregnant. I don't know when we will become pregnant. I simply don't know.

Barren & Bargaining

My maternity clock has rocketed into over-drive. I long for the pitter patter of little feet across the floor, for stinky diapers, for family traditions at Christmas time, for tea parties and fashion shows, for recitals and little league games, for fundraisers and girl (or boy) scouts, for stories to reflect back on when I am old and gray. Sometimes, my desire is overwhelming. I can only compare it to clicking on a light switch and suddenly flooding a dark room with blinding light. I used to joke with my husband that we'd have seven children; now, I feel like I'm bargaining with God to please bless me with just one. *Lord, if You bless me with just one child, I promise I will dedicate him/her back to You and raise him/her up to be faithful servants in Your kingdom forever.* I know you cannot bargain with God; that's not how faith works. But there are times when I feel desperate, empty, and at a loss.

Angry

There are times when I am like a child throwing a tantrum: "Are you freaking kidding me? Seriously? Why me? Why me? Why ME? WHY ME!" Or, maybe the real question is, why NOT me? There are times when my heart swells with the hope that comes with a late period, only to come crashing down around me in a sea of disappointment. On those days, I am angry and irrational and I question everything: *Does my husband have even the slightest clue what I am going through? Can he possibly understand what I am experiencing? After all, he has a biological son, so he can't possibly be able to relate.*

And just like that, my anger spills over into our relationship. I have an attitude. I'm short tempered. I indulge my anger in food. I feel worse. I try to change gears but overcompensate for my guilt by shifting the blame onto him: *perhaps there is something in his past that God is not pleased with and we are now both paying the price.*

Then God, in His infinite wisdom, reminds me that we—my husband, God, and I—are in this together. There is no blame; there is no guilt. God confirms for me that my husband's desires match my own: he too is praying for our future children. And I am comforted with the thought that even if we never have a child together, I have already been blessed with something I did not have before: we are a family. I will cling to him, and we will cling to God and to one another.

Patience

There are times when I feel sick and tired of waiting. Seriously! Everyone and I mean EVERYONE is pregnant! Even my neighbor's dog just had a litter. I am watching the world around me have babies. Married after me... Pregnant. Not married... Pregnant. Married, divorced, *then* pregnant. Didn't she just have a baby? ...Pregnant... again. She doesn't even like kids! ...Pregnant. How can you have seventeen kids (and counting) and I *still* not be pregnant?

It is bittersweet to watch all of your childhood friends, younger siblings, and cousins grow up and have families of their own. I seriously think I have been to a million baby showers over the years as they had their first child, then second, and sometimes a third. There is always the slightest twinge of sadness—and perhaps jealousy—as I attend baby shower after baby shower, birthday party after birthday party, and hit the "like" button on all of those cute baby photos on Facebook. I can't help but wonder when my time will come.

God reminds me not to covet. To be genuine in my well wishes, congratulations, and in the expressions of love I show others. I have to trust that God will fulfill his plan in my life through this exercise of patience.

Confused

God, why would you change my heart only to deny me? This doesn't make sense. Perhaps this is my own fault. What if the one thing I desire escapes me because many, many years ago I spoke it into existence? The Bible says, "Life and death is in the power of the tongue" Proverbs 18:21. But doesn't it also say, "When I was a child, I talked like a child; I thought like a child, I reasoned like a child. When I became a man [adult] I put away childish things" 1 Corinthians 13:11? I no longer think like that child, so *why do you deny me?*

I am confused, and today all I hear is silence.

Shame & Regret

I was fresh out of college, broke, living from couch to couch. I had nothing. *There are no excuses.* I had an abortion after undergraduate school. My decision fills me with shame, remorse, pain, regret…unforgiveness. I have never told anyone this part of my story. I refuse to talk about it. I often think that this is the reason why I have been unable to have children: forgiveness is an uphill battle. My husband lovingly reminds me that this is not how God operates, that God forgives us for our sins and that He will bless us with children in His own perfect timing.

"Mia," he says, "God's timing is always best."

Fear & Contentment

I fear that I will never have biological children. I fear that I will disappoint my husband. I can't help but wonder if I will be unable to give this wonderful man—whom I love so much—more children, especially after he has given me so much in sharing his son with me. I fear that I will dishonor God and be unable to fully love the son he has already blessed me with because I am not content. I fear discontentment.

Then God uses something as simple as a Facebook post from Joel Osteen to remind me—again—to be content and to trust in his timing. "When we are discontent, it dishonors God. We're so focused on what we want that we take for granted what we have. Being content doesn't mean we don't want change, we just settle where we are, or we give up our dreams. It means we're trusting in God's timing."

I plaster on a happy face. Today it is false but if I wear it long enough, perhaps it will become real. Happiness is a choice, right?

Surrender

I give up! I feel like I should stop trying. In fact, I've had people tell me that once I stop trying to get pregnant, that's when it will occur. I've even had people tell me that if God wanted me to have children, I would have them. Point. Blank. Simple. It is never *that* simple. Sometimes we are waiting on God, and sometimes God is waiting on us: to step out in faith, to surrender to His will, to sacrifice, to humble ourselves, to ask for His help, to get out of our own way. Women in the Bible like Hannah, Rachel, and Sarah give me hope. Sarah thought she was too old, but God gave her Jacob. Hannah poured out her heart to God, and God gave her Samuel. Rachel cried desperately to become a mother, and God gave her Joseph.

I will *never* give up.

I know her name. In my journals and in notes tucked into my Bible, I've written my daughter's name. I've written the name of her sisters and brothers. These are miracles, hopes, dreams, and prayers waiting to be answered. My vision has been written and made plain (Habakkuk 2:2). I am circling my future children in prayer: their health, their careers, their future spouses, their relationship with Christ, their contributions to society, and their impact on the world. My prayers will live forever. Prayers never die.

Finding Joy In Infertility

Infertility is heartbreaking: there are few words in the English language that can describe how it feels month after month of your menstrual cycle, declaring loudly, boldly, and unsympathetically that you are NOT pregnant. I sometimes have anxiety when I think of the possibility of never having biological children. I deal with it one day at a time. Today I'm okay, but tomorrow I may be curled into the fetal position on the bathroom floor with the shower running and my hands covering my mouth to muffle the sound of my cries. Dealing with infertility drains my energy, burdens me, taunts me, and threatens to steal my happiness… *if* I allow it. Amidst all of this heartbreak and pain, there is also joy.

My bathroom is often my place of solitude. It's where I go to cry and to pray. Tucked away in my bathroom cabinet, on a pink sticky note written in blue ink, are two simple yet profound words: FERTILE GROUND. For me, these words are God's promise and his assertion that despite medical prognosis (or lack thereof), despite the emotional exhaustion that comes from my day-to-day struggle with infertility, despite my confusion, my longing, and my perception of lack, I am fertile ground. I have already triumphed over infertility. The battle is won.

In 2015, God promised me that I would give birth. Only, it wasn't to a baby; it was to a book. And that book has given me a platform to help women heal from living in shame and the burden of unforgiveness. Through speaking about my experiences and sharing my testimony, not only am I honoring God and allowing Him to use me for His glory, I am also reaping the harvest of seeds sown in fertile ground.

In the last year, God has blessed me to connect with so many women who have not had children: sometimes by choice, most times not. This has helped me realize that God gives birth through us in many ways: through our books, our businesses, our ministries, our gifts, and our creativity. I am in awe of God when I consider that every time I create something, it is my baby: a fall-themed wedding card box for my mother's wedding, a keep-safe shadow box for a childhood friend for her baby shower, a Valentine's Day wreath for my mother. Even my ability to share my stories and experiences in books, blogs, and speaking engagements is an expression of my gifts and creativity and thus, my fertility. We are capable of giving birth every day in so many ways.

My struggles with infertility has helped me to see me in a new way and I truly have found joy. My joy is found in my unique gifts and creativity. My joy is found in the comfort, encouragement, strength, and unwavering faith of my husband. My joy is found in my son, who always knows the right words to say to flood my heart with love and my eyes with tears. My joy is found in the possibilities and dreams for the future. My joy is found in my connection to the Son. My joy is found in the fact that I have learned that I don't have to accept infertility as my final diagnosis; instead, I can accept abundance, forgiveness, grace, laughter, and love. I accept that my infertility is a temporary experience which God is using to grow me. I accept that I am full of creativity and original thoughts and that I am fertile ground.

I'm not saying that I am giving up on my desire to have children; my husband and I will exhaust every possibility available before we even get close to giving up, and even then we will explore options for adoption. But I am accepting that my journey to motherhood will be unconventional and uniquely my own. While I wait, I plan to continue focusing on being mentally, spiritually, financially, and physically healthy in preparation for the baby we have prayed for.

My heart breaks for my sisters who are also battling infertility. There is a silent bond, an internal sisterhood, that we share because we know the heartbreak, the pain, the anticipation, and the shattered hopes every time the pregnancy test says you're not pregnant. We know the anger and disappointment when your period shows up. And yes, at times, we may feel a tad bit jealous. But if I've learned nothing else from this experience, there are a few things that I know for sure:

- There is nothing taboo or shameful in admitting and sharing your struggles; you do not have to suffer in silence.

- You too are fertile ground.

I place emphasis on finding "joy" in infertility, but you could place any number of adjectives in place of the word "joy" as it fits your situation. You can find happiness in infertility, like the happiness of adopting a child and knowing you are caring for someone who may never have known the love and care of a family. You can find comfort in infertility, like the comfort of a supportive spouse. You can even find humor in infertility: I've discovered blogs that actually advocate laughter as a way to cope with infertility, as laughter can help to bring about healing. You can find hope in infertility, strength in infertility, peace in infertility, courage in infertility, and even greater intimacy in infertility.

I encourage you to write your journey, to document your story, to capture your thoughts and emotions on paper. Write to help get you through the confusing times, the fearful times, the dark times; I know it has helped me tremendously. Continue to pray, continue to accept and receive all the positive things life has to offer. Continue to live. Continue to cling to your spouse for support. And most of all, continue to believe in and explore all the ways that you are fertile ground.

WIPE EVERY TEAR: LIVING WITH DEPRESSION

BY ETTIE JEAN WHITFIELD

"You made all the delicate inner parts of my body and knit me together in my mother's womb."

Psalm 139:13

Today I sit on the patio enjoying the first really "nice" day of spring; it is April in Chicago. A joyous shout out to nature. It is time to spring into action; the birds are building their nests, the trees are sending out tender leaves, and the earth wakes up to begin the cycle of life all over. I am reminded of God's words that for everything there is a season.

My mind turns to thoughts of how all living things follow a pattern. I think of my grandchildren who are now in the spring of their life, reaching out to learn the joys and disappointment of new beginnings. Their parents who now are in the summer of their lives experiencing the joys, disappointments, and frustrations of daily living. Their experiences of having young lives now to guide and help prepare for the future. We are blessed in knowing that we have a God who created us and leads us in all ways.

"You, O Lord, reign forever; Your throne endures from generation to generation."

Lamentations 5:19

109

I was born in Jamaica, the third of four children. My sister is nine years older than I am, my older brother, seven years my senior, and a younger brother is five years my junior. As far back as I can remember, I spent all my summer holidays with my maternal grandparents on the land owned by the family stretching back for generations. As a result, the bond with my great grandmother, grandparents, aunts, uncles, and cousins were very strong and lasting.

My father was the head bartender at one of the major hotels on the Island, working long hours at a job he enjoyed. Later, as he retired from the hotel industry, he opened Caterer's Domestic Science Training Center, the first school on the Island to train bartender and domestic help to work in the hotel industry, on the Island and abroad. My mother stayed home until my younger brother started school, and then she started her own catering business within the school, with an emphasis on baking. My older sister and my younger brother looked like my dad and carried many of his characteristics. My older brother and I looked more like our mother and had many of her characteristics.

As a child, I was a loner and as I grew up I started to withdraw from the rest of the family. I became quite proficient in needlework, and could often be found lost in the pages of a book. Fortunately, Patrick, my older brother, recognized what was happening and stepped into the gap with love, encouragement, and guidance. We became very close and truth be told I idolized him. I felt able to tell him things that I did not understand, or situations which troubled me. He always had an answer. After an uneventful elementary school experience, I was successful with the exams necessary to enter high school, and entered just before my eleventh birthday.

The high school experience was a very difficult one for me. I was, at best, a mediocre student and preferred to stay under the radar as much as possible. It seemed all the teachers knew my sister who attended years ahead of me, and I just did not live up to the standards she set. It was easier to keep a low profile and just not compete.

Having very few friends, I spent a lot of time by myself and I was not good company. I found myself sliding deeper into a cloud of sadness and loneliness, crying a lot and wishing I could just disappear. In my mind nothing I did was "good enough." The feeling of worthlessness grew like a lump in my stomach, causing me to feel physically ill whenever I was called upon to do anything. Taking tests, taking part in church activities and piano recitals would find me vomiting for days before the event.

At about the age of 10, I joined the Girl Guides and was able to shine, as I was not competing with anyone else from the family. I enjoyed this period of time and became involved in the organization, eventually became a leader and mentor for the younger children.

Looking back, I realize that Mom and Patrick could not have put a label to my behavior any more than I could recognized it for what it was. Patrick made time to talk to me and in many ways tried to make me feel special.

Close to graduation from high school, my home economics teacher sat with me. She observed my behaviors throughout the high school years and was concerned. This was probably the first time anyone outside of the family ever showed an interest in ME, talking to me and allowing me to at least voice concern for my situation, thoughts, and fears. She suggested that I apply for scholarships from colleges out of the country in order to further my education.

I graduated at 16, doing much better on my exams than I anticipated, but I was too young to get a job, so I went to Patrick for advice. He suggested we go to Mama and discuss the possibilities open to me, and it was decided that they would pool their resources and get me enrolled in a 'Commercial School' to be trained in secretarial skills.

Little did I realize the road that would put me on, and how my life would be changed because of that opportunity. I always wanted to be a nurse, and for some reason the thought of being a secretary did not excite me, but my choices were few, and if I ever wanted to escape my present circumstances I would have to do what was necessary to help myself. So it was June 1953, shortly after graduating high school I started taking courses at the Durham Commercial School. I made a few friends and my life seemed to be on a fairly even keel. Six months into the two-year course, one of my friends wanted to take an entry level test to start a job. I went with her and while I was there decided to take the exam to see what was involved. I lied about my age and took the exam. Two weeks later, I was accepted for the position. Now I found myself in a real dilemma not having told my mother that I had skipped school to take the test. It was time to confess to Patrick what I had done and ask for help in making a decision. It was suggested I could take the secretarial classes in the evenings and on Saturdays to complete my year of Commercial lessons in order to get my certificate. I started working as the Junior Secretary to Mr. Tomlinson, the Senior Attorney at the Supreme Court.

After some time working with Mr. Tomlinson, I went to him explaining that I really wanted to go abroad to school but had no idea of how to go about applying. He started guiding me through the process of applying to Nursing Schools in England and Canada, as well as starting the process of applying for a passport. During this period of time I started seeing a gynecologist to get answers about the abdominal discomfort I experienced. I was told that my uterus was not fully developed and was sitting on my back instead of suspended. I was also told that I would probably never be able to have children. This did not really have much of an impact on me then.

"O Lord, I am calling to You. Please hurry! Listen when I cry to You for help."

Psalm 141:1

By the beginning of 1955, I had sent out many letters of inquiry and applications to many schools in England, Scotland, and Canada. All were rejected. At this point Mr. Tomlinson got involved.

He contacted a friend in Kansas who told him about a small Mennonite college in North Newton, Kansas that had a very good foreign students program and where he was acquainted with some faculty members. I completed the application, Mr. Tomlinson wrote a letter, and I was accepted, granted a financial package and the promise of opportunities of work that would keep me solvent. With summer jobs that sounded perfect.

My challenge was that I was accepted for the 1955 fall school year and had no idea how I would pull this off in such a short period of time. I had not worked long enough to save much money so that was another obstacle I would have to overcome. Only then did I find out that Patrick and Mom had decided to save everything I had earned. I was overjoyed to know that I was actually going to be able to pay for an airline ticket. I was set. I was excited. I was on my way to freedom.

I should have known there was a valley that would need to be crossed, and that the saying "nothing worth having was going to be easy" would be proven true. Somehow my dad found out and took exception to the fact that Mr. Tomlinson had been instrumental in helping me obtain my documents and withdrew his offer to assist with tuition. Patrick and Mama assured me things would work out, but I could not see how that amount could be recovered. Looking back, I can now see what I could not in the midst of my disappointments. We serve an awesome God and He had a plan, also there were people praying for me and God DOES hear and answer those prayers, sometimes not what we ask for but definitely what we need. Patrick withdrew everything he had saved and with the help of Mama and some relatives, I was able to get enough for tuition for the first year.

"You discern my going out and my lying down: You are familiar with all my way."
Psalm 139:3 NIV Study Bible

I was deposited at the foot of the stairs leading up to the Administration building where I was to register for classes and receive my dorm assignment. When I arrived, the staff were expecting me, their "Foreign Student," and I immediately was taken under the wing of freshman advisers to help me get registered. There was only one drawback...they did not speak Jamaican and I did not speak 'Kansan'. It really got pretty comical but helped lighten the transition as everyone tried to understand me and I tried to understand them. We eventually got through that process only to find out that we had a house mother, but five freshman girls had no house. Time for a backup plan; they emptied the first floor of one of the Sophomore Dorms, put in five beds, and we had a temporary dorm room, which, as a group, we chose to make a permanent dormitory. We worked well together and did not want to be separated. We now had three Kansans, one Canadian, and one Jamaican.

I had made inquiries about my trunk which should have been delivered that day to the campus. Needless to say that did not happen, so here I was with no sheets for making my bed and no clothes for the start of classes the next day. I sat on my bed not knowing what to do until one of the dorm mates approached and very slowly asked me why I was not making my bed. I explained the situation best I could and she immediately remade her bed giving me one of the sheets and a pillow case. She quickly went through her things and found a dress I could wear the next day to start classes. Hand washing clothes became a daily activity until my trunk was delivered a week later.

As a result of this incident, Marlene and I became good friends. As the weekend approached Marlene made arrangements with her brother, who was also a student, to go home for the weekend. They decided I could not stay at the College since all the classmates were going to be away, so they bundled me into the car and took me home with them. They introduced me to their parents who acted as if I had always been there and was a part of the family. It took no time for a very strong bond, which exists to this day, to be formed. It also gave me another side of white/black relationships to ponder.

The depression I still suffered from was not severe and I was able to hide it fairly well. The occasional crying and withdrawal from my classmates were considered bouts of homesickness and that suited me very well. I refer to this sadness and moodiness as 'depression' now, although I really did not have a name for it until I was officially diagnosed while in Nurses Training.

After a year in College, I applied to the School of Nursing associated with the College for admission, but was denied. The class was already full and I was told I should try the next year, I accepted this for what they said and determined to apply early the next year.

At the beginning of my junior year I was finally accepted in Bethel Deaconess Hospital School of Nursing after petitioning my counselor for advice about what I needed to do to be accepted. Apparently they had never had a Negro student before and did not know what the fallout would be, but the pressure from the College along with the acceptance of a Hopi Indian Student, forced their hand.

During my time in Nursing school, I saw my mother once as she came to my sister's graduation from Friend's University in Wichita, Kansas. It was a good reunion and I promised her I would return home for a visit after I had established myself and was able to do so.

"For I know the plans I have for you," says the Lord. "They are plans for good and not for disaster, to give you a future and hope."

Jeremiah 29:11

After graduation I worked in Kansas City then in New York. While in New York, I had a very traumatic breakup in a relationship which affected me both physically and emotionally. I applied for a job in St Louis, Missouri and promptly moved there. I was not in a healthy place emotionally or mentally when I left New York. Not long after I started working, I was able to develop a rapport with one of the doctors on staff who eventually diagnosed me with chronic depression and began the process of treating the condition in an effort to get my life back together. I was not able, however, to share everything that was driving it and soon wrote that off as something I could handle on my own now that I had a label for it and was sure I could now handle it.

At that period in time, depression was considered a mental illness and carried a stigma with it. The hospital was a large teaching hospital which I quickly learned was segregated and I would be working in the Colored section. I enjoyed working with the staff and patients, grew in my profession, and soon was promoted to Assistant to the head nurse, only the second one in the hospital. I worked as many hours as I could in order to stay busy so there was not much down time and at the same time earn and save as much as possible to get an apartment. My classmate from school with whom I roomed with in Kansas City also worked at the hospital and we again roomed together.

Of course she worked in the main hospital. After she got her first paycheck, I discovered that she was paid more than I was. Only then did I understand why we were cautioned not to compare paychecks or we would be fired. I learned that the black nurses were paid less than the white nurses and that was an accepted standard. We decided to fight that particular standard and within two months my salary was adjusted to match hers.

It was not long before she started dating. Since I was not in the position to meet anyone of color, I did not date at all. The feeling of isolation and inadequacy began to take over my thoughts again. I also suffered from insomnia and sought help for the insomnia and the depression and again approached my physician. I was still not open to see a psychiatrist as I felt the stigma of mental illness would define my employment and I was not open to taking a chance on that happening. The doctor prescribed an antidepressant which also helped me with the insomnia.

During my time working on the night shift, I met and became friends with a mature lady who worked as a private duty nurse. We spent our supper times together and before long she became my confidant. I really was interested in meeting someone I could date and maybe share a life with but the chances of meeting anyone in my present situation were not promising. I did not come in contact with many people of color. I shared all this one quiet night at work with my friend and she decided to have a party where she would invite some Interns from another hospital and some of her friends and relatives.

It was not a large group but there were enough young people to be able to mingle and enjoy the evening. As the evening drew to a close her nephew approached me to ask if I would be willing to go out with a friend of his who he thought would be perfect for me. Needless to say the answer was a resounding 'yes' and he promised to call me if anything could be arranged. Actually I did not expect anything to come of it so was surprised when he did call to arrange a double date. I looked forward to the date with a great deal of anxiety. I really could not imagine who would want to have a blind date and then what would they think about me. The date went well. I was totally enthralled by his manner and personality. Did I mention he was tall, dark, and handsome?

As the date ended, we said our good nights and he went on his way. Nothing was said about maybe going out again so I thought he was just not interested and that was that. However not long after he left, he called to tell me that he had really enjoyed meeting me and asked if I would like to go out again. I, of course, was definitely interested in going out with him and over the next three months we dated and got to know each other. I resumed my life working at the hospital. We got to really know each other, and started planning our wedding set for April 1967 in Jamaica.

> *For I am convinced that neither death nor life, neither angels or demons, neither the present nor the future, nor any powers, nor height nor depth, nor anything else in all creation, will be able to separate us from the love of God that is in Christ Jesus our Lord."*
>
> Romans 8:38 The NIV Study Bible

Death can't and life can't. The angels can't and the demons can't. Our fears for today, our worries about tomorrow, and even the powers of hell can't keep God's love away. Ken and I were married in a small wedding at the church where I had been christened as a baby, accepted Christ, and was received into the church family at age 13. This was a special time for me. My parent's gift was the reception and my mother made my beautiful cake. Many friends and family were able to attend, as well as some from the United States.

After a dream honeymoon, we returned to St. Louis to the apartment we rented. We were ready to face the future, whatever it threw at us. At least that was my vision and my determination. I returned to my job at the hospital which had now been integrated, and was promoted to Head Nurse, one of two black head nurses throughout the hospital. Things, however, did not go as smoothly as I would have liked on the job. I had a few obstacles to overcome, but I had the determination to be successful.

First of all, I was black and all the RN's were white. The Clinical Nursing Specialist (CNS) on the floor were black but they resented someone who was so much younger than them with much less experience than they had, telling them what to do. It was a battle but one that I eventually won. I found strength in my marriage; at last I had a friend with whom I could share my dreams and frustrations. Ken had a confidently strong personality which I very much needed to move forward in life.

Our first miracle was born in 1969, a beautiful, healthy girl. We had our second miracle in 1970, again a beautiful, healthy girl. The doctor swiftly put an end to trying for another, so we counted our blessings and settled in.

In 1969 we moved to a home in Rock Hill, Missouri where Ken quickly became involved in the politics of the city. After assessing the situation of his traveling and erratic work hours, I decided that it would be best served for me to be a 'stay at home' mom. It was a hard decision to make. I missed the adult interaction and the feeling of achievement I experienced in the workplace. It did not take long for all my insecurities to resurface and start me back down the road to depression. I was unable to express what was happening to me and since I had very few friends, no one to really confide in.

It was even difficult trying to explain to Ken why I was so sad and would cry at the drop of a hat. Everything just seemed to stay bottled up inside waiting to explode. It all came to a boil and exploded one morning as I tried to take care of the girls, who for some reason, were very fussy, probably picking up on my inability to cope, totally pushing me over the edge. I could not think, I could not function, I totally felt unable to cope any more. Sobbing, I looked at my girls and had no idea what to do. Finally, I was able to call my doctor, crying hysterically, asking for help. He must have sensed the absolute desperation, as within an hour he had called a pharmacy and had medication delivered with instructions to call him one hour after I had taken it.

I was eventually able to get the girls down for some quiet time and slowly got myself back together. I called him, calmer but knowing that I could not continue down the road I was on. I was able to tell Ken what was happening and we agreed I needed some professional help.

By the year 1970, depression was not the stigma it was considered in the early 1960's.

More people—many celebrities—were able to acknowledge publicly that they suffered from depression and expressed the relief they felt as they received treatment for the condition.

For three years I saw a psychiatrist, learning to come face to face with my perceived reasons for my unhappiness and inability to cope. It was not easy talking about what seemed to be deeply embedded in my soul, but in order to heal and get healthy for myself and my family I knew I had to express my deepest insecurities and low self-esteem and find some ways to cope. It was not easy and still will surface even now. I had to learn to accept myself for who I was, to forgive myself and those who I thought, and knew, had wronged me, which was very difficult to do. Understanding that the forgiving was not necessarily for the other person but rather to make me whole again was difficult to accept and near impossible to do. It took a concerted decision, and was difficult to let go of the hurts that I had held so close for so long.

After years of treatment I was able to express how I felt to my father and express the resentments I had felt asking for his forgiveness and asking that he accept my apologies for my reaction for the hurt I felt. I also had to learn that if I professed to a faith in God I needed to internalize that truth and live it. During this time my prayer life really grew, mostly out of desperation as I continued to learn to live with a low grade depression. I learned the place heredity plays in this illness and how to recognize the triggers that preceded a bout of sadness and using prescribed medication to control it. I realized that it's not something to be ashamed of, using my experiences as a tool to help others, and continue to control it as needed.

I started to dig deeper into scripture and become more involved in the leadership of our church, a job that taught me humility at every turn of the road. My prayer life became more active and as my faith grew I could better draw on that faith to be more stable for my family and those around me. With age and a secure relationship with Ken, my relationship with my sister improved, and I was finally able to interact with her. A big step for me as I still felt intimidated in her presence. I now regret the years I wasted being envious of her and living with the feelings of inadequacy. Ken and I decided early in our marriage that we would not allow our marriage to become stale, and made an effort to spend time alone each year to 'renew our relationship'. As we enter our 49th year of marriage I can truly say we have enjoyed each other and continue to do so with a special love. I have had the opportunity to share this bit of wisdom with young women who are feeling unloved and under-appreciated.

Our children, our gifts on loan from God, are now productive, mature young ladies. I give God thanks for them each and every day, sometime each and every hour. I pray that as they nurture their children they will realize that the love is deep and everlasting How we handle their situations are not always the same but at some time, at some point, one needs more than the other, and their needs have to be met where it is needed.

Our grandchildren, our double blessings from God, are now young people, some starting on the road to adulthood. I pray that the lessons they learned from their great grandparents,

grandparents, and parents will stand them in good stead and they will see the good in each other and strive to be a steadfast friend and advocate for each other.

To encourage our children to build their faith in the Heavenly Father, I started sharing scripture and a prayer with them on a daily basis. They in turn would ask for prayer for their friends and share the devotions I sent them. This ministry has grown and I continue to send out devotions to many people.

After my mother died, and in tribute to her, I published a book of devotions "Prayers From The Heart." I give God thanks for His continued direction and guidance and hope that this ministry will continue to grow.

From my experience, I'll share a few thoughts about depression:

- Depression is no respecter of gender, age, or social standing, and can be found in any socio-economic group.
- Parents, if you have been diagnosed with depression or have a family history of it, I urge you to be extra vigilant and aware of any unexplained changes in mood or behavior in your children.
- Depression can manifest itself at an early age but seems to be more prevalent as a child enters the teen years.
- Many are not diagnosed and the condition become more consuming as the young person enters high school and then college, experiencing the extra stress in a need to succeed but not having the energy to do so.
- Listen to your children, hear their hurt through silent or spoken cries for help. Pride has no place in the physical, mental, or emotional health of your child

and if not treated this condition can eventually lead to someone ending their life.

Here are a few signs of depression:

- Deep seated sadness that does not go away. Not the temporary sadness experienced by loss.

- Crying for no apparent reason, and usually unable to say why they are crying.

- A feeling of low self-esteem and a lack of worth often leading to tiredness and a lack of energy.

- Not getting pleasure from daily activities and the inability to experience joy.

- Treatment can involve therapy, counseling, or medication. Sometimes it involves all three to begin with until the condition can be controlled by one or any combination, and coping mechanisms are in place.

"Your eyes saw my unformed body. All the days ordained for me were written in Your book before one of them came to be."
Psalm 139:16 The NIV Study Bible

Thank You, awesome God, for Your grace and faithfulness. Whatever the future holds, I am in Your hands and I will praise You all the days of my life.

WITH NO REGRETS

BY KEAIRA ENGLISH

"As a single mom, you may feel the odds are against you. But with the help of God, you can raise up the next generation for Christ."

–Anonymous

As a child I had a pretty good life. I grew up in a two parent home; the only girl with three brothers. I got whatever I asked for and was hardly ever punished for anything. My dad said no boyfriends until after college, and no matter what never disrespect your parents because God will shorten your days. I lived by that rule of having no boyfriend for a while and thought all my friends did too; up until high school. Of course I liked boys but was always scared to date or talk to them. Plus, with having three brothers I had the fear of, "Oh Lord, what are my brothers going to think of him?"

I didn't date until my sophomore year of high school and I started talking to one of my friends' cousins who liked me. I knew he was in and out of jail but he was cute, and a little hood like I liked them. My mom and dad didn't too much care for me dating him but they trusted me so they would let me go to his house sometimes and let me ride around with him when he got a car.

He was my first boyfriend but I knew he had dated other girls before me, so I trusted he knew about relationships. It was new to me and I never wanted to disappoint him or make him think less of me. When I was 16, we had sex for the first time. I was terrified and knew I wasn't ready but I was scared to tell him no. After the first couple of times we had sex, I started hinting to my mother that I wanted to get on birth control. My mother didn't know I was having sex and she had no reason to think I was, either. She didn't want me on birth control because according to her that was for people having sex and I wasn't one of them. I would make up lies and tell her that I was experiencing heavy bleeding from my period and some of my friend's moms had let them get on birth control to have lighter periods. She wasn't budging and never put me on birth control. I couldn't tell her I was having sex, so I just continued trying to "be careful." It wasn't but a month or so after we started having sex, my mom came to me saying she had a dream that I was pregnant. I quickly said, "No, it couldn't have been me that was in your dream." And for a week or so she left it alone. I was working part-time at Old Navy and remember working at the register feeling like I was about to pass out. I've had seizures since I was five years old and I can feel when they are coming on, so I thought that's what was happening. I called my manager to the front telling her I needed to sit down in the back for a little while. As soon as I made it to the back, I passed out. I don't remember much of what happened after that but my mom and dad were called to come get me. I went to the hospital and they confirmed my pregnancy. I couldn't believe it.

I was beyond scared, and my parents were furious. I couldn't tell my boyfriend right away because he was in jail. My dad did not talk to me for about two months, and my mom had an attitude every time she saw me. She was mad at me and I was mad at her because I tried to tell her to put me on birth control. Nobody in my family would talk to me, and my feelings were hurt. I felt terrible inside, knowing I'd messed up, but I had to deal with the consequences.

Once I got the chance to talk to my boyfriend, I told him that I was pregnant and of course he was ecstatic. He already had a son and thought it would be perfect for us to have a little girl. Part of me wanted to be as excited as he was but since my family wasn't, I couldn't enjoy the moment as much. Plus I was young and didn't know anything about babies. I continued to go to school every day as I was barely showing, but I was stressed and miserable. I was just ready to get everything over with. I figured once I had the baby, my parents would be in love with the little person and everyone would be fine.

A couple weeks passed by and one evening, I was lying in bed and woke up to excruciating pain. As I got off my bed to go to the bathroom, I noticed I was lying in a pool of blood. I was bleeding badly and could barely walk. I panicked. I yelled for my mom and she rushed in. She saw the blood and said, "Keaira, I think you're having a miscarriage." I didn't know much about miscarriages but I knew that meant something wasn't right with the baby. She called 911 and I was rushed to the hospital. There were about four nurses in the room. It was confirmed, I had a miscarriage and I was instructed to push the baby out. I was confused and in pain. Everything was happening so fast, I couldn't even gather my thoughts. I pushed the baby out and the nurse asked me if I wanted to see the baby. To this day it still haunts me and I wish I would have just said no. Seeing a fully formed baby, with tiny fingertips and features come out of me, not knowing if it were a boy or girl, distressed me. I was mentally disoriented; deep down I was hurting and mad at God for taking my baby away. I just didn't understand why other girls I went to school with got to have their babies but I didn't get to have mine. I questioned what I had done to deserve this. Before the nurse left with the baby, I was asked if I wanted to be added to the "Angel tree" where other mothers who experienced similar losses were put up on a tree for support and counseling if need be. I wanted so badly to say yes because I felt that would be the only way to keep alive the memory of my baby but my parents were in the room. I knew they weren't happy from the beginning and I saw their faces when I was asked. I declined the offer so they wouldn't think that I was trying to hold on to something that I had no business with.

Now that the baby was out, I was required to have a D&C (a surgical procedure performed after miscarriage). I had a fear of going under the knife and felt certain God was punishing me since I was having sex, got pregnant, my parents hated me, lost my baby, and now I have to have surgery. I was sedated, and then they performed the surgery and about two hours later I was able to go home. The ride home was quiet. I was embarrassed and didn't have much to say. My parents told me they loved me and that they were glad I was okay.

That was August 2005 and we didn't talk about the pregnancy or the baby after that. May 2007, I graduated high school and found out the guy I had a miscarriage by was sent to prison with a 30 year sentence. Although I felt sorry for him, I thanked God for not allowing me to have the baby because this man would not have been around to help me raise it.

When going through the midst of our storms we feel as if God is punishing us and we seem to question His doings. God says, "You don't understand now what I am doing but someday you will."

Once I graduated high school, instead of going off to college I stayed home and went to the local community college. I worked part-time and went to school full-time and was enjoying life. I hung out with friends every weekend, going to the club and partying. One of my close friends at the time had just gotten an apartment with her boyfriend so I spent a lot of time there while her boyfriend worked. I remember walking into her home one day and saw a guy who caught my attention. He was dressed nice and was handsome. We caught each other's eye and later that day after I left my friend's apartment, he gave her his number and asked me to call. A day or two later, I called. We met up and spent time together, when he could. I knew he lived in the same apartment complex as my friend but we never met at his apartment; instead, at a local park or a grocery store parking lot and we would go out to eat or sit at the park and chat for hours. I didn't pay attention to the red flags. I believed him when he said he was single, lived on his own, in his mid-twenties, and had two cars. In my eyes he was a grown man, independent, and seemed to have it together. I liked that. I knew he had two kids because I had seen him around the apartments with them and he seemed to be a good father. After a while he invited me to his apartment. It looked like a female decorated it with fluffy, furry pillows, a lot of candles, a fluffy rug, plants, lots of décor, but I didn't think much of it; another red flag.

I was young and I felt privileged to be in his apartment so I didn't make a big deal of anything. We started having sex frequently and I remember every time we did I prayed to God I didn't get pregnant because I knew we weren't protecting ourselves. I had no reason not to use protection. I was listening to him and just did what he asked and he didn't want to use a condom.

One day, I was standing outside my house talking and laughing with my best friend when my mom pulled up after getting off work. She asked me to come to her and told me she'd had a dream that I was pregnant. I lied and told her I had just got off my period, knowing I haven't had one. My period has always been abnormal so I just knew it was going to come soon. My mom said she made me a doctor's appointment that morning and I better not be pregnant. I was PISSED! The fact that I was 18 and she made a doctor's appointment had me heated. I walked back over to my friend in tears telling her my mom had a dream I was pregnant (again) and I had to go to the doctor in the morning. I knew last time she had this dream... I really was pregnant so I knew the possibility of being pregnant was 95 percent with the five percent of praying to God to give me another chance.

The next morning, I was a nervous wreck as my mom drove me to Planned Parenthood. She told me to go inside and ask for a pregnancy test and told me she wasn't going in with me. I went in and was out in fifteen minutes. I got back in the car and she asked aggressively, "What did they say?" I looked at her and told her I was four months pregnant. I felt like dying. She was yelling, "What are you going to do now? How are you going to raise a baby? I'm not telling your dad. You will have to tell him." And "Who is going to help you?"

I sat in the front seat in a daze. Knowing I'd messed up... again. I didn't want a baby. I didn't know how to care for a baby and was really enjoying life, going to school and clubbing on the weekends. I knew a friend who'd had an abortion so she was the first person I called when I got home. I asked her to schedule an appointment for me to abort the baby as soon as possible. She agreed and said she would call me back. The following day my child's father called me to find out how the appointment had gone. I cried hysterically telling him I was pregnant and talked to my friend about getting an abortion and that's most likely what I would do. As soon as I mentioned abortion, he said I would not be killing his baby and that I really had nothing to worry about because he already had two kids and he had experience.

I was sick to my stomach. A part of me wanted the abortion and the other part of me was scared of going against his wishes. I was always against abortions and said I would never get one because I felt God would never forgive me. I couldn't believe I was thinking about going against what I'd always stood by. Later that night my best friend called to tell me I was scheduled for an early morning appointment to abort the baby. As much as I didn't want to, I knew I had to do it. I just couldn't have a baby. That night I didn't get much sleep. I cried and talked to God. I apologized for being disobedient and asked him to please put on my heart the right thing to do. The devil was telling me to kill the baby. God was saying do not kill my child. I woke up the next morning having faith, no longer doubtful of what God was doing and determined to go on with the pregnancy even though I didn't know how I was going to do it.

As the months went by I grew bigger and accepted the fact that I was going to be a mother. After my first sonogram my mom was excited and interested in being a grandmother. I still had not told my dad; I was hiding my belly from him every time I saw him. As long as my mom was happy, I was happy.

It was the day before my baby shower and I had not heard from my child's father in two weeks. I was worried, hurt, and in disarray. As the day was coming to an end, he showed up at my house unexpectedly. I was extremely angry because he thought it was okay to just show up knowing I hadn't heard from him. It did not sit well with me. We were arguing and I demanded that he not attend the baby shower. He respected my wishes and from that day forward I had a feeling that I would be raising my baby alone. Two months later as I was sleeping, I started feeling a sharp pain in my abdominal area. My initial thought was contractions but I wasn't sure because I still had three weeks until my due date. I rose up to try and walk off the pain and saw that I was lying in a pool of blood. My heart started pounding and I cried out to God saying, "No, Lord, please don't let me come this far to have another miscarriage." I was terrified. I yelled for my mom and could see the worry in her eyes as she entered my room. She called the ambulance and they came and rushed me to the hospital.

After getting settled in and the pain under control a nurse came in and said she has good news and bad news. She asked which one I wanted to hear first. As fearful as I was I probably told her neither one! She went on to say, "The bad news is you won't be going home today. The good news is that you will be leaving here with a baby." That wasn't good news to me. I was terrified! My eyes were so big and I felt like I was about to pass out. *Is this really happening?* I thought. My due date wasn't for another three weeks. I had told my dad a couple weeks before that I was pregnant. He was hurt that I had not told him earlier, but said he would be there for me no matter what. Now it was time and I wasn't mentally ready, but with my parents by my side I had the support I needed and was ready to get it over with. I tried contacting my child's father to let him know the baby was on the way but couldn't. I called his mom to relay the message.

Two hours later on May 7, 2009, I gave birth to my beautiful daughter. I thanked God a million times that I made it through labor without any pain. The first time I looked into my daughter's eyes I was so scared. Thankful that the labor was over with, but scared because I was now responsible for a human being. I knew it was time to grow up and I did not want to let her down. Not long after I had her, her dad showed up to the hospital. Our families met for the first time and congratulated us on the baby. It was getting late and my mom and dad had been at the hospital since I had checked in that morning and decided to go home to get some rest and come back in the morning.

Once they left, it was just my baby, her father, and me. Not long after my parents left, he asked if I was okay and told me he would be back in the morning. I couldn't believe it. *I just had our child, don't know what to do, and you're going to leave me here alone*, is what I was thinking. I wanted to go off on him but I was exhausted and knew it wasn't worth it. As soon as he left tears started running down my face. My heart hurt so badly. I wanted to call my mom and ask her to come stay with me but I didn't want my parents to know that he left me alone. As weak as I felt inside it was time for me to be strong on the outside. I was released from the hospital the next day.

I remember the day I brought my daughter home; it had been a long day. I was tired but thankful to be back at home. The first night I remember my daughter crying so much. My mom was in and out of my room, coming to get the baby and walk around the house with her to calm her. My mom finally got her to go to sleep and I was able to lie down. Just when I laid my head down, I got a call from a number I didn't recognize. A woman asked, "Is this Keaira?" and I said, "Yes, who is this?" She told me her name and said she was my child's father girlfriend and she saw my name in his phone while they were at the hospital with their six month old baby and she wanted to know who I was.

As tears streamed down my face, I was heartbroken and in disbelief. As she talked, all the red flags I decided to ignore were coming together—the female decorated apartment and the two different cars were theirs (one his, one hers). And he was actually 12 years older than me.

I was shocked and had been fed so many lies. I felt like a fool and deserved it because I had no business messing with him in the first place. He called the following day apologizing and lying some more and I didn't know what to do. I wanted to talk to my mother but there was no way I could tell her that her 19 year old daughter had a baby with a 30 year old man. I wanted my daughter's father in her life but I was so disgusted with him.

The first couple of days of being a mom got real, really fast. I was learning to change diapers which I had never done before and was frustrated because I couldn't differentiate her cries. I could not tell if she was crying because she was hungry, crying because she wanted to be held, or crying because her diaper needed to be changed. I couldn't do anything without my mother having to step in and help me. It was embarrassing and I wanted to give up. Everything was a challenge. This was not for me and I wanted to quit. I felt like a failure and kept telling myself I'd made a bad decision to keep her. Mentally my mind was not in it and honestly I just did not want to do it anymore.

As I reflect on those days, I know I only made it through because God kept me, and I know that if my mom had not been there to help me I would have lost my mind. Honestly, I was having thoughts of committing suicide and thoughts of leaving her with her dad and never coming back. I can't believe I could have even had those thoughts. I was so selfish then.

It took a few months to get used to being a mother and it took so much of my time. I stopped going to school to work full-time and take care of her. Co-parenting caused nothing but problems and difficulties. If it wasn't his way then it was no way at all, and if I upset him he was quick to say the baby wasn't his.

I eventually moved out on my own, struggled to pay for day-care, and rent was late every month. I didn't want to ask my parents for help because my daughter's father was supposed to help. I was angry at him because neither he nor his family offered to help. I worked to make everything look good from the outside as if I was doing well, but deep inside I was angry and depressed. I was angry at myself for having a child with a sorry man, I was angry at him for not helping me care for her except for when he wanted to, and most of all I was angry at God. Even though I was young I knew I was a good woman and I felt like it was God's fault that I was dealt this bad hand. I was tired of doing good yet nothing was going right in my life.

Since I was so upset with God I woke up one day and decided I wanted to "try" living my life without God. I made up in my mind that I would be just fine without knowing God and I knew that I could live a joyful, meaningful life without Him. So what did I do? I stopped going to church, I stopped praying and talking to God, and every two weeks when I got paid I was at the club. I was hanging out and barely spent time with my daughter. I would have really bad dreams at night but refused to pray them away because I did not want to talk to God. Being a mother wasn't my first priority. Partying was. I felt love for my daughter but I didn't know how to really love her. I didn't know how to be a mother, and I was unhappy with my life. I wanted to be in school. I wished I had not gotten pregnant, and I couldn't talk to anybody because I felt they wouldn't understand.

My mother called me one day and asked me to take her to work. As soon as she got in the car, she started going in on me, telling me how terrible of a mother I was, how I didn't spend time with my daughter, that I was selfish and I needed to get my life together. We yelled back and forth at each other and I said some disrespectful things. I couldn't wait to get to her job to drop her off. As she exited the car, I called her a B***h and sped out the parking lot. I turned onto the street and another car came out of nowhere, hit me, knocked me across the median and into a tree. I thought I was dead.

All I could remember was hearing my dad's voice saying, "You disrespect your parents and God will shorten your days." Glass shattered from the impact and the left side of my face was cut open. And the top part of my left arm was burned by the airbag. Seeing the damage of my car, I could not believe I was alive. And as much as I wanted not to believe, I knew it was only God who kept me and saved my life. I made it out because God spared my life.

I went to the emergency room where they cleaned up my face with Iodine, an antiseptic to help heal the wound. When I got home that night, as I looked at my face half gone, all I could do was get on my knees and thank God for saving me and not letting my daughter grow up without her mother. I was so broken without Christ. As ashamed as I was to go before God I went to church that Sunday and asked God to forgive me. Forgive me for even attempting to live without him, forgive me for being disrespectful to my mother, and being a terrible mother to the child with which He blessed me.

The following Sunday, my pastor preached a message on letting your past be your past, forgiving, and living with no regrets. I knew the message was from God and intended just for me. From that day forward I decided that I was going to make a shift in my life. I dedicated my life to Christ and let go of everything that was making me angry and stopping me from receiving my blessings. The gash under my left eye reminds me every day how much I have to be thankful for. I had a weak mind for a moment, and was angry for so long, constantly blaming others and refused to accept responsibility for my own life. But, it was God who restored and redeemed me. I thank God for never giving up on me and believing in me to fulfill my purpose of motivating other teen moms and single parents to never give up on their dreams. I am an aspiring journalist and have dreams of telling the world what God has done for me, and I give Him all the Glory.

With everything I've learned along the way, it's important to remember who you are, and that you never fall too far that God's grace can't lift you up. Here are a few more lessons:

- Lesson 1: Ignoring red flags—Red flags are not the problem. It's what you do with the information you're faced with that matters. Ignoring the red flags is what gets us in trouble.

- Lesson 2: Until you start changing the actions you take in response to red flags, you're always going to get the same results.

- Lesson 3: Trust yourself by knowing who you are and knowing your worth.

- Lesson 4: I did not know how to be a good mother. I developed the discipline of discernment. I started spending time forging intentional spiritual friendships with seasoned believers who have helped me grow into the God fearing woman I am today. Ask God to continue showing you discernment.

- Lesson 5: Learn how to say No or to tell your significant other that you aren't ready (to have sex). Saying NO and waiting until you are ready and responsible can save you from having problems with the other parent. Make smart decisions so that your children do not have to reap the consequences later.

Today, I am a better mother because I have forgiven my daughter's father. I was broken, hurt, ashamed, full of sorrow, and more. But this journey brought me from a place of questioning my future to helping me discover my purpose. Today I am still tackling being a single mother yet I am motivated by my own experiences. I volunteer around my community and mentor teen moms as a part of my vision to stop the cycle and help women realize their worth.

With my love for writing, I am currently pursuing my degree in Journalism. I want young women to know that as a single mom you may feel the odds are against you but with the help of God you can raise up the next generation for Christ. Everything I experienced has made me the God fearing woman I am today. I am now the best mother I can be to my daughter and I instill the word of God in her daily. We pray together before she heads off to school every morning and at night before she goes to sleep. My past is just that—my past. It hasn't been easy but it was worth the life lesson. I am embracing the life I have been given and doing so with No Regrets.

FORGIVE AND LIVE; LETTING GO OF THE PAIN

BY CHRISTINE ROEBUCK

*"We cannot change the past, but we can change our atti-
tude toward it. Uproot guilt and plant forgiveness. Tear out
arrogance and seed humility. Exchange love for hate, thereby,
making the present comfortable and the future promising."*
                                        —Maya Angelou

I was child number five of seven children raised in the midst of the
1960's, in a small community outside of Marianna, Arkansas.
My parents and grandparents were sharecroppers. Sharecroppers
worked the land for the landowner in exchange for a place to live.
We were a poor family, but were content; our parents made sure
we had everything we needed and some of the things we wanted.
There was a lot of love given to us daily by our mother.

Our family lived in a three-room shotgun house, rectangular
shaped, where you could see straight through the house from the
front door to the backyard. Looking out the back door was the
out-house and a water pump. Our parents slept in the front room,
the girls slept on one side of the second room in a twin bed (head
to toe), the boys slept on the other side of the room the same way
and the kitchen was at the rear of the house.

I was a "knee baby." Meaning, I was old enough to baby-sit the twins and my brother who was 13 months older; too young to hang out with my older siblings. It was normal for sharecropping families to share the responsibility of taking care of the children not old enough to attend school; it was a real village in those days.

The landowners hired the children and grandchildren of the parents who worked their fields when they became old enough to chop and pick cotton, or whatever the owner of the land needed. In exchange for working, we were allowed to live off the land, farming it, planting vegetables, fruit, raising hogs and chickens. Between the ages of two and three years, I remember being in the cotton field with Mama Emma (grandmother) and others that were hired to pick cotton. I don't recall how long it took to pick the entire field, but it seemed like forever. When I was sleepy my grandmother allowed me to lie on her cotton sack to sleep while she picked cotton and pulled the sack with me on it. There I lay with my little cotton-picking sack, made from a flour sack. Now, I realize that I was being conditioned to repeat the cycle of my parents and grandparents. It seemed as though when you are a product of a certain environment it's possible to repeat whatever that is. However, understanding choices and building upon what my parents exemplified coupled with God's Favor changed the landscape of what my life could have been.

My father had an eighth grade education and worked from sun up to sun down in the fields and at the lumber mill, when a position there became available. He was a master of managing the family finances. I recall many times my father called me to the kitchen table where he had the bills, money orders, and envelopes laid out with stamps. He would ask me to write the names of the creditors on the money orders and the addresses on the envelopes. Although I did not understand the importance of what he was teaching me, this was a very important time of my life that taught me how to manage my finances responsibly.

When I was seven, we moved from the three room shotgun house, into a three-bedroom house with running water and an inside bathroom. This was an incredible blessing in our young lives. The children in my family were taught to be responsible, hardworking, to love God and to get a good education. All of us siblings had chores from washing and folding clothes and hanging them on the line, cleaning the house, mowing the lawn, feeding the livestock, working on vehicles, attending to the garden, and so many more. But, helping my father with the finances was one of my favorite things to do. There was no yelling or shouting condescending remarks. He was patient and willing to teach me.

In contrast, even though my father was a fierce provider, he was also a strict disciplinarian who wasn't open with his affection and at times released his displaced anger through fights with my mother after having too much to drink. Watching the fights as a toddler affected my ability to be comfortable with voicing my opinion in relationships as an adult. I often feared the ramifications of speaking up; thus feeling that both my opinion and I were insignificant. Have you ever allowed your past to haunt you to the point that you walk on eggshells—trying to avoid making someone angry? I know now that I am significant to God and I do matter.

Learning to become responsible at an early age was the norm in those days. I helped my mother in the kitchen with cooking, washing dishes, occasionally breaking them and being yelled at by my father. I was called clumsy and butter fingers which crushed my spirit and self-esteem. My father seemed easily frustrated when I didn't do things quite right, but my mother was there to literally pick up the pieces and tell me that it was okay. At the time, I did not understand that people could only offer what was within them. Whatever is inside of a person will soon come out, good or bad. However, as I grew older, I believed God can change the heart of any man and that was my hope for our father-daughter relationship. I dreamed of having a close-knit relationship with my father, feeling comfortable with approaching him without being belittled, but being embraced and verbally hearing him express his love towards me. When my father started going to church and becoming more committed to living for the Lord, the abuse subsided.

However, prior to my father's deliverance from alcohol and abusive way of communicating, a seed of low self-esteem and lack of confidence had already settled within me. I sought the approval of others. I focused only on the things I was doing wrong, not remembering to celebrate the good things that were happening in my life. For example, I was an "A" student, that earned a "C" in one of my classes and I cried rivers because my brothers teased me saying I was dumb. Even though my mother told me I was smart, the implication of not being smart enough penetrated and followed me throughout my adult life. Not smart enough to finish college, not smart enough to interview for promotions, not smart enough to open and run my own business.

Have you ever felt as though you could not shake a seed that was planted from your childhood, even though it was a joke? What I learned from allowing words to interfere with every area of my life, is that I can kill the seed as sure as it was planted. My past alike, drives me to be the best that I can be and encourage others to be relentless at rising above whatever situation that seems to have defeated them. My brothers were doing what brothers do—tease. The way that I have dealt with the "dumb" or not smart enough skeleton when it rears its head is that I rely on the word of God to help me to overcome every obstacle that presents itself.

As a teenager and later as a young adult, I found myself seeking the love and approval from others that I didn't receive from my father. For example, as an athlete I desired to hang out with the popular teammates outside of practice, but was not invited into their circles. While sports was an important and fun time of my life, I often felt unpopular. I didn't voice my feelings to my teammates because I feared rejection on an even larger scale.

As I grew older, I trusted the wrong types of people and it pushed me into a deeper state of pain. At the age of 17 while hanging out with my younger sister and our two friends, I found myself separated from them as we left a nightclub. I saw one of my brother's friends who was a popular guy in school and I thought it was kind of cool that he asked to drive me home. I only knew of him from school, but didn't know much about him because he was three grades ahead of me. He gained my confidence by using my brother's name, saying he was with my brother the weekend prior and offered to let me drive his car to seal the level of confidence I needed.

I told my friends that I would be driving, trailing behind them and as soon as my sister and our friends drove off, he took the keys and told me to get on the passenger's side. Everything about that felt wrong but I did what he told me. Before I knew it, we were riding down a dirt road in the middle of a field where no one could hear me scream and fight. He showed me his knife and said, "You'd better stop screaming or I'll kill you." I was sexually assaulted at knifepoint right there in his car.

After what seemed like hours, he drove me home and told me I better not tell anyone. My sister and our friends were in bed when I arrived home around six A.M., but were awakened by the scolding from my father. He was angry, yelling and asking where I had been and my mother was asking what happened. The only thing I could say repeatedly was, "He wouldn't bring me home."

I was devastated, traumatized, and exhausted. My mother stood next to the bed where I was sitting and ask if the guy hurt me, that she would tell the police. I was afraid to say yes, because I had already been threatened and the thought of going to the police frightened me even more. I had been violently violated and was scared and humiliated. To make things worse, my assailant showed up that morning at the retail store where I was employed to invoke fear in me. I was traumatized all over again and asked the manager to relieve me from the register before my assailant got to the front of the line.

The sexual assault haunted me for the next eighteen years because I never told anyone other than my husband. In the meantime, the low self-esteem, un-forgiveness, trust issues, and relational atrocities were at its best emotionally draining. I heard a preached word by Dr. Melvin O. Marriner at Grove Church, Portsmouth, VA in 1998, on forgiveness that literally changed my life. He said,

"There is someone here that has been raped and you won't even call his name. You are carrying him around your neck by harboring unforgiveness." Dr. Marriner had no knowledge of the details of my life. I believe God gave him a prophetic word just for me, to set me free from myself.

The shift in my life took place that day; I went to the altar crying rivers and for the first time in 18 years, confessed that he was speaking to me, confessed the person's name, and I was on my way to being delivered from being muted, afraid to say that it wasn't my fault and that my assailant was wrong. Most importantly, I forgave him for what he did to me and my healing began. I was no longer stuck carrying the burden of the secret and plotting what I would say if I ever saw him again. Or if he were married, how I'd embarrass him by telling his wife what he had done. I was not able to help others who had gone through the same or similar things over the years or be healed in my heart enough to say the word rape, until I had forgiven myself and my assailant. God got the glory out of a tragic situation that happened to me; I am no longer a victim, but a victorious survivor.

I learned how to be resilient, a woman of God, and at the same time decided that I would expect and demand better treatment from others and my husband when I became a wife to someone. My promise to myself was to never allow anyone to hit me. I won't put up with that. My mother was my foremost role model. She was a sharecropper turned lumber worker, shrewd entrepreneur, successful at everything she put her hand to, influential in the community, church, and was a lover of God, teaching her children to love God, too.

My first marriage, I was 19 years old and by the time I was 21 I found myself experiencing verbal and physical abuse that I promised myself I wouldn't put up with. At the age of 31 the marriage ended in divorce. I was functioning in a depressed state of mind and with low self-esteem.

My family had no idea what I was going through; I became good at hiding what was going on behind closed doors. I learned how to get through certain challenges quietly and for a while believed that everybody had similar experiences; at the same time I refused to believe that would be my destiny. I was not perfect by any stretch of the imagination, but still believed that I deserved better.

I encourage you to stay alert! God will send help to walk with you through difficult times in life. My godmother, Mama Gene, was sent into my life when I was 19 to help me rise above the low places. She helped to build my confidence and reinforced what my mom told me all of my life: "I can do anything that I put my mind to." In other words, there was nothing that I could not do. There was always a way so, try again. Don't allow your fears to stop you. Do it!

The important things I have learned are to refuse to allow past hurts and pains to stop me from living out my purpose in life, and I encourage you to do the same. You might ask these questions: How can I move past my hurts? How can I avoid allowing my pain to hold me hostage? Our past hurts and pains do not equal our future.

In a nutshell our parents never quit, but dreamed that their children would have more in life than they had and do more than they did. They wanted to expose us to greater opportunities that we may not have had if we had stayed in the sharecropper's house. My view of living in a share croppers house today is that it served its purpose, but thank God that my parents had vision. They did not allow the naysayers and haters to prevent them from moving forward in life and give their children options. Although neither of my parents graduated from high school, they were two determined people with incredible work ethics and God-given vision with a strong will. My belief is that their past caused them to be more determined to ensure their children had the opportunity to get a good education, great job, and accomplish whatever we aspired to.

My gifts of encouragement, teaching, and giving as well as my purpose to be a catalyst to help people to find their way out of the wilderness of debt as I know them now, were cultivated by both of my parents, but in different ways. Having experienced some things that God could have allowed to kill me, I stand on His promises that all things work together for the good of those who love Him and are called according to His purpose (Romans 8:28).

God is getting the glory out of my life, the good and the bad. At the age of 28, I sought out counseling for myself because there were things that I could not tell my family; I didn't want them to worry. Again, the independent, survival personality type in me was determined to work through the hurt and pain on every level of my life that I was facing. Therefore, I remained in counseling until I made significant progress, all the while I allowed God to clean my life up.

One day when my father and I were ending a phone call, he said, "I love you." I was stopped in my tracks when I hung up and thought, *Did he say what I think he said?* From that day forward, God blessed us with a close bond. For seven years, we ended our conversations with "I love you" and there were hugs when I went home for visits and when I departed. My father was a man of integrity and when God saved him, he became a devoted Deacon of our home church, caretaker of the church grounds/cemetery, and sought to live his life pleasing God. I am grateful that I was given a gift of having a close, loving father/daughter relationship, hearing and experiencing his love and affection before his passing.

My current conviction concerning my life is that I love who I am. My life experiences have prepared me to become the fierce, responsible, passionate, bold minister of the gospel and business-woman with a strong work ethic that I am today. I would not change my upbringing or any other experiences in my life; I mean that with every fiber of my being. My view is that to experience victories or successes, there must be valleys, hurt, pain, and failures in my life.

I am a student of my own life. However, at times I take life or myself too seriously and feel as though I have to take care of the world. I have people in my life that helps to keep me balanced, namely my husband, Ken. He has an incredible sense of humor that makes me laugh out loud and he is a prayer warrior. When the little girl that had to grow up quickly peaks her head out from the weight of responsibility, I have to tell her, "Today is not the day to be serious, but to have fun." These are some of my takeaways for embracing my life experiences:

- Forgive—Avoid holding grudges. Un-forgiveness weighs you down and gives the other person control over your life.

- Faith—Place your life in God's hands and believe in an intangible outcome. Trust that things will work out no matter what you've been through. It was ONLY by God's Grace that I am still here. The low places in my life caused me to seek Him.

- Pull the skeletons out of the closet and shut the door—Re-living a muted past and imprisoning yourself in this great future promised to you is self-torture. Refuse to allow the silence to speak louder than your right to "speak up." Being free is a process—don't rush it or abort it.

- Seek out a confidant and godly counsel—The first instinct is to keep things to ourselves, hence carry hurt and pain for many years. Cultivating pain and hurt lowered my self-esteem, therefore lowered my level of expectations of being loved the right way and destroyed my ability to trust.

- Being healed is a choice and a process—Give yourself permission to be healed. It takes time and effort to get there; so please don't allow others to rush you and by all means don't rush yourself. The process is necessary and can be grueling, but worth it.

- Celebrate you—Don't feel guilty about your success. Speak well of yourself; accepting compliments and celebrating accomplishments. As your relationship with God becomes more intimate, celebrate your growth.

FROM FEAR TO FAITH

BY LURA HOBBS

"Courage faces fear and thereby masters it. Cowardice represses fear and is thereby mastered by it. Courageous men never lose the zest for living even through their life situation is zestless; cowardly men, overwhelmed by the uncertainties of life, lose the will to live. We must constantly build dikes of courage to hold back the flood of fear."
  –from his sermon, "Antidotes for Fear" in "Strength to Love" by Dr. Martin Luther King, Jr.

The water was heated to the perfect temperature. I dove in the deep end of the 12-foot deep Olympic-sized pool and glided to the surface. After taking a breath, I swam slowly to the other end switching between strokes. Since there weren't a lot of people in the water, it was fairly still and peaceful and I didn't have to swim against someone else's current. When I reached the other end of the pool, I smiled and thought to myself, *That was awesome!* That day is etched in my memory. Although I haven't been back to that pool in years, I can close my eyes and see that afternoon as if it was yesterday. Just months before that day you couldn't convince me to put my head under water because I was terrified of drowning and I didn't know how to swim.

My mom put me in swimming class as a child at the local YMCA but I was slower to learn the skills than the other kids. The instructor thought she could help me get more comfortable by putting me in the deep end of the pool. The exact opposite happened and a fear of water was hard-wired in my mind and heart. And now, more than 20 years later, it took everything I had to show up for that first day of swim lessons. All types of questions were racing through my mind. How many people are going to be there? Am I going to be the oldest? Will I be the only woman? What if I can't learn to swim? How hard is this going to be? Why am I doing this… to myself? I've lived this long without knowing how to swim, clearly I can live without it.

This is how irrational my fear of water is: I have been on a cruise, I have been on a small sailing boat, and I've been on a little paddleboat. Growing up, I would race to the car to go out fishing with my dad. All the things someone who is truly afraid of water probably wouldn't do, I did them. Ask me to get out of the boat and into the water, that's a completely different scenario.

I started swim lessons because I was living in the midst of one of my fears already and I figured I might as well get a two-for-one out of this season. At the time, I was unemployed and trying to figure out how I got there. So, tack on conquering my fear of water. No problem, just add that on. Somehow, taking focus off my current situation and onto a different fear gave me a way to gain a sense of accomplishment. Facing my fear of water, my fear of drowning, helped me face some of the lessons I needed to heal from my layoff.

There had been a layoff rumor for months. Widely known, it was going to be a significant number of employees impacted across the entire organization I worked for. All of us who managed teams were equally in the dark, not knowing if we would be let go as well. We all knew the structure was going to be very different but we had no idea who was on the "in" list and who was being left out. Recent senior leadership changes reshuffled the deck on who was in the inner circle and who wasn't. One of my most beloved bosses had recently left the company so I had no idea where I stood.

The day came and the meeting was a blur, "Your team has been eliminated and your role will not exist in the new organizational structure."

Before I could even process the conversation, I was packing up my office trying to get out of there with some level of dignity. Afterwards, I sat in my car in the company parking lot in shock, realizing I was just laid off from a job I loved. Along with many colleagues I considered friends, we had no plan for the future. It would have been a different scenario if I thought I was on the chopping block and had my resume out looking for a job. In hindsight I was immediately questioning why I had not prepared for this moment.

The next few weeks were long and tough—I was on an emotional roller coaster from being pissed off to really sad. I didn't know how to process all the thoughts and feelings I had—where was I, and why didn't I have a plan? In between being angry and sad I had all these questions both for my former bosses and for God himself. Truly, the questions for my former employer didn't matter, although at that moment the questions seemed so important, questions about why me and not someone else and why this structure and not a different one that was being debated. None of that really mattered.

My questions for God were much more significant. What are You trying to teach me? Why am I having this experience? What have I done (or not done) so that You had to get my attention this way? After questioning God, I traced back my steps and asked myself some tough questions. Had I become too prideful? Was I not spending my discretionary income in a way that was responsible? Did I treat my team well and had I been a good boss? Did I deliver on what my goals were and how did I end up on the short/cut list? Had I done my job with integrity? I questioned myself and God endlessly. *Why?*

All those questions led me to spending a lot of time journaling, thinking, praying, and reading, needing to put my soul at ease.

None of my questions for my company were ever answered, and in the end those didn't matter. My questions for God led me right to looking myself in the mirror and to His word. Some of my questions for myself were easy to answer, others weren't and all they did was make me angrier rather than give me a sense of relief. I had just finished a banner year as far as corporate life in marketing was concerned. My prior year annual objectives—nailed them. Millions of dollars delivered to the bottom line. Count it. My immediate concern wasn't because I was thinking about my salary. It was much deeper than the financial impact. My fear kicked in. I was ashamed in that moment like I was naked. ME... unemployed?!

I'm a type-A personality. A bit of a control freak. A natural planner—there's usually Plan A, Plan B, and Plan C swirling through my mind in any given situation. A bit of a work-a-holic, competitive, and someone with constant timelines for everything, that's who I am most of the time. Being idle isn't something I do. I don't sit still for long periods of time. But, when God took my busyness away, I had to face the stillness, the quiet, and learn from it.

In the quiet, I realized I was living in a period where I had no control—that alone caused anxiety. Fear. Being unemployed has always been a fear of mine which is part of the reason I work so hard. Fear of moving out of my comfort zone. Fear of being completely out of control. When I "peeled back the onion" it came down to a **fear of losing part of my identity**. I had failed in this instance and I feared significant failures like the plague—it's shameful and embarrassing in my mind. Successful people don't fail. All in my own mind, that's so untrue!

Inventors, entrepreneurs, scientists, you name it, they failed often in the pursuit of excellence. This level of failure, in my opinion, was new for me. I was afraid and I didn't like the overwhelming sense of fear and shame. Afraid of not getting another job, of not being qualified, of my career being over, of being irrelevant, of starting over.

The fears were compounded but I kept asking myself why, so I could get it all out on paper. I felt like I had failed myself, my family, my team at work. Through reading more about entrepreneurship, start-ups, and watching the careers of people I admire, I had to learn to accept that failure happens as a part of growing. I had to reframe failure as a moment of pause, not an ending point—a comma, not a period. It doesn't matter that I failed (in my view), it's whether I was willing to get up and start all over again.

There were so many people excited for me in ways I didn't understand. "This is your chance for a break," was usually how those conversations started. I didn't want "a break!" I got really pissed when people approached me that way. Clearly, you don't know me very well. "Who am I if I'm not working?" is really the question that kept swirling in my mind. Although I wasn't able to say that aloud to anyone until months later, that question surfaced early on.

Who am I if I'm not working? That question is based in fear and identity. Fear because I was completely and totally anxious about not being in control, being in a situation for which I had not planned. Fear because I really had no idea how to move forward and what I truly wanted: identity because work was such a big part of who I was on a day-to-day basis. The two—fear and identity—weave together.

Over the course of the next year God held up a mirror to me in so many ways and I didn't like the woman I saw at that time. The relationship between my true identity and the fear I was wound in became evident. My identity was too linked to my career. I DO have a life outside of work as a wife, mom, daughter, sister, and friend. However, if you heard how I used to introduce myself to someone, one of the first and maybe only things you would hear about was work. My career defined me beyond what I realized.

So, I had to dig into my fear. What am I afraid of, and what is it robbing me of? What would I try if I wasn't afraid to fail? What "comfort zone box" have I unknowingly erected around myself? Why was I so unwilling and unable to take a break? There were people who actually wished they were laid off and wanted the break. Yet, there I was miserable in it. So, there were days spent journaling, reading, and really spending time alone to dig deep.

It's amazing that none of this surfaced until I was in a situation I had not planned to be in. Planning is my artificial zone of feeling like I'm controlling things. God truly has a sense of humor. Put me in a situation that I hadn't planned for—at all. Make me sit in that unplanned situation much longer than expected. My comfort zone was completely shattered. Close the escape routes where I could get out of this uncomfortable situation quickly.

Yes, that's where I was—forced to face my fears. I was afraid of being irrelevant because I wasn't working and had no career. I was afraid I wouldn't find a new position equivalent to what I had left. I was afraid I wouldn't find a new job at all. I was afraid of who I was without a career. I was afraid that I was letting my husband down because it was taking longer than I expected to find a new position. I was afraid to tell people I had been laid off and they think I was a lazy worker. I was afraid that financially things wouldn't go back to the way things were. I was afraid of telling anyone the full story...

Through months of bible study and examining I realized I had to make the shift from fear to faith and to an identity based on who I am full circle, not just what I did for a living. I had to admit I was afraid because I didn't want to be idle. I didn't like the idea of not being able to say I have "X" title at "X" company. These are mind shifts that have reframed so many areas of my life. For every fear and doubt that surfaced I had to go to God to get the answers. Eventually, there was a scripture for nearly every question or doubt taped in different places around the house to remind me of God's answers. I had to actively choose faith over fear.

It was a roller coaster ride and a boxing match all at once. From the high of getting phone calls unexpectedly for these absolutely fantastic positions, to the lows of nearly every phone call or interview for a job that required my family to relocate out of state. Networking and interviewing got old fast and there were only so many projects to do at home. The old me wanted to find a path back to the way things were—comfortable and known. The new me is down for whatever—ride or die—let's go for the path forward to whatever is ahead—FEARLESS. Let's try it, if it doesn't work, no big deal.

The boxing match was between the old me and the new me to see who would win, and I was on a perpetual roller coaster of emotions. I remember sitting on the floor staring at the wall one day because I didn't get a position I interviewed for that I knew was mine. The location was right, a company fairly similar to my last, a job I could succeed in—no questions. Months of interviewing at several places and I knew this was my blessing. Then the call came, one of those thanks but no thanks, you're so awesome but we've decided to change our direction and not fill this position but create a different role in another group.

Why did I want that role so badly? It was in my comfort zone. Again, wanting to move backward instead of forward.

The ugly truth was the ball of fear stuck in my chest did not go away for months. I didn't wake up one day and it wasn't there. For me, faith gave me the courage to keep moving forward. I journaled about all the things I was grateful for—there were still blessings happening every day. I fed my faith by surrounding myself with a small circle of friends, praising God even though there were days I didn't feel like it. I immersed myself in God's Word every day and journaling how things were going so I could clear my head. Eventually my faith covered the fear—faith strengthened over time and fear weakened. If a few weeks went by and I wasn't actively feeding my faith, the fear would start growing again. I learned to feed my faith daily so my faith would cover my fear. Both were still present but I had to feed one and not the other.

Within a year I had a new full-time position—a role I would not have even considered before being laid off because it was nothing like any of my previous positions—it was completely out of my comfort zone. It turned out that the person who hired me for this full-time role, I had met prior to being laid off. When I traced back the people I had met that led me to getting this job it had started months before my layoff. God had already laid the foundation for how the story would end, I just couldn't see all the pieces coming together over time. But, I had to be off long enough to stop trying to put myself back into the same place/role/situation I had just left. Without the learning experience of the layoff I wouldn't have taken the different career opportunities that God has provided. I would have kept looking to do the same thing and follow the same path that my peers were on. I had to stop doing what was safe, known, and similar to everyone else.

Through this experience my fear of getting out of my "comfort zone box" has diminished over time because I've now seen God move me into new situations and completely provide whatever I need—it's less about me being in control and more about me being willing to learn and adapt to whatever opportunity He provides while asking Him for whatever I need to be successful.

Moving from fear to faith meant redefining in my mind who I was. First, I am a Woman of Faith, although a work in progress, I'm moving toward the person God desires me to be. My relationship with the Almighty had to be primary to everything else. Second, are all those important relationships we so often take for granted. My work and career came after my relationship with God and family. I had to cement my priorities and truly make better choices based on my life view. Third and most important I had to cement in my mind and spirit—*My career is WHAT I do, not WHO I am!*

My struggle in building my faith to overshadow my fears may not be the same as the next person's, but I believe there are lessons in my struggle that could be a blessing to anyone. We all have fears driving our decision-making in ways we don't realize. Often it takes an event like a layoff, or other life-altering action to bring it forward. Why not proactively dig up those fears that are stopping you from moving forward and address them head on? Here are some of the lessons I realized along the way:

- <u>Yes, I am afraid.</u> That truly was step one—admitting where I was. My key was to stop trying to act like I wasn't afraid and face it.

- Embracing that <u>my divine path is just for me</u> was a tough lesson. What I envisioned as Plan B, C, or D was God's Plan A. Submitting to His plan required enough faith to keep moving forward past the fear. My planning will never beat God's divine plan. I can't see from His perspective. My Plan A is usually from a self-centered view of what I want and that usually means it's a plan that keeps me comfortable.

- <u>It's okay if my path is different from everyone else's.</u> I can't be afraid to do something different, just because no one else around me is doing anything similar. It's so easy to fall in lockstep with whatever your peer-group is doing and think that has to be the right path for you. I can't measure my success based on anyone else's.

- <u>Time off is not time wasted.</u> My break was a gift from God to help me align to His purpose and plan. In the quiet I was able to ask myself some life-defining questions. I had to get to know the woman in the mirror better—alone—not in the perspective of others' opinions. My time off was time to tune into my life marathon and to set my personal pace.

- <u>God provides.</u> No ifs, ands, or butts. Although my initial fear was not financial, that challenge eventually came front and center. He gave us exactly what we needed when we needed it, in His timing, not mine. My role was to be ready, knowing and expecting Him to come through right on time. I had to be willing to let go of my "want" list and

> know that God was going to give me just what He knew I needed.
>
> - <u>My identity is in Christ</u> not in a company, title, or an office space. Although God has allowed me to achieve some level of business success, if I don't have any of that I am still a Woman of Faith in the making. If I get myself out of the way, He will move me steadily towards the person He desires me to become. My inner being is most important.

What are YOU afraid of?

FEAR. We all have it in some area(s) of our lives, but we rarely talk about it. Fear is not discussed and debated, yet it's there, every day, robbing us of something. We're too spiritual, too grown, too accomplished to have fear. Fear of public speaking. Fear of being alone. Fear of being known for who we truly are. Fear of taking that mask off at work. Fear of being too (fill in the blank), for someone to love. FEAR. We try to dress it up as something else. Fear robs us by keeping us locked in tight "comfort zone boxes" afraid of what's on the other side of what we know or see. Fear keeps us doing the same thing while expecting different results. More than anything, fear stops us from becoming all we were created to be. Stop thinking and talking about "haters." What's really in the way is the fear inside.

So often, fear is not something we talk about, especially people who believe in God. If we're honest with ourselves though, most of us have some deep-seated fears. Move past those big, life-threatening, or obscure fears many of us think of like bungee jumping or parachuting out of a plane. Most people are afraid of those. Lay that aside. Which fear is robbing you from moving forward? Is there something you've been procrastinating about for a long time and haven't faced? That may be fear. Unwilling to walk into a situation you're not sure you can absolutely win in? Probably fear. Stuck in a place you know without a doubt you should have left months or years ago. Fear. The other thing fear stops us from—asking for help—because we're afraid of being "found out."

So, I'll ask you to stop for a few minutes and just answer the questions in the previous paragraph. Are there any underlying commonalities? What is truly holding you back? What are you *really* afraid of?

The fear to faith shift is a battlefield of your mind and spirit. Unable to transition from one position to the next as quickly as I wanted, I was forced to see who I was in that year of being still. Why not proactively dig into what's stopping you? What "comfort zone box" have you erected in your life? What if the very thing your heart desires is just outside of your comfort zone? We have to walk through fear to grow. It's not an 180 swing from fear to faith, it's tiny steps put together over time. The myth is that fear completely goes away; it doesn't, we just learn to keep walking through the fear.

Just like my 10-year-old self gripping the side of the pool hanging on for dear life, I am too often tightly holding onto my plans with a white knuckle grip. Like the swim teacher who wanted me to trust her and let go, God, the ever perfect Teacher, asks us to put our plans, desires, and hopes in His ever capable hands. Although His plan may be different than ours, and cause us to face our fears, if we place our plan in His hands, the results will be more than we imagine. I hope you'll join me in releasing your grip, slowly but surely, and dive into deep waters of whatever fears you have, believing He will not let you drown.

GOD'S GUIDED MOMENTS

BY DEEDRA JORDAN-EVANS

"It takes courage...to endure the sharp pains of self-discovery rather than choose to take the dull pain of unconsciousness that would last the rest of our lives."

–Marianne Williamson

I lived in Atlanta for almost 10 years. I thrived in its experiences, its diversity, its energy. But once my parents started getting sick, I was confronted with the reality of my parents' health failing and what had to be done to take care of them. In Atlanta, I was working full-time in addition to being involved in church-related activities, singing and acting in film projects both independent and big-budget. While doing all of this, I was trying to help my parents from afar but it wasn't working all that well. Not to mention during all of this, I had been invited to attend the graduate program at SCAD—the Savannah College of Art & Design—to pursue a Masters in Fine Arts. Attending SCAD would mean moving to Savannah, GA. Decisions, decisions! I had been wanting to take advantage of an opportunity like this for years. To be able to be in an environment where I could further cultivate my skills and talents and rub elbows with some of the most influential players in film, television, music, and the arts was like a dream coming true. A degree from SCAD would help take me to the next level in my career as an artist. And all the while, I felt like God was leading me home to Oklahoma which was depressing because I loved Atlanta so much. Going back to Oklahoma felt like starting all over again because I hadn't lived there for what seemed like a lifetime. It brought to mind the story in the Bible of Boaz and Ruth. I felt like the mother-in-law Naomi going to the land of Nun—I wasn't going to get none, have none, or see none. I was moving back to a place where work was scarce and the dating pool was in even worse shape. I was very upset dealing with the prospect of not only being very single but VERY unemployed.

But I complied. I made the move back to Oklahoma, and to my surprise, it was worse than I had imagined.

I moved from a place where I was rarely sick to a place where I was chronically sick because of either the weather or my environment. It was horrible. I was living with family that was completely clueless to the vast hidden abundance of dust and/or mold in air conditioning vents or other places just out of sight. All of that was contributing to me being constantly sick. You know, it's amazing what you get used to in your environment. I remembered my mom asked me if I was ever that sick when I lived in Atlanta. I told her, "No!" and that I had NEVER been that sick in my life up to that point. I questioned God and His plan as I was at my wit's end. I had made the move from Atlanta to Oklahoma in obedience to take care of two parents that absolutely didn't want any help from me while my body was completely breaking down, and to make matters worse I couldn't find any work!

I felt like I had traveled from the land of milk and honey to the wilderness. I just assumed obedience would feel so different...I assumed it would feel a lot less like suffering and a lot more like victory because when you're following God in obedience you feel like you're going to be rewarded for that obedience. It's one thing to read stories in the Bible of heroes of the faith, those who followed the Lord in obedience. It's an entirely different thing to walk in it yourself. It's in this place where doubt set in. Now I began to doubt my decision to make the move. It made me think of Moses when he led the Israelites out of Egypt into the wilderness. Over time they began to doubt and quarrel against Moses and the God who led them there…the same God that led them on dry land through the Red Sea away from their Egyptian captors. There I was doubting that same God that had led me to this place in my life. It seemed like the only thing I could do at this point was cry out to God. In all of my frustration, loneliness, anger…I kind of let God have it. In His infinite patience, He allowed me many opportunities to come to Him just as I was—crying, pleading, praying, asking, "Why, God? Why me?!"

I'd love to tell you at this point in the story that the heavens opened up right above my head and the Holy Spirit immediately descended to speak directly to me to tell me His plan. He did not do that. I'd also love to tell you that life got easier from here on out but it didn't. Don't get me wrong, things started to look up a bit. I was able to finally find part-time work. I had also gotten close to one of my cousins who was playing basketball, which was a lot of fun for me having played basketball during my college years. But it was also painful because I sustained a back injury during one of the workouts that led to hospital visits, steroid injections, and chronic pain. That part-time work I mentioned was spread across two different jobs—one was a position at a downtown office in Oklahoma City where I had to park several blocks from my office and walk there, and the other was working at Dillard's which involved me standing the majority of the shift. It was excruciating…some of the worst physical pain I've ever felt in my life. Emotionally, this was a difficult time as well. On top of dealing with all the feelings that come along with dealing with chronic pain, loneliness, doubt, and lack of direction, I had received word that another one of my teenage cousins I was close to had received a cancer diagnosis. I just wanted a little bit of light, anything that could give me something to hold onto—a spot of relief in this wilderness journey.

With everything that was going on, I got to the point where I really wondered what I was supposed to do with my life. Before leaving Atlanta, I felt like I was on the verge of realizing so many dreams as an artist and performer. Now living in Oklahoma trying to figure everything out and dealing with the trials of life, there was nothing at all it seemed that was leading back down that path that I thought was my destiny.

So I simply asked God, "Is this even something you want me to do anymore?" I felt guilty for even asking the question given everything that was going on at the time. But through all of that, God saw fit to answer me. One day during a lunch break while working downtown, I walked to the location where I had to go to pick up my payroll check. An older black man—worth mentioning because it wasn't a common occurrence to see a black man walking around in that area of downtown—saw me walking and asked me if I happened to know where a nearby FedEx Kinko's was because he needed to make copies of his headshot and bio. He happened to be in town from Kansas City because he was preparing to go to an audition near the downtown area. Now it was customary for me to go on a brief walk during my lunch break. By this time, I had gone on a few dozen walks at least. Those times were spent having conversations with God asking for direction or talking to myself. But this—running into an actor needing help with directions so that he would be ready for an audition—had never happened before. I started talking with him because I immediately saw the open folder with the headshot. I thought to myself, *Why is he even down here from another state? For acting, really?* But not too long after talking with him, I learned that he was truly an experienced actor and a genuinely good guy who was needing help. I also learned about an agency he was working with that was based in Oklahoma—the agency that had booked him for the audition he was prepping for. He wanted to make sure that I was a seasoned actor before he gave me any solid information, which I understood. He wanted to make sure that I was prepared. We exchanged contact information, and a week later, he sent me information about the agency and a referral. I contacted them, went in and met with Margie, the owner of the agency. She signed me that same day and gave me encouragement. I thought to myself, *I hear you God, I hear you.* From there, I started to get bookings—at first I was booked for local commercials and then I started to get the chance to audition for roles in films. I ended up with roles in a few independent films that were shot in Oklahoma. One of them was called *Bringing Up Bobby,* directed by Famke Janssen (*X-Men* franchise) and co-starring with Milla Jovovich (*Resident Evil*) and Bill Pullman (*Independence Day*). Can I tell you that Famke was not only gorgeous but so kind and nice to me, like I was one of the main actors! And Milla and I had times where we would both be getting our hair done in the trailer and we'd giggle like little school girls for what seemed like hours! How crazy is that?!

The next film project I was part of was *Home Run,* starring Vivica A. Fox. It was amazing to get to work with such incredibly professional, talented actors and crew. And yet probably the most significant encounter I had working on a shoot was for a local commercial. It was a public service announcement for young mothers, providing them with tips on breastfeeding and safe sleep for their newborn babies. I was cast as a young wife and mother who had just given birth to a newborn son, but got there only to find out that the shoot had been cancelled because the mother of the baby who was to be in the shoot with me and my "husband", decided not to bring the baby out due to the possible EF5 tornado threat. So we were looking at a cancelled shoot because there was no budget to extend it out to a second day. But it just so happened, Gods Guided Moment, that the person who was directing the spot was a director I had worked with before who loved working with me. He fought for the shoot to be extended to the second day.

The producer of the commercial wanted to make sure that it represented a family and wanted to make sure that my "husband" could stay because he was from Texas. I hadn't had a chance to talk with him but just was able to observe him from afar. He was tall, well-spoken…and fine, but I didn't allow my thoughts to go much more past that. The decision was made to extend the shoot to the next day. They decided to put my "husband" up in a hotel to spend the night.

I went home and came back to the shoot the next day. I changed into my costume for the shoot—grey, silky, long-sleeved pajamas—to coordinate with my "husband" and his attire, also adorned in old-people looking pajamas.

The shoot was located in an upscale, older, large home and the scene was shot in the master bedroom. So while the crew set up for our scene, me and my "husband" began talking. He introduced himself to me and the conversation went from there. It was very easy talking to him. Once the crew finished setting up, filming began. We only needed 2-3 takes to get the job done.

As we were leaving to go our separate ways, I had been noticing the weather reports and received an urgent call from my stepfather to seek shelter immediately, that the tornados were headed our way. I mentioned to my departing "husband" that it wasn't safe for him to get back on the road to head back to Dallas, that instead to follow me to the mall nearby where I work to take shelter. I knew the mall was close and we could take the back roads to miss the piled up traffic. Within a few minutes, everyone in the mall was evacuated. We—me, my "husband," and co-workers—all went into the basement, hunkered down for three hours, talking and sharing peanut-butter sandwiches while tornadoes swirled about. Once we got the all-clear to leave the mall, I exchanged numbers with my "husband" so he could let me know he made it home safely. Sure enough, I got a text late that night that he made it home safely.

Then intermittently over the course of the next few weeks, I got calls from him but didn't take them because he was going through a separation/divorce and I didn't want to get in the middle of that. As time went on, he came through town because he had commercial shoots he was booked for. Over time we would cross paths through work and a friendship developed. After his divorce, my friends and I were there for encouragement, as well as healing. As more time passed my friends encouraged us to date. I begin to reflect on the notes and the prayers I had written over the years about Gods Guided Moments and thought, *Could this be one, too?* Again I asked for direction.

More time passed and things became more clear, more defined. I revisited a spouse list that I had created after reading the book "The Five Love Languages" by Gary D. Chapman and he matched. But I wanted to be sure. Still more time passed and our friendship developed even more. Would you believe that I married that same man? My "husband" had become my HUSBAND.

Little did I know how this path—a path I would have never chosen for myself, one fraught with pain, loneliness, doubt, and disillusionment—would lead me to, of all things, my husband. All of these moments were absolutely essential in leading me to the love of my life and to a place where we're building an amazing future together. It's not perfect but it's ours for the making. I can't imagine my life any other way. In spite of everything, I thank God for those Guided Moments—that He GUIDED me to this place.

GOING FROM GOOD TO GREAT!

BY NECOLE D. TINSLEY

"In the midst of your storm is your biggest blessing."

–Anonymous

In 2005 I had a booming career as a therapist, I worked at the number one hospital in the country, and I graduated from a top Historically Black College and University (HBCU). I was super independent and self-made, but I felt like there was more out there for me. I had always wanted to start my own company but had no idea how. I was feeling burnt out and very overwhelmed with life. I was already 30, so my biological clock was ticking and there were no prospects in sight. One day I woke up, looked at the ceiling, and said, "Lord there has to be more out there for me than this." My answer came when I was offered a position that was unrelated to my career of choice. I saw this as my ticket, my way out of the mental health field, so I took the position. I would be working evenings and weekends. I thought this schedule would allow me to start my writing career. I got into mental health because of my own issues with being molested at nine, distant family dynamics, and never feeling like I fit in. I always felt different from everyone else in my thinking and how I saw the world. I was always told I was a utopian thinker. I just saw the good in everyone and everything. Now I felt I was healed so I didn't need my career anymore, I was free to be who I had always wanted to be. Sadly I didn't really know who that was. I was so super happy; I gave away all my mental health books. Anything pertaining to my "past career" I was getting rid of. I was committing career suicide and happy to do it! My going away party was emotional because a part of me loved helping others uncover why their behaviors were the way they were, and I loved helping them discover their own path to recover. Then, there was the other part that was tired and burnt out, tired of feeling alone, being alone, and feeling like my only success was career success.

The position I accepted was a sales position. I was promised to make a lot of money in a short period of time. As I left my going away party, I took a deep breath and secretly said good bye as I slipped out the door, I didn't want anyone to see me leave or cry. I didn't know if I was making the biggest mistake of my life; all I knew was there had to be more out there for me then just this, and I was determined to find it.

The next couple of weeks were challenging for me at my new job. I was used to a more professional environment. I was on a sales team with what the company called the strongest closers in the industry. We got folks to buy the product when no one else could, but everyone hated us for our skill level. It was our job to "save the deal," put people back in the ether, and re-sell them the perfect package. It was perfect because it was a thoughtless position, but it was frustrating because it was a thoughtless position!

I was on the same team as this guy that I thought was the rudest and most immature guy in the world. He was very inappropriate; he had no filter with his words, would lift girls skirts up when they walked by, and even talked about his family being from LA and being in a gang (all which later I found out wasn't true). He was definitely not educated or polished, and very annoying. I did my best to stay away from him but the further I distant myself from him the more intriguing he became with me which in turned intrigued me. Finally during a difficult close of a client's deal he asked me for my help and as I had done in the past, I helped. This sale required thought, quick strategic planning, and teamwork, all of which we brought and after several hours we closed the deal together. It was amazing and I was on cloud nine as he sung my praises.

Closing deals had become a high for me so this one just took me to a whole other level! To celebrate, he asked me to grab a drink with him. Thinking no harm, I did. We talked and I felt like for the first time I got to know the real him; I liked the real him. It was a softer side, a kinder side, and a thoughtful side. Shortly after this encounter we started hanging out more after work together and I became his unofficial "therapist". As he shared stories of his life, family, kids, and dysfunctional relationship or lack of relationship, we grew closer. Shortly after several "hangouts" we started dating. I quickly met his parents and spent every weekend after work with him; it was great. His behavior started changing and those at work who knew (although many didn't) stated that it started changing for the better. Those compliments made me feel good, feel better about my decision to leave the mental health field, and I was happy with my decision to date him. I looked to the heavens and thanked God, thinking this was the more I longed for.

After a year of meeting and six months of dating, he proposed to me; I happily said yes. On January 13, 2007, I would start the perfect life, secrets and all.

The battle inside of me after getting married was real. Right before I walked down the aisle my girlfriend looked at me, took my veil, pulled it forward to cover my face, and said, "Good-bye, Ms. Tinsley!" My heart dropped, and then stopped. At that very moment I wanted to run. I wasn't ready to say goodbye to Ms. Tinsley. I wanted to run out of that church, run very fast, so fast no one could catch me, but as always, the voice told me that behavior wasn't socially acceptable, so reluctantly, I took a deep breath, swallowed my feelings, and allowed the doors of the church to opened.

I took one look at my soon to be husband and said, "He adores me; it's going to be okay." We had a ball during the reception, and the honeymoon was perfect. It was all okay. I took a chance and made the right decision. Once again, I thought, I was winning!

Shortly after returning home from the honeymoon, our challenges started. He had children and I hadn't shared this with a lot of people, mainly my parents. I didn't feel like I could either. They never wanted me or my sister to date anyone with kids. I think this was mainly because of their feelings about their own half siblings and family issues. They thought life would be easier if we all started at zero. Also, sales started going down and the market eventually crashed; our incomes decreased greatly. We had money saved but didn't realize times were about to get hard. I started to miss the independent woman I once was but I was of age now and "Society" and my "Family Values" said I had to settle down, have kids, and be happy with "this" perfect life. This was the more I longed for, right!?!

A year into the marriage, we experienced a miscarriage, unemployment, and from there we started to grow apart. Two years into the marriage, infidelity, separation, more job loss, verbal abuse, and eventually physical abuse were alive and well. I never thought I would be in a relationship where I was spit on, stomped on, and told how fat and ugly I was daily.

By August 2009, he had met another woman and started hanging out with her. I didn't know in the beginning but I knew something was off. Once he decided to move out of our home, the same weekend I lost my job, I knew then there was someone else. That weekend was Labor Day, and it was an extremely long and hard one. I wanted to curl up in a corner and die. Instead I partied like a rock star; it wasn't like I had work that Tuesday morning to go to. I had been fired. I drank my sorrows and ate my feelings that weekend he left, although eating my sorrows was nothing unusual for me. I started doing it more often after this experience. My friends experienced the lows with me that weekend. They kept me safe but allowed me to get out of control. Reality set in Tuesday morning and I quickly slid into a depressive state. I wanted to fight to keep my marriage together, but didn't know how. Two months prior to all this happening, God showed me I was about to go into the valley but would come out happier and made new.

During the separation, I kept my vows because that's what I was taught. I started looking for materials that would improve who I was as a woman and a wife. I watched the Christian movie called "Fire Proof" that showed a failing marriage and the steps the couple took to get their marriage back on track. I even engaged in the 40-day love dare challenge that accompanied the movie where you read scriptures and followed instructions on how to do nice deeds for your mate. It was great; we started improving our communication and even started talking about reconciliation. I was falling in love with my husband again and welcomed him back home.

By November 2009 he returned, well, his body did, but the person I once knew and fell in love with didn't. The person who returned was nasty, unkind, deceitful, and had a lot of hate in his heart. Within two weeks he had started hanging out as if he was a single man, then the calls started to my phone. Late night nasty grams as I called them. He would get up in the middle of the night, disappear, and refuse to answer his phone when I called or texted. A month went by and I became resentful of the man who returned. Between the late night calls and text messages, along with the increased partying and hanging out all night, I wondered why he returned, what we were doing, and was it just over.

The New Year came, and with that brought new demons. By now I knew about her and of course she had already known about me. On New Year's Eve, we decided to go to church together to start the year off right. After church we headed to a friend's house for cocktails; we stayed till about three A.M. On our way home, he got a text. He didn't answer, then the phone started ringing; he didn't answer. Once we pulled up to our house, he said, "You can go in, I'll be back."

Ummm what? I was confused. We just went to church together, had a wonderful evening, and agreed to rebuild together. I was so hurt, I got out the car and jumped into another car and followed him to his destination. That morning, a different side of me came out and she and I met for the first time. It wasn't a pretty encounter; cops were called and she tried to press charges against me, but the cops told her that if I went down everyone was going down. Being as though he knew this encounter went further than he expected, he agreed to take his mistress to her house, and I was left driving home alone, with anger, hurt, and resentment in my heart while he stayed behind to console her.

He made it a point to tell me how worthless I was, that I wasn't worth being loved by him or anyone else. We didn't even celebrate our third wedding anniversary together. As the months went by, my depression increased which made it harder to find a job, nonetheless get out of the bed. I started believing the nasty words that came out of his mouth. I started believing I wasn't worth it anymore, she was better, and I had wasted my life. The verbal abuse continued until one weekend when his children were visiting. We had been waiting for him to return from getting the truck gassed up. He was taking a long time so we called him, he didn't answer, then his oldest daughter went outside to find him in the car talking on the phone. She caught a glimpse of the conversation which angered him. He returned into the house. He approached me in a way no man should. So much was said in such a short period of time I don't remember but what happened next I'll never forget. He took his fist and punched me right in my lip. I was shocked, angry, and hurt. I ran to his kids, then to the bathroom and saw all the blood dripping down my lip. The kids were crying and his friend, who was living with us at the time, just stood there. The next thing I know I balled up my fist and hit him as hard as I could in his face. It was a long and emotional night. Sadly his children had to witness everything. It was the first time he had hit me but sadly it would not be the last. I never felt safe with him again.

One day I looked in the mirror and I didn't recognize who was staring back at me. I had gained 80 pounds, face was broken out because of my bad diet, and my self-esteem was at an all-time low. I had fallen, and in the worse kind of way.

I was married but was alone; he would leave the house every night but wouldn't come back till the next day. He said he was going out "with the boys", but I knew better. I could smell her on his clothes. The smell of cheap perfume made my stomach curl. He would walk into the house like there was nothing wrong with him coming home 24 hours later. He acted like it was okay with what he was doing, but I guess it was because I had no energy to fight him anymore. I was willing to accept defeat. I just knew I had to figure a way out. I couldn't take the cheating or the abuse anymore. I couldn't pretend everything was okay when it wasn't, and I didn't want to fake it anymore. I left my home in the middle of the worse snow storms I had seen, and I checked into a hotel for the weekend. I cried and prayed for strength from God above. I started hearing Him speak to me. He showed me my future, gave me my vision back, and poured His strength inside of me. That weekend, I was ministered to by Mary Mary's Thankful CD. I played "Can't Give Up Now," "Shackles," and "Yesterday" over and over. I played "Shackles" the most. The words went through my head over and over: "In the corners of mind I just can't seem to find a reason to believe that I can break free, Cause you see I have been down for so long feel like the hope is gone but as I lift my hands, I understand that I should praise you through my circumstance..." and so I started praising Him!

I couldn't help but playing the words over like a broken record: "Everything that could go wrong all went wrong at one time so much pressure fell on me I thought I was gonna lose my mind..." then I heard God's message: "...but I know you wanna see if I will hold on through these trials but I need you to lift this load cause I can't take it anymore..." Right then, I asked God to give me strength, make me whole again, and use me for his kingdom.

Once I left the hotel I decided I had cried my last tear. Either I was going to trust God, or I was going to walk away from God. I couldn't believe in God but have no faith in His plan. I started working on my escape plan, only to find out I was pregnant with my husband's child.

I spent most of my pregnancy sad and alone. He had once again left our home. A month and a half before my son was born, I was put on bed rest; the stress had caused me to be monitored weekly. I allowed him to return back into our home, him vowing to change and commit to our new family. He never kept his promise. The day my son was born, he was at the hospital with me. He was colder than the stirrups I placed my feet in. My son was born around 10 A.M., cleaned up by 11 A.M., and my husband was out by noon. I had gotten very sick so I wasn't able to hold my baby or even see him. They wheeled me into a recovery room as I went in and out of consciousness while throwing up from the epidural. He returned that night; even in my sickness I could tell he had gone to see her.

I broke my fever and held my son almost 24 hours later. I bonded with him and whispered to him I was going to keep him safe. I told him he would never know the struggle. I was released from the hospital and that night he left me and our newborn to spend the night with her. My parents stepped in when they could, along with my friends. One particular weekend one of my friends left her husband and three kids to come and stay with me during my recovery. She took care of my newborn while I slept, cooked food for us, and cleaned up. It was hard for me to lift my baby at that time because of my stitches. I'd had a C-section due to my child's placement in my womb.

As I grew strong, his hate for me grew deeper. Months earlier I had returned back into the mental health field working as a contractor. At six months pregnant I found a job. After eight weeks of delivery, I returned back to that same job and started my hustle. By summer I was growing in the field and obtaining clients on a consistent basis. I was doing well and my bounce back was fierce. This angered him and one day the hitting started again. He attempted to destroy my property, pulled my hair once, and the final straw was when he hit me in front of my babysitters' house. This time there were adult witnesses. I couldn't play it off anymore. I was tired of the cops coming to my house weekly. I had to face the embarrassment I felt while my friends and neighbors witnessed the demise of my marriage. I was at the end of my rope wanting to end it all only for my child to save me.

I grew stronger in the months leading to his final move out. During the process I lost friends, dignity, self, and pride. I gained strength, a sense of self, and a family—my family. Over the years my family had become distant. During this process I learned to lean on them, reach out to them, and trust them. My sister and I grew close, cousins spoke more often, and parents started respecting me for my individuality. My ex's final move was on October 31, 2011. My son was 10 months old. This time was different. That night, I asked my dad to come over, I changed the locks on the door of my house. November 1, 2011 began the healing process. I wrote, and journaled, cried, and got angry. I allowed God to speak to me.

New Years' 2012 came and once again I went to church. I made a conscience decision that from here on out I was going from good to great! Over the next couple of months I went in and out of depression, but I continued to fight my way back by finding and writing positive thoughts on sticky sheets and plastering them on my bathroom wall so I could see them every day! I set daily and weekly goals for myself and checked them off as I accomplished them. My circle of friends changed, I gained new skills to increase my income, and I prayed daily if not hourly at times. I was determined to win! I even started exercising which made me feel better about who I was on the inside and out.

I started the forgiving process by journaling; I journaled a lot. I wrote down my role in these situations and why. I did self-examinations and search for understanding through prayer. I prayed a whole lot. I asked God to show me my faults, errors, and help me to improve. I asked God to create a better version of myself. I bonded with my son and poured every effort into making sure he didn't know the struggle. I worked a whole lot during this time as well. He saw me cry and took on my emotions. It was unfair, but he became my keeper. My son saved me and gave me something to live for. The process of forgiving was hard, lots of sleepless nights and long talks with God. I realized that the first person I had to forgive was myself. Then I could forgive everyone else. I worked through the embarrassment I experienced, the hurt I harbored, and the pain that the scars left behind. I would be forever reminded of that life but I would be forever changed. With each passing month I grew stronger and wiser, I changed for the better. I grew up mentally and discovered who I was. I developed my own thoughts and feelings and learned to love and believe in what I stood for, not being influenced by others thoughts, views, and opinions.

The road to recovery wasn't easy and it came at a cost. During 2013-2015, I experienced several setbacks. My past haunted me and I almost gave up, but my friends and family wouldn't let me. One particular evening, I went to the store to purchase a couple of items for myself and my son to eat for dinner. My bill had come to $10.54. I swiped my card and it was declined. I was confused so I swiped my card again. Once again it was declined. I paid for my items with cash and left the store. I went to my car and checked my account. It had been frozen. This angered me because I didn't know why. All I could do was cry while sitting in the parking lot of the grocery store. The next day I got dressed for work, got my son dressed, and took him to his daycare center. I returned home without telling anyone I had no plans to go to work. I called out sick for the day, and then I called the bank. I found out the IRS had frozen my account due to a back bill we had filed together. I once again got angry and questioned. *Why does this always happen to me?* I took my clothes off, poured me a glass of wine, and got a bottle of pills. I couldn't do right and I was tired of trying. At the same time I did this, a good friend called me and could tell something was wrong. I told her what had happened with my account. She assured me everything would be okay but I was mentally gone by then; she could tell. Before getting off the phone she said, "Necole, don't give up, you'll get through this. Promise me you won't give up."

I told her to give me a day; I just needed to rest. I drank the whole bottle of wine but never took the pills. I picked my son up that evening, and he ran to me and gave me a big hug. He said, "Mommy I thought you had died." That hurt my heart. We were so connected, he nor anyone else had known I wasn't going to work that day nor planning to say goodbye. That night, I fixed him his

176

favorite meal and vowed to continue this fight. I might have bent but I wasn't made to break!

Just like the day I woke up and said to God there has to be more out there for me than this, I realized there was more out there for me. One day it didn't hurt as much anymore. One day someone said you have a glow, you look happy. By journaling, forgiving, and working on my goals, I stopped hiding, stopped making excuses as to why I wasn't showing up, and I started showing up. I started being present and living in the moment by interacting more with people, laughing more, and engaging in conversation. I stopped playing small and started dreaming big. I started a vision board club where I held/hold vision board parties at the start of each year and send monthly motivational text messages to help my group and myself stay on track and achieve their goals. I prayed often and relied heavily on God's word, listened to His voice, and allowed Him to order my steps.

In the healing process, I realized it wasn't his fault. I needed to be needed, loved, and to feel like I belonged. I tried to take someone and create the perfect image, the perfect fantasy, the perfect man. It wasn't his fault he couldn't live up to my fantasy, heck, it wasn't even mine. Honestly, it wasn't anyone's fault. He entered my life at a time when I was stuck. I wanted more out of life but was afraid to fail, was afraid to take chances, and instead of learning from my mistakes I beat myself up for them. Through my parents, I was taught how to be perfect, appear perfect, and live perfectly. My sister and I was taught to avoid situations that would create adversity and show our flaws. I was to never talk about my molestation because it would put shame on our family. Sadly, that part of my life created the desire to want to fit in. I always felt that if I didn't have any flaw, and made no mistakes, someone would want me. I always lived for the moment when I was chosen because I was perfect! This experience taught me God uses imperfect people for his kingdom.

After being in the valley for seven years, I discovered the more was about the journey, taking chances in life by following God's purpose and being okay with failing. The more was about self-discovery, self-love, and self-expression. I finally started my writing career and am telling my story through my writing. The more was about making mistakes and owning them, learning from them, being okay with them, and believing in them and its process. The more was about healing and rebuilding. The more I was longing for was always inside of me, I just had to step outside of my comfort zone and stop playing small to appear perfect. I had to allow God to use me, and not be afraid of the process. The more, WAS ME!

I CAN LOVE, AM LOVABLE, AND LOVED

BY AUDRA R. UPCHURCH

"After you've done all you can, you just stand."
                                        –Donnie McClurkin

I can't believe I had to go to school on a Saturday! *Well, at least it's a beautiful day*, I thought to myself as I stepped out of the building into the parking lot. Returning to school in my 40's while working a full-time job was tough. I was exhausted but couldn't help but smile because spring was in the air and for the first time in a long time, I felt hopeful. Even the thought of the 45 minute ride home from Chesapeake, VA to Suffolk, VA didn't seem so bad today.

I drove home paying close attention to the road. I trained myself to keep an eye out for deer because Route 58 was notorious for them. Trust me, drive long enough and you'll see them any time of day, and this Brooklyn girl wasn't taking any chances. As I drove down the Virginia highway, heading to Suffolk, the scenery was absolutely beautiful. This is the kind of view I would have never had in Brooklyn. The trees were full bloom, the colors were bright, and the sky was clear; just breathtaking. Just then another thought hit me. What would happen if I got in an accident right now? How long would it take someone to realize that something had happened to me? I had pretty much isolated and distanced myself from everyone in my life, so at that moment, the answer to that question scared me and I wondered how I let things get so bad and then my heart saddened as I remembered....

"Push, Audra! Push!" I could hear one of the nurses in St. Mary's Hospital yelling at me. I was 17 years old, about to give birth to my baby, and I was homeless. Words can't explain the terror I felt at that moment but as I pushed and heard my son cry for the very first time, my fear was replaced with so much happiness; for a little while I forgot how bad my situation was, but that wouldn't last for long.

When I came home from the hospital with Sean, my 7lbs 3oz son who was born a month early, I moved in with his father, let's call him John and his mother, let's call her Jane, in the 3rd floor apartment in Breevort Projects in Brooklyn. I slept in the room with Jane and she was incredibly helpful. She would get up with the baby and allow me to rest at night. She would help me dress and bathe him too. I even started calling her mom and for the first time in a while, I enjoyed having a mother figure in my life. Too bad it was short lived.

A couple of days after my son was born, Jane planned to move to North Carolina and was clear that she was not leaving me in the apartment with her son. I contemplated what I would do as I held my beautiful son in my arms and the tears started to roll down my face. The weight of knowing this perfect little angel could be born to a mother that couldn't even care for him was too much for me to bear. At that moment, John walked by and saw me in the room crying and went to get his mother. They both tried to console me but I was inconsolable. Sean was only a few days old and I was already a failure as his mother. I wanted to give him more but felt at that moment that I had nothing to give.

John and his mother both talked to me and assured me that I wasn't in it alone. We agreed that I would go with Jane to North Carolina for a while so that she could help me get on my feet. As they talked I could feel the weight lifting and began to feel hopeful. Having been homeless since I was 14 years old due to my mother's mental illness, it had been a long time since I truly felt safe and loved. Although I knew, somewhere deep inside, that my mom still loved me, her mental illness had escalated to such a point where she was no longer in touch with reality; it had been years since she maintained a home or took care of me. So after talking with Jane and John, I felt relieved.

However, it seems like after that moment, everything changed and not for the better. Jane did everything for Sean and I was demoted from being his mother to being her assistant. When I tried to step in, I was scolded like a child. I didn't want to risk upsetting her and losing the roof over my head, our head, so I complied. I felt extremely vulnerable and alone. I tried to talk to John about it but at 21, he was 100 percent dependent upon his mother financially and wouldn't dare speak up for me. John graduated high school three years prior and was no closer to getting a job than the day he graduated. He attended a trade school for a little while but gainful employment never materialized. It seemed as long as John kept his mother happy, ran her errands, and kept the house clean she wasn't too bothered by his employment status so he wasn't going to bite the hand that fed him. The writing was on the wall but I just didn't see it. One day, a good friend came over to see my new baby and went to pick him up, but Jane wouldn't let her. My friend looked at me to say something, after all, I was his mother but I didn't. I could feel Jane's eyes piercing at the back of my head, so I just put my head down and my friend took it as her sign to leave. As she walked out, she whispered in my ear words that would haunt me for 20 years…"That lady is going to take your baby from you."

Two years later as I stood in front of a North Carolina judge and heard the gavel hit the sound block, my heart simultaneously broke. The judge had determined that it was in the best interest of the child, my son, to remain with his grandmother in North Carolina. He was now two years old and no longer knew who I was. I was dazed and confused. I looked at my friend Laverne, who was standing next to me, in disbelief. Did I just lose custody of my son? How did this happen? I could hear my friend's words echoing in my ear. How could I have not seen this coming?

When my son was three months old, Jane convinced me to return to Brooklyn to have a medical procedure. After receiving abnormal test results during a physical exam and not having medical insurance in North Carolina, it seemed logical for me to return to Brooklyn for treatment. She promised to take great care of my Sean and somehow talked me into leaving him there until I finished school. As I was walking out the door, she suddenly remembered that she needed me to write a letter authorizing her to take him to the doctor if he got sick. I was running late to catch the Greyhound, so she pulled out a blank piece of paper for me to sign and promised she would write out the letter for me later so I wouldn't miss my bus. I signed that blank piece of paper not knowing that too would haunt me one day.

I returned to Brooklyn, found an apartment, had my treatment, and decided that I wanted my son. I felt like a part of me was missing so I lined up a babysitter, got a job at a bookstore near the World Trade Center, and prepared to bring my son home. I decided finishing high school would just have to wait. I talked to Jane and told her my plan to get Sean and bring him back to Brooklyn. She kept finding reasons to push my date back further and further. When I finally returned to North Carolina to get Sean, Jane politely told me that I could not take him without a North Carolina court order. The law was on her side as Sean had now been there for six months and six days so he was no longer a New York State resident; now North Carolina law applied. She also pulled out the piece of paper that I signed which was no longer blank. It now stated I was giving her full custody and control of my son. How could I have been so naïve to sign a blank piece of paper? How could I have been so trusting? I vowed that day I would never trust anyone like that again.

"Snap out of it. Snap out of it now!" Laverne said as I looked around and noticed we were the last two people in the courtroom. Then she looked me square in the eye and said, "If you let these people see you cry, I will beat you down right here and right now. They want you to fall apart but that will NOT happen today if I have anything to do with it." She used some other words but I will spare you the profanity. She grabbed my arm and led me out of the courtroom. From that day on, we were thick as thieves.

My friendship with Laverne was weird to most people and I guess still is. Laverne is the mother of John's oldest son, who is only four months older than my own son. Yes, that's right, our sons are brothers. When Laverne heard what was going on and realized I would be going to North Carolina to court alone, she risked losing her job, left her son with her mother, and came with me. After all, she felt that it could have been her son that was taken.

When I returned from court that cold December day in 1989, I was not the same person. A part of me died on the way back to Brooklyn. I had given birth to my second child, Alyssa, that summer so I now had a four month old daughter waiting for me when I got home and I was completely empty. I had nothing to give her. The mother that left for North Carolina was not the mother that returned.

Sadly, Alyssa's relationship with her dad was ruined from the start. Todd was someone that I met at work and distanced myself from soon after I found out that I was pregnant. I was jaded by what happened with John and his mother and had no intention of letting Todd or his family anywhere near "my" daughter. Then one day when I was around six months pregnant, Laverne helped me realize that I was punishing Todd and his family for what happened with Sean and that my daughter would suffer because of it, so I reached out to his family. His mother has been an amazing support to me every day since and we have been blessed by her unconditional love.

When I returned from court, I started partying hard which was completely out of character for me. I grew up in church but this "new Audra" that returned was no church girl. I partied from Thursday to Sunday every week that I could. When I wasn't partying, I was working. When I wasn't working, I was sleeping. There was no time for church. I mean, why bother, right? It appeared that God wasn't listening anyway and I was angry. What did I do to deserve a mentally ill mother, to be homeless at 14, abandoned by my family, and now to lose my son? I prayed and prayed and still returned home without my son. So what did that mean? Did God feel I wasn't good enough to raise my own child? Did God feel that I was a bad person? Did God not love me too? Was He even listening? The music in the club drowned out those thoughts, so I went on an endless partying spree.

I worked off and on, lived in Section 8 housing, and survived minute by minute with no preparation for tomorrow. I was extremely distrustful of people so I never made new, lasting friendship. I would befriend someone for a while but eventually find some reason to let it go. I kept in touch with Laverne and adopted her friends as mine but still kept my distance. They were fun to party with but we never really talked about anything serious or how I felt about what happened in court that day. My life was lived on the surface. That went on for years until one day I enrolled in New York City Technical College to pursue my Associates Degree in Accounting. Then slowly everything changed for the better.

I had reluctantly taken my GED exam a few years earlier and looked forward to sitting in a classroom again. College was a breath of fresh air. I studied hard and was able to excel. Soon I ran for student office, mastered Robert's Rules of Order, and learned I could work my way around a board room. I figured, if I couldn't be successful at life, I would be successful at business. I began reading my textbooks like they were novels. During Spring Break, I would work as if class was still in session and all the Accounting professors knew me well as I aced all my coursework.

Then in 1994, the Work Experience Program (WEP) started. It took students from welfare to work, even if they were currently in school. I was close to graduating and was fearful that I too would be pulled before I finished. I had no one to watch my daughter in the evenings to attend night school so if I was pulled to attend the WEP program, that would be the end of school for me. I watched as some of my classmates had to leave school and I prayed. One day I got a letter from Social Services stating that I needed to come in.

My appointment was scheduled for 10 A.M. but the caseworker didn't get to me until 4 P.M. By that time, I had waited all day and was a nervous wreck. I just kept praying that she wouldn't pull me from school to go sweep a park, which was the typical WEP assignment given.

When the social worker finally walked up and called my name I couldn't look at her. She guided me to a small, bare cubicle in the back of the room as I braced myself for bad news. I was so nervous, I didn't notice that she had a text book in her hand. Once we sat down, she said, "I have seen you around campus and I hear you're a strong student." She placed her Accounting textbook on the desk and said, "I think we can help each other."

I looked up confused. She said, "I need an accounting tutor and you need to graduate," then smiled. Without saying another word, we had an understanding. The Work Experience Program was no longer a concern. Looking back, I didn't give God any credit at the time but my prayers were definitely answered that day.

Shortly after finishing school, I packed up my daughter and we moved to New Jersey. Two years later, much to everyone's surprise, I got married. It was one of the least thought out decisions I've ever made. At the time I figured, if it doesn't work out I'll just get divorced. That's pretty much what everyone else in my family did, so what was the big deal? Little did I know...

Living in New Jersey was great because I was able to land well-paying jobs almost immediately but as a single mother, I felt like I stood out in a negative way amongst my colleagues. I thought that getting married would at least give the illusion of normalcy, even though I wasn't fooling anyone. When I told one of my co-workers that I had gotten married, she asked me without hesitation, "Why?" Baffled by her response, I didn't answer, so she said "Well, we all know that he doesn't keep a job so I'm just wondering why you would marry him. I thought you were smarter than that."

Shocked by her response, I walked out of the break room without saying a word. The truth is, she was absolutely right. We lived together for two years prior to getting married and he would get fired from every job he worked. The truth was that he didn't want to work…at all. He even admitted that to me once. Things only got worse once we were married. The first year of marriage, he did not work one day for a whole calendar year. Not one day. And would show up at my job all times of the day. So who did I think I was fooling?

But although he didn't work, he wanted to be with me. So what did it matter that he didn't work a steady job? At least I was married now. After years of feeling abandoned by my family and rejected by God, I welcomed someone wanting me, no matter the cost. Even if that someone couldn't or wouldn't hold down a job. Well, at least I had a good job so maybe success at work was all I was ever going to have.

Unfortunately, the more money I made, the more he spent and the stress became way too much. As my daughter grew she had no respect for the man I married and little respect for me as she saw me take care of everything while he did nothing. He convinced me to leave New Jersey and move to Florida with the promise that new surroundings would motivate him to work. We spent thousands of dollars on the move but in the end, it didn't change anything. He took his bad habits there, too. After three months I left him in Florida. I moved to Virginia to stay with my cousin in Norfolk and felt completely overwhelmed. I was 31 years old and my daughter and I were sleeping on my cousin's couch. How could I be home-less again?

Looking for answers, I started going back to church and felt that maybe I could give my marriage one last try. He made me so many promises and called me every day, several times a day so I finally agreed to give it another try and he came to Virginia. After all, he was my husband. We rented a house in Virginia Beach and he got a job, for a little while at least but eventually went back to what was familiar to him. Unemployment. This time the stress took its toll and I soon started having heart palpitations. After three years of marriage, I asked him to leave but for good this time. Two years later the divorce was final and I had a divorce party to celebrate.

Two years to the day after my divorce I pulled up into the driveway of my first home. I bought it all by myself. After my divorce I went into overdrive going after higher paying jobs. I also enlisted in the Army National Guard at the age of 34 and was accepted into Officer Candidate School. A year prior to filing for divorce, I filed for bankruptcy but I systematically went to work rebuilding my credit so I could purchase a home one day. When the loan officer at the bank looked at my file, he was impressed with how quickly I increased my credit score so I qualified for a conventional loan with ease. The closing on my house was complete in 20 minutes from the time I walked in the door.

Everything was great on the outside. I had a home, I had a brand new job, my credit score was on the rise but on the inside, I was just going through the motions.

My daughter graduated from high school on a Thursday and it fell on her 18th birthday. She moved out the very next day and the last bit of my emotional connection to the world went with her. We always had a turbulent relationship and that day was no different. My cousin that I stayed with in Norfolk eventually moved back to New York so I was in Virginia alone. When I left Florida, the main reason I came to Virginia and didn't go back to Brooklyn was to be physically closer to Sean. I had only seen him four times since that day at court but somehow knowing he was only living two hours away seemed to comfort me, but now, that no longer worked. An opening came up in our San Diego office and I went to my boss and volunteered to go.

I moved out of my house and rented it out so I could save some money for the move. The San Diego office wouldn't be ready for quite a few months, so I had time to save and was excited about the change as it gave me something to look forward to. After my divorce, I stopped attending church and had become a Buddhist. To me, it seemed like the intellectual thing to do at the time. I first studied Buddhism in college courses and became intrigued with the religion. I never understood why God allowed me to suffer and struggle as I did in my youth and I was still angry. Also, I was incredibly isolated and my new friends at the Buddhist center embraced me. Most importantly, they all seemed genuinely happy and I was puzzled by that and thought maybe if I hung around or chanted long enough, I could one day be happy too.

But it wasn't meant to be. Buddhism, that is. At least not for me. One morning as I chanted, tears started rolling down my face as I realized that I was never going to get the happiness the folks in the Buddhist Center had. When I chanted I felt absolutely nothing. I did it because it was a part of the ritual. I didn't feel any of the things I would hear others talk about they felt while chanting. Then it hit me. I didn't feel it because I was not a Buddhist. Right then, I felt God's presence in that room and He reminded me that I was His and that He had never left me. I fell on my face and cried for hours. Finally I got up and jumped in my car and drove to a friend's house that I hadn't seen in over seven years. When I pulled up to the driveway, the house looked empty. I motioned to leave a note on the door but then it opened. She was there and all I could say was "pray with me" as tears ran down both of our faces. You see, it had been so long since I had prayed, I no longer knew how to utter the words and drove there hoping she would help me. As cleansing tears poured down my face, she prayed with me and I finally understood that through all the awful things I had been through and felt so alone, it was then that God was carrying me.

A few weeks later, as I drove from school on Route 58, accepting my role in how I isolated myself from the world I said, "Lord, a few weeks ago these tree branches were bare and now they bloom with Spring. If you can change them, why not me? I don't want to be this person anymore. I want to live and I want to love." So then my journey began and it hasn't been easy. I've had to tear down walls that were built so many years ago. But you see those walls stopped me from giving love, receiving love, and living free. I've had to learn how to make sound decisions; not based on past experiences or guilt but guided by love and with a free heart. But most importantly, I've had to learn to accept my authentic self, flaws and all. I had to put in the work!

Not long after the drive on Route 58, I went back to my boss and explained that I could not move to San Diego. I was not leaving Virginia. After my tenant's lease was up, I moved back into my house and reached out to Sean to actively build a relationship with him. He is now married to a wonderful woman, Jasmine, and has two beautiful children, A'mir and Amayah. I am so blessed to have the joy of watching my grandbabies grow up. They affectionately call me GiGi.

In 2012, I married Tony Upchurch, a retired Navy Veteran and the love of my life. We run a successful business together in Virginia Beach and he supports my dreams and is my biggest cheerleader. We can do anything together.

My relationship with my daughter is still shaky but I love her dearly and pray that one day we will reconcile.

I can't go back and undo the mistakes I've made but I can move forward inspired daily by the opportunity to live my best life. I've established boundaries so that I can feel comfortable loving people without fear. I can be myself knowing that I can love, am lovable, and loved.

I've learned to accept that there are consequences for mistakes made due to poor judgment. That doesn't mean that we should dwell on our past but it does mean we should learn from it. Here are a few things I discovered on my journey:

- Stay connected. My worst times were when I mentally and physically isolated myself from family and friends.

- Ask for help. So many of us let pride stand in the way of us getting assistance from someone waiting to bless us with their knowledge, expertise, and resources.

- Believe in yourself. Stay true to who you are and never underestimate your own self-worth.

LAUNCHED INTO DESTINY

BY ELLA D. CARROL

"Hardship often prepares an ordinary person for an extraordinary destiny."

–C.S. Lewis

I was born and raised in the church. Part of me felt like so much was expected of me to be the perfect kid or to do great at everything. My first act of rebellion took place my senior year of high school when I fell for a guy who was cute and I got pregnant. Not that my pregnancy was intentional because I thought it would never happen to me—but it did. He warned me if I ever got pregnant, I would have an abortion no question about it. And I did, twice; because I couldn't shake the physical attraction I had for him. Shortly after the second abortion, I was involved in a car accident which gave me a wakeup call to get myself together. I decided to rededicate my life to Christ, continue to focus on my education, and move on with my life.

Part of me liked the "bad boy" type, too. I remember like it was yesterday. I saw a photo on a co-worker's desk of her brother, Nelson. I went from complimenting the man in the photo to becoming his pen pal, and later phone calls and visits, since he was in prison. He always shared a scripture with me in his letters and we wrote back and forth about the Bible, our visions for the future, and general business ideas. We connected through our conversations. Even though I was working on my master's degree during this period, something in me was looking to fill a void. Mind you, I thought I was whole and fulfilled.

Initially I thought I was cool not being in a relationship and after much reflection I discovered when the opportunity presented itself, all that changed. I thought, *"Who am I to judge him in his current situation?"* Right? I was reminded of the Word of God, "For all have sinned and fall short of the glory of God" (Roman 3:23 NIV). I thought I could relate to him because I too had done things I was not proud of. Thinking back to my abortions and feeling like I should have served time for what I had done—murdering two lives before they were given a chance to fulfill their destiny. And I did it in the name of pleasing a man.

I accepted Nelson for who he was. During our courtship, I did not try to change him because I never thought I could. Part of me felt he was a womanizer because of the way he looked at other women when I visited. When I mentioned how I felt, he would say or do something to suppress the insecurity within me. In actuality the insecurity I felt was a red flag. Part of me thought I was helping him. I can't count how much money was spent on gas for visits, phone calls, as well as funds to get him daily necessities. I also invested in his education while working on my own degree.

When we got closer, it became more sensual, even to the point where I'd do things I had never done before. He made me feel like a woman, so I thought. Physically, he knew how to make me feel good without touching me. I needed to be accepted and I thought he loved me unconditionally, or with Agape love as I learned in church. But his was more of a sensual, or Eros type of love. He made me feel needed. I brought him his favorite foods, like fried chicken and spaghetti. I was on cloud nine, and my sister brought me down to earth when she said, "You are living in a bubble because when he gets out of prison, it will be different." I felt she was on the outside looking in and judged him, not realizing she was sharing from her personal experience. I realize she was one of my gatekeepers.

My Pastor, Bishop Steve Houpe of Harvest Church International, advised us to wait a year before getting married to make sure we knew we were ready. And I was cool with waiting because I felt that would give Nelson time to rebuild his relationship with his son as well. I shared the feedback with him. As the man of the relationship, I looked for Nelson to take the lead. He was ready to get married so we went through premarital counseling and read some books in preparation.

I felt I had something to prove to all of those who I believed were against us. Because others were telling me he was not who God had for me, I thought, *I can pray and hear from God, too.* To be honest, I was not praying like I should have been at the time and I didn't listen to my gatekeepers who were looking out for my best interest. I overrode all of the feedback and didn't guard my heart. The Bible is clear when it says, "…for everything you do flows from it," (Proverbs 4:23 NIV). Nelson was a good person in spite of circumstances, but he was not the man for me. Yet because of my insecurities I was going to make our relationship work. A part of me felt I had to settle because I was getting older and wanted a family.

I got sick one year, while we were still courting, and that was my exit from the opinions of others in the church about my situation. I left the ministry and thought I'd go to another church where I wasn't known and no one knew about me being engaged to a man in prison. I thought I could start over with my soon to be husband somewhere else. Nelson and I were married and we stayed under another ministry, but I never felt that connection like I did at Harvest. Going back to Harvest was the best thing Nelson ever did for me. However, it was hard returning because in my mind I was thinking about the opinions of people who knew or thought they knew my situation.

Life after marriage was cool at first; the first year was a blur with a few happy moments. For instance, for the wedding, I wanted to make sure we had a limo. We drove to the Boom-Boom room at the themed hotel in Kansas, which was my gift to him because it had a spiral staircase with a Jacuzzi upstairs, and a his and her shower downstairs with a waterfall. We even had our wedding pictures on canvas for display while the tent was being converted from the wedding to the reception. Then off to our honeymoon in Branson, Missouri.

I remember there were some issues too, such as financial problems and red flags. As wife number two, I was concerned by his ties to his ex-wife. Here we are, newlyweds and he is overly concerned with her medical condition. Part of that I found admirable. The problem was he did not show me the same level of concern at the same time. I couldn't understand why he felt the need to be there for her. Several months later I became pregnant with our first daughter. During this period, he was attentive, cleaned the house, and was helpful. I was diagnosed with gestational diabetes and needed to eat better, not just for myself, but for our baby. Nelson stressed for me to take care of myself physically, but I was dealing with hormones, tired, and frustrated.

I was concerned about our financial future. I am taught a Godly man covers his household and I felt uncovered. We were married about a year before I realized he had been unfaithful in our marriage. He told me about two instances—both were emotional affairs. An emotional affair is where nothing physical transpires, but one's heart connects with another person's heart because of the emotional attachment through conversation. However, the second led to a kiss. I felt betrayed in both instances so when he claimed to work late or go somewhere, I believed he was with someone else. He lied so many times I felt I could not trust him again. Although I forgave him, I still could not trust and he did nothing to build up my trust again. I wanted our marriage to work and thought going away together would help.

When we returned to Branson, Missouri, the place we had our honeymoon, I gave him a chance for us to have a fresh start and rebuild the trust. I didn't believe he would allow another affair to take place. I was naive in my thinking and wanted to fight for my marriage. This was when I should have prayed more for my marriage and we should have prayed together because there is power in agreement. Despite our problems, he was determined for us to have another baby and I got pregnant with our second daughter.

With all the problems we were still facing in our marriage, Nelson's son was murdered and shortly after that so was his nephew. While he was grieving, our marriage was dying a slow death. During both of those episodes, I was trying to stay strong for him while carrying our child. I had developed a relationship with his son but didn't know his nephew all that well. However, I didn't have a chance to grieve because that particular year, there were multiple deaths in our families. It was either a murder or natural death taking place seemed every other month. It was just too much going on with me emotionally. In spite of the fresh start, Nelson became more distant and less interested in me—in our family, and eventually we separated. He came to the house to get a few of his things one day and I noticed his hygiene was not up to par. I knew he was dealing with personal matters but he always took care of himself physically and that's when it hit me. I realized he was dealing with depression and it dawned on me I may have too. The pregnancies, financial stress, and deaths caused an overwhelming weight of responsibility for me. I was trying to figure out the right way to handle the load and prayed to God to reveal anything hidden from me about Nelson. I often say be careful what you pray for. Little did I know God answered my prayer very quickly.

During one of his visits, Nelson used my laptop to check his Facebook account and afterwards when I pulled up Facebook it asked me to sign on as the last user, which was him. I signed in using the same password I originally assigned to his account, and saw all the women he had become friends with and I read the messages. I noticed a conversation with one woman, which started off friendly, but when nicknames were added in the mix, it became a bit more personal. I made a copy for my records, in case I needed evidence for divorce court.

I confronted him in a calm and solemn demeanor—not ghetto fabulous or violent. I had to keep it classy. All he did was listen but did not respond to my questions. I wanted to know more about his involvement with this woman and he refused to answer. After further investigation by talking to other family members, I saw she was involved with helping him with the business too. I even asked if we could all sit down and talk like adults. Of course he refused, and called my request childish so I sent her an email asking her to call me. When she did, surprisingly, the conversation went better than expected. She first shared with me she was just asking for his feedback as a friend. I simply asked her did she not have a dad, brother, uncle, or cousin to get advice from instead of talking to a married man? She apologized and I told her she was forgiven. At that point it was between her and God.

Even after all that Nelson still hung out with her and allowed her to come to the house to pick him up or drop him off for his visit with our girls. The boldness of his actions really hurt me, leaving me upset and angry. It was like a movie was running in my mind about all I did was love him, wanted the best for him, and wanted to be the best wife I could be for him—yet no matter what I did, it was not enough. I felt like I was not enough. Depression was really taking shape during the separation. I isolated myself. I stopped going to church and surrounding myself with other believers because I thought everyone would look at me and say, "I told you so." The enemy even put suicidal thoughts in my mind on more than one occasion, but I focused on my daughters and it kept me from going through with it. This is when my shift took place.

One nice Saturday afternoon, Nelson came over to visit the girls. He pretended he was taking out the trash but was really waiting for the other woman to pick him up. I was sitting in the office seeing all of this. He even told me he was going to hang out with "his friend" at the park while I was at home with my oldest daughter and pregnant. All I could do was laugh and say, "Lord, you know."

I truly believe what really kept me from having a nervous breakdown was not only the grace of God, but my praise and worship. I was hot but had to keep my cool. I believed we were trying to work it out. We went to counseling and he acted as if he wanted to save the marriage. The kicker for me was when we went to a counseling session with our Pastor as a last resort, he still went back to the other woman.

The straw that broke the camel's back was his infidelity. We met one day and I asked straight up, "Who do you want to be with? Me or her?"

He flat out said, "I want to date her."

I said, "What?"

He said, "I want to pursue a relationship with her."

I said, "Okay." After that we had to file for a divorce. That's when I thought about a message my Pastor preached, "Faith, Foolishness, and Presumption." I was in faith for God to heal my marriage but at this point I would have been bordering on foolishness. I desired to be married because I believe in marriage and all it stands for. I was willing to do whatever, within reason to make the marriage work. At the same time, I believe it takes two to make a marriage work no matter how much you pray.

Emotionally—I felt so stupid. I couldn't believe all I had done and all of the relationships I sacrificed to be with this man—when in the end he chose another woman. I felt like such a fool. I thought about what my mom and others said: he just wants to be with you because of what you have and what you can do for him. Initially, I felt numb spiritually. Then I thought about the grace, mercy, and forgiveness of my Lord and Savior and especially the blood of Jesus. However, I didn't forgive myself for quite some time. Physically, I felt like a ton of bricks had dropped on me. I realized that I got caught up in having the perfect wedding without making sure I had the right person. Yes, I loved the thought of being married and being committed. In reflection, I think I was more committed to the idea of marriage than actually the person. When Nelson approached me with the idea we needed to "blow things up and work it out," his words for getting to the root of our problems, I was ready to do just that. I was willing to take off work for a family emergency because my marriage was in a bad place and I wanted to make it work. Instead, he wasn't committed and kept putting off our conversation. Looking back, that may have been a way to stall for time while he was trying to decide what he wanted to do. I am of the mindset, if a person doesn't want to be with me, don't keep me locked in so you can have your cake and eat it too. I had the desire to be married and finally realized I was married to the wrong man. Like someone said, sometimes you have two good people in a marriage and neither person is bad, but they are just not right for each other.

As a result of this episode in my life, I learned I should:

- Stop putting me last. I won't neglect doing something special for myself and I won't feel bad when I do.

- Look for signs of depression in others, especially after traumatic life events. For instance, watch when they isolate themselves, or don't take care of their physical hygiene when they normally do.

- Cover my marriage more in prayer because it is a spiritual battle.

- Pray with the man I marry because of the power of agreement.

- Listen to my gatekeepers because they truly have my best interest at heart.

- Know my future husband's strengths and see his weaknesses as areas of opportunity.

My healing began when a friend invited me to a prayer retreat in Denver. I learned to commit myself to prayer and self-care. As a result, I am stronger. I've learned and am still learning not to be so judgmental. My experience helped me to be more sensitive to others who may be experiencing a life episode. I am that much more sensitive when I see a single mom with children. You really never know what a person is dealing with and you never know what led them to where they are in their life—hardship, transition, death, or molestation. When I hear older people make certain comments under their breath about young women, my heart cries. I've become more sensitive to listen to others who may want to share their hurt. I'm more apt to share my story and not feel bad about it because at the end of the day, the Bible says, "They overcame him by the blood of the Lamb and by the word of their testimony" (Revelation 12:11 NIV). It brings freedom because I am sharing my authentic self with transparency, and I'm not worried about the opinions of man.

This experience launched me into my destiny! I started developing my business and networking with like-minded individuals. Currently, I work with small to mid-sized businesses to make them more manageable by offering services to keep their organization efficient and on task. It's done through process improvement and promotional services to market their brand to the world via social media and then measuring the success of their marketing strategies. I've also created two brands — Love Is My Swag (#LIMS) and Giving Is My Swag (#GIMS). These brands are used to support nonprofit organizations where their mission aligns with my company's vision, LockBox Strategies, LLC. We come together via events to help raise funds for various initiatives and scholarships for area youth based on criteria including ethnicity, socioeconomic status, single-parent household, and/or homelessness.

More than ever, I am committed to taking care of myself so I can be there for family and friends. I am committed to being present and leaving a legacy for my daughters. Just know, no matter how far you have fallen, you will come out stronger. You will make it through! Everything you go through is a stepping stone in your journey, and it all leads to fulfilling your destiny.

LEAVING MYSELF ALONE

BY STEPHANIE PAYNE WILLIAMS

"All of our unhappiness comes from our inability to be alone."
                                                    –Jean de la Bruyere

I *don't like leave,* I remember thinking this to myself as a child. I have a memory of sitting on the floor as my mother prepared to leave the house. When the wig was adjusted correctly on her head, her makeup applied perfectly, I knew it was almost time. The last thing was for her to put her purse into the crook of her arm. Nooooooo! I would yell inside my head. I was afraid to say it out loud. I knew, even at a young age, that it was a mistake to express my true feelings. "I'm leaving now," she would say. "I don't like leave," I'd say under my breath. She never heard me.

My whole life I have said phrases like "I don't like leave," and other expressions of my true feelings in whispers and muted words. I used just enough breath to get them out, but not with enough sound to mean anything or have any impact on the person or situation at hand. I'm not sure how I came to be this way. Was it a spanking I got after doing something I like to do and was told it was wrong? The smack across my lips when I spoke out of turn? Or, was it just the normal insecurities of growing up second behind my beautiful, light-skinned older sister, my golden boy twin brothers, or the little sister who came along after my mother's second marriage. I don't know. But, what is more troubling, is that I am a grown woman who still struggles to express herself in truth. Not just to others, but to myself. And I am determined to figure out why.

Now, don't get me wrong, I say things. I say a lot of things. Ask me how my date went last night, and you'll get every nook and cranny of the details. I can be the Queen of "Too Much Information" on light hearted conversations with friends. But when it comes to things that really matter, I have a problem expressing how I really feel. Especially if it affects someone else. If it will cause another person pain or discomfort, I pause. I debate. I lie. I would like to get to the point in my life that during any and all situations, I can look down at my hands and they not be wet from me holding my tongue.

My true wants and needs fought against my fear of "leave" and other words that I have wanted to express, but put other people's feelings, thoughts, and needs ahead of mine. Now, when it came to my children, I don't regret the decisions I've made that were in the category of a mother's sacrifice.

It was the 80s, I was 26 years old when I discovered my husband was addicted to crack cocaine. When I found out, my children were one and three years of age and I decided to leave him. I know in my heart, had it not been for them, I would have stayed with my husband. I would have stayed, thinking I could love the addiction away. I would have toughed it out believing that giving back rubs and baking homemade biscuits could make it all better.

I hated drugs. I was afraid of them. To this day I have never so much as smoked a joint. Do they still call them joints? Well, they did in the 70s. I started seeing joints show up at neighborhood house parties. I saw my friends separate the stems from the seeds that would pop out and burn holes in their clothes. There was a lot of polyester and rayon being worn by teens and pre-teens in the late 70s and if parents would have looked really close at their teen's clothes, they would have most likely found some small burn holes. They said smoking marijuana wasn't addictive or harmful. But I didn't believe it. I thought I would be the first person to take a puff and die; THEN they would find out it really kills you. And my mother and grandmother would be on the news and the front page of the Memphis commercial appeal because their daughter and granddaughter was smoking "that dope" and died. Embarrassing them to the highest. That fear kept me sober.

Had I not had my boys, I would have put my true feelings about drug use aside and tried to save my husband. Well, I did stay for a while. I mean, he was my husband. My father walked me down the aisle, my best friends put on those god-awful dresses I picked out because they reminded me of the dress Princess Diana wore when she married Prince Charles. We had taken vows in a church. But, when I saw that rehab, a new job, and starting over in a new city didn't change a thing, I knew I had to leave. I had to save my boys. I refused to let them grow up in a household where I was chasing their father down every payday trying to make sure he didn't blow his paycheck on crack. Hiding our valuables and lying to the kids about everything because they were too young to be told what was really going on.

When my son asked, "Mommy, what's wrong?" Of course, I would say, "Nothing, baby." I told myself I was saving them, but they really saved me. Because of my inability to be my authentic self, and speak my truth, happiness played hide and seek with my life. And I was sick of chasing happy. Well, it's not like I'd never felt happiness. I had moments of happiness, and I try to have a sunny disposition most days. But, there were times when I just couldn't bring the sunshine. And it's hard for me to admit it. It's like I don't want to burden someone else with what's going on with me. I'm supposed to **be** the sunshine. Even if the sunlight is manufactured with stage lighting and mirrors.

When I was going through the drug use of my husband years ago, a lot of my friends didn't know at the time. I hid it. I kept it all deep inside of me; even the time when I attempted to confront him at a crack house. You would think holding all that inside would be extremely difficult, like trying to not sneeze in a field of fresh cut grass. But, at this particular time in my life, it was easy to hold my true feelings in. I had so many years of practice doing it when I was a child. By the time I reached my 20s, my true feelings were delicately contained. Like a shard of glass inside a marshmallow. You couldn't tell it was there. You really had to look for it. Or make it hot enough so the spongy layer of marshmallow melted away. But, no one looked for it. No one called me to the carpet on my "acting" like everything was fine and dandy.

It's hard to be truly happy when you feel like most days you are "acting." Putting on a performance. When you are performing your life instead of living it, you really aren't living. Every time you stifle your voice for the sake of someone else, you lose a little bit of your true self. And I had been doing this for a long time. Covering my feelings with performance after performance. But when the performance ends, who was I then? There's no crowd, no spotlight, no applause. End scene and fade to black is a lonely feeling and existence when you don't know who you are.

I couldn't stand being alone with myself because the person I was with was a stranger. It was difficult to get to know myself when I was hesitant about expressing the real me. Not the actor. The real me still had that child-like fear of speaking out when it would cause someone else discomfort. I was the type of person who wanted to make sure everyone around me was comfortable, no matter how my day was going or how I was feeling. I wanted people to feel when I walked into a room, like the temperature would rise. I would be like a warm front moving in. A tropical breeze that you just wanted to lean into. Lie against. Never want to leave. Because remember, "I don't like leave."

Being left leads to loneliness. And being lonely is what I try to avoid at all costs. Of course, God knew this about me because recently, I'd been forced to spend a lot of time alone. I was not comfortable with it at all. The frequent time alone started when I was laid off my last job. While I was working, my life was busy and loud. Lots of different people, lots of talking, meetings, music, comedy, and laughter. And when I was laid off, my life got eerily quiet. It was shocking to my system. The first couple of weeks were okay. It was like I was on vacation or just taking some time off. But when the days kept going, the phone stopped ringing, the interruptions didn't come, the random people stopping by my office was no more, I was forced to spend time with myself. All alone. I couldn't handle it. I couldn't face myself without the distractions. Not without a buffer.

So, what I have come to realize, my "I don't like leave" statement was still a force in my life. I didn't want to be alone as a child and I don't want to now. I performed in my own life so people would always be around me. There. I said it. I did it so they wouldn't leave—so I wouldn't have to be alone. Being alone made me feel worthless. Like in a world of billions of people, there is not one person willing to be with me: share an afternoon; split a pizza; steal a fry off my plate. I know it's not as dramatic as I made it, but it honestly felt like that to me. I fought feelings of not being worthy or good enough my entire life. And when I was alone for too long, the voice of loneliness was loud and clear. I made many poor life choices by living my life so someone won't leave me. I would make it really comfortable to stay. Warm. Kind. Loving. Non-confrontational. But behind that were lies, resentment, and inner turmoil.

Yes, I do mind that you live with me and don't pay your share of the bills. Yes, I do mind that I found a receipt from a Christmas present you bought with two ladies suede coats in different sizes; and the other one was not for your mother. Yes, I mind that you have sex with other women and come home and climb into bed with me and spoon. No, I don't want to live with a drug addict.

So, most times, I was quiet. I pretended everything was okay. I pretended to be supportive. I accepted apologies I didn't believe. I pretended I wasn't dying inside because I denied myself the true expression of disgust. I risked my health, my sanity, my God given right to be myself, all so I wouldn't have to just be **by** myself. Crazy, right?

Once I committed to a relationship, I stayed. Whether it was personal or professional. I stayed longer than I should. There would have to be some type of catastrophic event taking place to force me to leave a situation. I ignored the signs or found a way to rationalize them. My focus was always to do my best and be there for everyone else. Even when I made the rare decision to leave, it wasn't for my own good. It was for the good of another person. When I finally left my crack addicted husband, I didn't do it for me, I did it for my sons. I had to make a choice; to do what was best for my then husband, or my children. I didn't at one time think about what was best for me. Or, ask God what I should do. I just jumped face first into Mama Bear mode, and rode it out. Once I lifted my head and looked around, I had made it through the storm. God took care of me when I wasn't paying any attention. I was stepping blindly off of cliff after cliff and He was there with a drawbridge each time. I wasn't looking where I was going and God knew it. He covered me and protected me from my own ignorance.

There was one night in particular that I know it was only by the Grace of God that I am here today. I was home with my two boys who were toddlers at the time. We had no money and not much food in the house. My husband had a part-time job and was getting paid that night. I had a conversation with him before he left for work. I begged him to bring his check home so we could buy groceries and pay bills. As the time passed that night, I knew he wasn't coming home. I asked a friend to babysit and got in my car and drove around the city. I didn't know anything about crack. Where to get it, how it was used, how addictive it was. I just knew I needed money for my children.

I drove around aimlessly and just happened to turn down an unfamiliar street. And there it was, my husband's car. Parked in a driveway at a house I didn't know. I pulled into the driveway directly behind the car, got out, walked to the home, and knocked on the door. A man answered and I asked if my husband was there. He said no and slammed the door in my face. I knocked again. I heard some muffled cuss words coming from behind the door, then nothing. I knocked again. The door flung open and before I saw the man, I saw the knife. He told me to leave or get hurt. I returned to my car. But didn't leave. For some reason, I wasn't afraid. I started blowing the car horn. I leaned on it with my elbows. Constant blaring. I wasn't leaving until I had money to feed my kids. Neighbors started coming out from the surrounding homes and I kept blowing the horn.

Eventually, my husband emerged from the house, his whole paycheck had been spent. I could have been killed that night. I didn't know what I was walking into, who these people were, or what they were capable of. God had that drawbridge ready just for me. And I was too stupid to notice. I was so worried about my kids and my husband's feelings, I wasn't aware of my own danger and God's blessings and protection.

You would think going through situations like this would cause me to change. It didn't. I think I actually closed up more. My true feelings and voice got buried deeper.

I think back again to my childhood. Past the toddler "I don't like leave" stage, to the elementary school stage when I learned about keeping up appearances. Not just the take a bath, comb your hair, brush your teeth stuff. It's the "What will people think" appearances. I was taught you have to always keep in mind what other people think of what you do, and what you look like. My hair couldn't be nappy even if that's its natural state. It would be hot-comb pressed within an inch of its life at all times. I wasn't supposed to get my school clothes dirty, walk on the backs of my shoes, or listen in on grown folk's conversations. I was supposed to keep quiet when a grown male friend of the family gets too "handsy" with my 10 year old body. And I was to never ask why Daddy don't live with us anymore.

I had to act like I was told to act. Say what I was told to say, be who I was told to be. This type of behavior caused me to be in a constant state of second guessing my every move because I had become so accustomed to someone telling me how I was supposed to feel or what I should do. And on top of that, I worried about what everybody was thinking and how my life appeared to others. And this morphed into sometimes just lying about how I felt or pretended I was okay with certain situations. Along the way, I thought that if I did everything I was told, life would be better. Even though looking around, everyone else was far from perfect.

In raising my sons, I started out like my mother and grandmother before me with the same mentality. But one day, after the divorce papers were filed, something changed. Shifted. And I wanted to break the cycle. I believe it was the realization that I was solely responsible for two innocent souls. I wanted my sons and me to have a different relationship with each other. I wanted them to think for themselves and be able to make decision without a dozen family members putting in their two-cents. I wanted them to have the confidence I wish I had at their age. I wanted them to have a voice. Their voice. I started talking to them. Listening to them.

When I could afford it, we would have family day and go to a restaurant with cloth napkins and spend time together. I was trying to get to know who they were and in the process, maybe I would get to know myself too. I tried, and it seemed like they had a better grip on their true selves than I did. I didn't realize at the time that the shift had started. Even though it was my children, I was still putting someone else's feelings and well-being before my own.

I did the same thing with the man in my life that I started seeing after my divorce. Everything I did was about him and my children. If I was a good enough mother, my children would be around. If I was a good enough girlfriend, he would be around. Well, now the children have grown up and the relationship ended. No matter how much or little you do, there are reasons and circumstances that cause relationships to end. Things happen that cause one of you to tilt your head to the side and look at your partner and realize you don't know who they are. They are doing things to you and around you that cause you pain. Someone once said that when God is trying to get your attention, He'll start with a pebble, then a rock, then a boulder if you are hardheaded. Well in this relationship, the first serious one after my divorce, I was getting pebbles pelted about my head and body for years. I deflected them. I couldn't face being alone. I rationalized, I forgave, I was stupid. Then the boulder came. It landed right in front of me where I could not deny seeing it and I couldn't get around it.

I finally left, moved to a new city, and spent all of two weeks alone before I freaked out. I could not stand it. The alone was so foreign and uncomfortable. I would feel lost at home. I went to work every day and was happy. I could skip-to-my-lou down the halls and through the studio. I was fulfilled. Then, I went home. Head down, shoulders slumped. This was really the first time in my life that I lived alone and I was over 40 years old. All my friends told me I would love it. I grew up in a house with four other siblings, married at 19, and had two kids by 23. I was going to love living alone. And I thought I did—for about two weeks. Then I was miserable. It was quiet. Even though I had furniture, it felt barren. There is something about another person's energy in a space. I think I may be addicted to other people's energy. Whether it's good or bad. It's like I needed it to survive. Like some type of booster cables for my own energy. My energy by itself was weak. When I was alone, it barely generated enough power to turn on a flashlight. But bring in some other people and I lit up like a Christmas tree. It's an addiction. Straight to the vein. But, staying lit is a job in and of itself.

Now, the job was gone. With all this reluctant alone time I had, I was forced to face my issues with leaving and loneliness. I had a lot of time to think, contemplate, realize, and wonder. Some good, some bad. And one day, I just decided I had given enough time thinking about the bad. Maybe I needed this time to get it all out. I kept myself busy and loud so I wouldn't be able to remind myself of the bad things in my life. But, I needed to face them. Ask myself the hard questions and come up with the difficult solutions.

One of the things I found difficult was hearing God. Oh I prayed. I have always prayed. But seldom had I felt like I actually heard God. I knew He was there and that He loved me. But I couldn't hear Him in my spirit. And once it was quiet, I thought I would automatically hear everything God had to say to me. But it didn't happen. And I replaced the noise that was my life with fear and anxiety. Faith and fear cannot coincide. So now, it even felt like God was silent to me. And instead of clinging to my faith, I chose fear. So, I started to unconsciously create more time alone with myself. I didn't want to be around anyone.

I was depressed and sad and started to crave isolation. The isolation didn't ask me what was wrong, I didn't have to explain my sadness. It was a vicious cycle and I made a bad situation worse. At night, I was afraid of every sound and creak the house would make. I slept with the door to my bedroom closed and locked. I would even position a chair under the doorknob. I started to feel my mortality. I felt like I wasn't going to make it to the next morning every time I turned off the bedside lamp at night. In the morning, I was surprised every time my eyes opened, I was still here.

So, since I was still here, I had to find an answer to my life-long struggle with being alone. I needed to remove my fear and find the faith I had abandoned. I started to think of all the good things about being alone. There had to be something good about it. And after a while, I looked down and noticed I was without pants. The first thing I do when I come home is remove my shoes and whatever is covering the bottom half of my body. Yes! Being alone means no pants! I found one good thing about being all by myself. When I lived with my younger sister, she would always complain about my no-pants-inside policy. "Can you cover that up? I'm blind!" she would say.

Now, I could be pantless, walk around the house and not have to answer to anyone. It was a minor victory, but it gave me hope. I started to find a few small things that made me smile about being alone. A long shower. Leftovers. Then it became a game. What's good today about living alone? Nobody asked me why I was saving one chicken strip. Or why I ate a half slice of cheese and put the other half back in the package. Or why the stick of butter had crumbs on it because I rubbed it on my toast. Yeah, I started with nakedness and then food. It helped.

Once I relaxed, I started to feel different. I was able to appreciate my time by myself. I still slept with the door closed, but no chair under the doorknob. Baby steps. And one day, when I wasn't doing anything special, not paying attention, I felt a pebble. And I listened. And in a soft loving voice, in my spirit, this is what was revealed to me.

Being alone doesn't have to mean no one wants to be with you. It just means **you** need to be with **you**. My unhappiness was only because I denied myself, of myself. And the result was not hearing God's voice in my life. I needed to be with the real me, the person I am when no one is around, because I can't do God's work as a performance. God has some things for me to do, and I kept myself surrounded by people and distractions so much, that I couldn't hear what He was saying to me. My focus was not on God or His work that He assigned to me. My focus was on doing everything in my power so I wouldn't end up alone. Being alone was not the life I'd dreamt about. But what I didn't understand was the dreams I had for myself were nothing compared to the plans God had for me. Who could create a better life for me than God? He knows my heart's desire. He put it there. So why would I think if I truly desired to share my life with someone, that He wouldn't allow that to happen? I had friends who absolutely loved being by themselves. They had no desire to get married, have children, or live with anyone. That's not me. I wasn't created like that. But I had to trust that what's best for me, God will provide. He would put the right man right in my path. He would allow me to give birth to the most wonderful children and He would allow my life to be filled with all the things I loved. Music, conversation, laughter, and the love of family and friends. And when I needed to get quiet and still so God could reach me on the main line, I would be obedient and do so. Just me and the Almighty. One on one. And the best part of all, He would never leave.

LIVE WITH PASSION AND PURPOSE

DR. DEBORAH STARCZEWSKI

"Just do it"

–Nike

You are here for a reason and have a purpose. Mary, the mother of Jesus, said words we would do well to remember, "Whatever He says to you, do it" (John 2:5). Nike didn't come up with the phrase first—JUST DO IT. I have learned that obedience is like a key that opens new doors, saves lives, and unlocks destiny.

I recently heard the phrase, "This will be a walk in the park." It means something will be easy, but I began to ponder that statement and realized that good and bad can happen in the park. While the grounds may appear beautiful with flowers of all colors, there can be thieves in the park too. While the grounds look perfect, there can be holes and places that are not level. Many things that look easy in life aren't as easy as they seem. Life is also much like a roller coaster—it can be fun, but it can frighten you as well.

The morning I heard the cardiologist tell my husband that he had less than a week to live *if* he didn't have open-heart surgery was a real eye opener. My husband's response to the news would seem unbelievable. Dan said, "I need to wait till after tax season." I remember thinking, *This is the epitome of stupidity.* But, since my husband has an accounting firm and he needed to stay on schedule, it made perfect sense to him. The doctor responded, "No, Dan. You will be dead by Friday. You can't wait till after tax season."

My mind was flashing back over the entire year my husband had a horrendous cough and wouldn't go to the doctor. I remembered waking up at night seeing him in an open-vision as if he were dead in the bed, lying there like a pale corpse. It was like a picture on a television screen coming across my mind. I knew we had a serious problem. I prayed and asked the Lord to speak to Dan himself one morning because he wasn't listening to me. Many wives can relate to this. Even though God may use a wife or husband to speak to their spouse, that is the last person he or she usually wants to hear it from. I was extremely aggravated. Only a few hours after that prayer, my husband called and said five different clients told him that he needed to get his cough checked out. I realized God had answered my prayer immediately and had sent other people to tell him.

Like most men, my husband is stubborn and would not go to the doctor. But on this occasion, he asked me to call and make an appointment. Imagine that! He wouldn't listen to me, but would heed the warnings of five clients. It didn't matter and I was happy that he was finally going to the doctor.

My mind reflected on all the ways the Lord had spoken to me through dreams, visions, and warnings and we were now sitting in the cardiologist's office with a death sentence. In the dream, I saw a four-sided plexiglass machine with a beautiful stream of light colored purple liquid that appeared to be coming from the Mercy Seat in Heaven with the sun shining through all the way to me. I knew in my heart what the Lord was revealing to me because I have studied the Mercy Seat and the Old Testament tabernacle. Because of the finished work of Jesus Christ on the Cross at Calvary, His precious blood was shed for redemption for all mankind. His blood is the ultimate sacrifice forever, and applied in heaven as the final sacrifice. The Mercy Seat is at the right hand of God in Heaven, just as it was in the Old Testament tabernacle. When the Lord Jesus Christ went into the tabernacle in Heaven, He sat down on the Mercy Seat because His work was finished. The Mercy Seat is symbolic of the Throne of God and a reminder to all believers that God raised the Lord Jesus Christ from the dead and set Him down at His right hand—far above all principality and power (Ephesians 1:21).

When we come to the throne of grace, we find mercy and grace to help us in our time of need (Hebrews 4:16). Dan and I were definitely in a time of need. God always gives a natural manifestation of what is happening in the spirit realm. The Holy Spirit of God reveals all hidden truth and shows us things to come. You need to know anything that is hidden and thank God for the Holy Spirit, who is our comforter, teacher, and our help in time of need.

A few days after the dream and my husband's initial trip to a regular physician, we ended up in a pulmonary specialist's office and were escorted to a room for Dan to have a breathing test. There was the machine the Lord had shown me before in the dream. I shared the dream with my husband and it brought comfort to him as well.

Having experienced heartache, pain, and rejection in my life, I can appreciate any help from God and others. I know that the enemy of your soul comes at a very young age to cripple you emotionally to set your life on a path of disaster. Because of real life issues I have walked through—pain, heartache, walking through divorce and severe betrayal—I have come to learn that God is our refuge and He will never fail you, nor leave you, nor forsake you. This came through developing a relationship with Him, not just knowing about Him in my head, but a heart change. He is our help in the midst of storms in life, and storms come to all. He wants you and me to live with His supernatural power and wisdom in our everyday natural life.

I know what it feels like to have the sweet confirmations from God, to receive a phone call with an encouraging word, or to see a personalized car tag that confirms what God has spoken to my heart. It is in intense times—times of anxiety, fear, not knowing what to do in the natural in the midst of a storm—that God is the I AM in the eye of the storm. There is calm in the eye of a storm. You overcome by the Blood of the Lamb of God—Jesus Christ, and by the word of your testimony, so it is vital to share encouragement with others.

Some of the instructions God gave me from that day forward may seem strange to you but what I learned is that God has a sense of humor and can get your attention in any way He sees fit—right in the midst of extreme circumstances. He makes it plain and simple so you get the picture. Even in the midst of life and death situations, God has a way of encouraging you to keep moving forward and to fully trust Him.

While the enemy was trying to take my husband out early, God had a different plan. No matter how fear tried to grip my heart, the words of the Lord were far greater than any fear or doubt the enemy was sending. I made the choice to stay in peace.

One of the ways God so beautifully encouraged me was through a bronze sculpture of a tree. Early each morning my mother and I would go home to shower and change clothing and return before the doctors would make their rounds. As we crossed over the *threshold* of the double doors, I kept noticing the tree sculpture but didn't stop to pay much attention to it because I wanted to get back to my husband's side. One morning, I chose to walk over to investigate the bronze and learned it was named THE MERCY SEAT. What a natural manifestation of the hand of God at work in our lives. He was making me aware of His divine presence at every turn and confirming the warning in the dream I shared earlier.

I began to think about the threshold experience we were facing with Dan's life and death sentence. Liminality is a term used to describe a threshold experience. It is from the Latin word *limen,* meaning "a threshold." In Anthropology (the science of "humanity"), liminality is the quality of ambiguity or disorientation that occurs in the middle stage of rituals, when participants no longer hold their pre-ritual status but have not yet begun the transition to the status they will hold when the ritual is complete. We are all in a state of transition in life. It is composed of danger, marginality, and disorientation. I was facing it all with my husband.

Right in the midst of the storm, I saw God confirming at every turn and I grew in my faith to a whole new level. So did Dan. I shared the details with Dan and his eyes were opened to see God at work in the midst of the life and death situation. My mother and I never left Dan's side, with the exception of going home for a shower and to change clothes. We prayed the Scriptures over him, and turned him over every two or three minutes due to the pain because he couldn't get comfortable. I walked with him down the halls holding his hand so he could regain strength and lung capacity. My precious husband had two open-heart surgeries due to his mitral valve being worn out, experienced two strokes, and was in Mercy Hospital for 25 days. That is intense training.

After the Great Physician does surgery on any of us, He wants us to walk again as well. I wrote the full account of what happened in my second book *A LEAP OF FAITH (25 Days at the Mercy Seat)* and it will encourage you to take your own leap of faith in every area of life—from personal to business. I speak on taking your own leap of faith at conferences, churches, and in the marketplace to inspire others because life does not always go as planned.

When real life hits, it becomes personal. I learned that it is important to obey instructions if you want to succeed in life. Obedience is key. When you know that God is for you and He sees all, it is easy to listen and obey. It doesn't matter what you are facing, He is with you. However, when facing a life and death situation, it is imperative to stay in peace and heed God's warnings.

I can assure you that we had intense experiences at Mercy Hospital, but the amazing ways that God encouraged and led us are both practical and supernatural. God delights in putting His super into our natural. God can take ordinary and make it extraordinary.

As I reflect back on the day, after leaving the cardiologist's office, Dan had a decision to make. He wasn't a happy camper. He went to work and I took Mother to lunch. My phone rang and it was the cardiologist calling to tell me he hoped Dan made the right choice. I figured the doctor called me because he knew how Dan reacted to the death sentence, and knew I would respond with urgency to inspire my husband to move forward immediately. He also asked if I thought Dan would be willing to have a heart catheterization on the same day he was scheduled for a TEE (TransEsophageal Echo-cardiogram)—the next day, February 24th. I told him that I would ask Dan and since he was going to be a captive audience, I didn't see why he would mind.

A Transesophageal Echocardiogram is an alternative way to perform an echocardiogram. A specialized probe containing an ultrasound transducer at its tip is passed into the patient's esophagus to allow imaging and Doppler evaluation which can be recorded. It uses echocardiography to assess how well the heart works. When we have a problem, we must have a diagnosis in order to solve or fix the problem, and then act on it.

Dan chose to have both procedures and as we walked down the hall of the hospital, I remembered taking the same walk with our son a few years earlier when he had the same test prior to open-heart surgery. My son, Landon, Dan's stepson, had open-heart surgery seven years earlier. I will never forget the phone call when Landon told me he had collapsed while running on the treadmill. I told him to go to the emergency department at the local hospital. I was at Bible College when the call came and I called my husband at his office in Winston. We both had a one hour drive to make it to the hospital.

Landon was born with aortic stenosis at birth, but when he saw his pediatric cardiologist at age 19, the physician advised he was fine. He made a mistake as we all do. My mind began to race and reflect on the details of that storm we had walked through seven years earlier. I remembered the intensity and the fear that tried to overtake me, but how God gave me the word *bicuspid* and the word *onyx,* and how He confirmed the problem with my son's heart and even showed me the type of valve replacement that was brand new in the United States. I remembered how the cardiovascular sur-geon asked how I knew about the On-x valve since it had just been introduced only a couple weeks earlier and he just learned about it.

I have learned to pay attention to details and listen for the still small voice of God. I remembered hearing a teaching series on the

Old Testament Tabernacle and how the onyx stone was placed on the shoulder of the Priests. Then I came inside our home and when I walked through the door, across the threshold, I noticed a show on the television with a bathroom that had been redone with solid onyx. Because I kept hearing the word, I knew God was up to something. Our son, Landon, received the first On-x valve in the USA. You can see with the few details I have shared how God reveals and guides you to stand strong in the next storm. What we walked through with our son was great preparation for this storm. We grow stronger in life as we weather real life storms through turning to God and trusting Him.

I have also learned that what we do most in life is wait. I waited by my husband's side as they began to prep him for the procedure, kissed him, and said the three words we always say, "I love you" before I walked back to the waiting room. The surgeon who did the TEE came out and told me there was a scheduling problem and they were going to wait till Monday to do the heart catheterization. I didn't have peace so I called Sanger Heart and Vascular and asked to speak to a manager. I shared my concerns and the fact that it wasn't our fault there was a scheduling problem. They chose to send another surgeon over who did the procedure. I thank God I was not afraid to step up and make the call because I remembered the words from the cardiologist—"Dan has less than a week to live."

Time passed and then I heard my name called and stood up to speak with the surgeon. I walked out in the hall where he informed me Dan had gone into heart failure and they lost him, but were able to use the paddles to raise him up. They were not even able to finish the heart catheterization. They were admitting him to CCU through the weekend to get him stable for surgery. I had a calm assurance that only comes from God in the midst of a storm. I chose not to allow fear and anxiety to overtake me and stayed in the place of peace that only comes through a personal relationship with Jesus Christ. I also felt and knew we were in intense times—again.

What is also amazing is how God walks through storms with us, matures us for the next one, and how even at the time of this writing, I am receiving texts with pictures of a newborn baby I am praying for that has had open-heart surgeries right in the middle of the editing process. You can see how God prepares us, propels us to walk through storms, and positions us to share and pray for others walking through the same. God equips us to help others. It is also amazing how I was able to share the pain that comes from open-heart surgery with my friend, the grandmother of this precious child, and gave her hope to believe God because of what we have walked through already.

Just as the pain of open-heart surgery is like being run over by a Mac-truck, the pain of heartache, betrayal, cancer, loss, and all of life's problems are just as real. It is natural to feel pain, anger, and all sorts of emotions, but you must make the choice to respond and not react. God uses what you walk through to equip you and empower you to reach back for others. He teaches you to trust Him, much like the power of resting in the arms of a loving parent gives you a glimpse of the power of resting in the arms of our Heavenly Father. Just as a natural parent watches out for a child, the Lord watches out for you and me as His children.

Thank God the Holy Spirit reveals all hidden truth and shows us things to come. He had warned me through a sense of urgency not to wait. If I had waited and trusted the first surgeon's words that Dan would be okay to wait till Monday, Dan would have gone into heart failure in the car on the drive home. If I had listened to some of the people texting me and wanting me to move him to a different hospital, and trying to give advice, instead of trusting the peace in my heart from God, my husband would not be alive today. Always trust the Holy Spirit and His promptings and put your faith and hope in God, not people. You must shift from the fear of man (being a people-pleaser) to the fear of God. When you have the fear of God, your faith will be in Him as well. It is vital to put your faith and trust in God.

I will never forget the stop sign outside Mercy Hospital that read STOP WORRYING because someone had put a sticker with the word "worrying" on the sign. I saw it each time I drove home and came back to the hospital. God used practical ways to encourage me to stop worrying, to believe, and trust Him. I shared them all with my precious husband, who by the way listens to what God says today and heeds the early warnings. It is vital for life that you learn to hear God, and obey His instructions.

I remember how the Lord spoke to my heart that Dan's surgery would be on Leap Year Day and it would be like it never happened. The heart surgeon scheduled Dan for February 28th and then later changed it to March 1st. I shared what the Lord had spoken to my heart with my husband about the date. The next day the heart surgeon came to inform us that he wanted the right team in place so he was changing the date to February 29th—Leap Year Day in 2012.

There were lots of changes, times of waiting, and a sense of urgency where I knew I had to totally trust God. I have learned that what we do most in life is wait. Sometimes you are waiting on people to get into divine alignment with God to have the right team in place. Other times, you have to stand up and know it is dangerous to wait any longer.

I also know that the longer the preparation in life, the greater the calling. The more severe the attacks, the greater impact you can have in life. This is why the enemy tries to stop, block, distract, and destroy people. The enemy doesn't attack you because of your past, he attacks you because of your destiny.

Dan made it through the first open-heart surgery but was not healing properly. On March 5th, the Lord spoke a very funny, yet strange word to me. When I went home to shower and change clothes, the Lord spoke to me to put a particular sweater on that has ribbons with two balls made of fur that you tie into a bow. The Lord whispered to my heart that I would need to have balls that day and stand up to people. I know that may sound a little strange, but that is how He got my attention.

Another morning, the Lord spoke to my heart to wear a black skirt, a particular blouse and sweater and high heels—because I was going to have to step into a new level of faith. It is imperative for you to make the shift from fear to faith. That morning Dan was complaining of a headache and said he felt anxious. I asked his nurse to check on him because I knew these were warnings of impending strokes after surgery. I recognized the symptoms because I had worked in the medical field for seven years in my twenties. My mother and I drove home early each morning to shower, change clothes, and return before 7 AM so we could see the doctor when he made rounds. Most of the mornings, we changed into comfortable, casual clothing, but when God gives an instruction, your part is to obey and "just do it."

While those instructions were humorous and may make you wonder, God will use whatever way He sees fit to give you a specific instruction and encouragement along the way. Before we made it back to the hospital that morning, my daughter-in-law called to tell me that Dan wanted us to hurry because he was seeing what appeared to be a screen closing over his eyes. By the time we returned, my husband had two strokes and was being sent for a CT scan to determine the damage. He had two strokes to the frontal lobe of his brain and had short term memory loss. I realized God had warned me through the instruction about Leap Year Day—because it was like it never happened to Dan because he didn't remember. I am thankful God didn't share that detail with me ahead of time. The doctors were in the room and I began to declare God's Word over my husband and told him that he was not leaving me down here by myself. I remember declaring that Dan would have full memory and God's healing power works. I had to take a stand…right in front of the medical team, doctors, and surgeon. That was exactly God's instruction. He warned me, confirmed it, and I had the choice to obey—or not. I obeyed, prayed God's Word over Dan, and watched God heal him, time and time again. It wasn't automatic with the strokes, but healing to his memory came back over a few days. At first, he thought he was in the hospital for our son, Landon, who had open-heart surgery a few years before.

Intense times cause you to focus, reveal what is important and necessary, and teach you to pay attention. Obedience comes easier when you have experience with God. He teaches each of us in different ways, but wants all to learn to hear, listen, and obey. When you learn to trust God in small things, it becomes easier to trust in larger things. God teaches through life in practical ways.

We all have struggles in life. There is always a solution. We all experience times of heart-wrenching pain and intense times, from daily challenges to life and death circumstances. It is what you do in those times that either help you or harm you. You can choose to be a victor in life. You don't have to live as a victim. You can choose life. You don't have to die before your time if you will heed the warnings and obey instructions.

My hope and prayer is that you will realize how valuable you are, that God has a good plan for your life, and for you to take your own leap of faith and believe for God's best. I personally know about the resurrection power of God because I have experienced and know it. I pray that you will choose to turn whatever you are walking through into a platform of purpose—and extend a helping hand to others, who might otherwise give up on life.

Life has peaks and valleys. We all experience them. I have often heard that time heals all wounds, but I don't believe that for one moment. It is what you do with your time that either brings healing and a newfound celebration for life, or you can choose to stay stuck in the past of defeat, distractions, and despair. When you turn to God, He is there to help lift you up out of the dirt and decay of life. You are God's priceless treasure. He wants to heal you, bring you out of struggles to success, and position you with a new platform of purpose.

The more you walk through, the stronger you can become if you choose to connect with others. You can bury the past, but learn from it, choose to bless others, build others up, network and do business and life together. The enemy wants to isolate you and make you feel like there is no hope. God wants to position and empower you to help lift others out of despair and hopelessness. He wants you healed and made whole to partner with Him.

We are all divinely connected like a beautiful tapestry. When you turn it over and look back, you will see the tied knots that don't look so nice, you will recognize the divine connections, and the finished product is worth every connection and place you have walked.

Dare to dream again. Find out what's blocking you and move forward to success. True success is advancing God's kingdom… leading our families, our communities, and ultimately the nations back to God. My third book is "THE MIDNIGHT HOUR: Will America Turn Back To God?" I chose to obey God and do what He has put in my heart to do—write and publish books, preach, speak, and teach people how not to miss heaven by 18 inches. I have often heard the distance between the head and the heart is 18 inches. It is not knowledge about God that gives us eternal life, it is having a real heart change.

Don't carry your gifts, talents, and story to the grave. Dare to dig in the dirt and push back against every obstacle by forging ahead—fully knowing you have a divine destiny in God. His light shines brightest in the darkness. God will use you to help others make the shift—to put aside their past and replace it with the great plan God has for them.

You can own your own business, start a company, go back to college, or run for political office. Whatever God tells you to do, do it. I have people ask me how I write books. My answer is simple—I start. I wake up at night with the Holy Spirit speaking to me and I come downstairs and write. God will put thoughts and dreams in your heart. He will give you new ideas for a business or venture.

Life brings problems no matter if you are doing great things or hiding out on the sidelines. Do you want problems from doing nothing, or do you want challenges that face anyone as a choice of stepping up to open that new business, start that new marketing firm, or becoming a social media expert?

Even in the midst of change, chaos, and unrest across America and the nations, you can dare to dream, step up to the plate, and learn something new. You may have failed at something personally, but it doesn't make you a failure. You can dare to dream, turn your passion into purpose, and pursue a larger platform to impact the lives of others for success.

Don't be consumed with your struggles so you can see your success. Turn to God and receive His plan for your life. The very thing you've walked through is what the enemy is trying to use to destroy someone else. Choose to connect with others and build your life while living it. Your passion will propel you into purpose to leave a legacy of serving others while doing what you love. You are an overcomer...so share your story to encourage someone else not to give up, and give all the glory to God.

Just as God raised my husband up from earthly death, He can resurrect your dreams to life (or destiny). Keep moving forward in faith...greater things are ahead. The God of all creation—the only God who is alive—is for you! Keep moving forward with your eyes fixed on Jesus. Don't focus on the temporary struggles...keep your eyes on the Savior and watch Him give you success—His divine way.

God's ways are always best. If you don't know God's plan for your life, you can come to know it and do it. Hold true to what God puts in your heart. If I had been swayed by man's opinion, my husband would not be alive today. Don't allow fear and anxiety to overtake you. Choose to live in the place of peace and rest through developing and nurturing an ongoing relationship with Jesus Christ.

Tips for spiritual growth that will help you with everything in life:

- First and foremost, don't get hung by your tongue. Speak life over yourself and others.

- Choose to forgive everyone—including yourself. Choose not to be offended and always remember, the person God will bring in your life for your next assignment, the enemy will try to create strife to get you offended. Make the choice not to be offended at anyone. Choose to respond and not react. You will notice a difference as you make the choice each time and sense God's strength in your weakness.

- Read books based on the principles found in God's Word. Read the Bible, connect with other believers, and listen to sound, biblical teachers every moment you have free. Instead of picking up a magazine, keep a book with you, your Bible, and a great tool: *Prayers That Avail Much*, which is a book of prayers packed with Scripture for every need. When you sense a warning, stop and pray. There is no time like the present. Prayer changes everything, saves lives, opens doors, and slams the door shut on the enemy.

- Develop a love relationship with the King of kings, and the Lord of lords. He wants you to be in good health and wants to prosper you in every area. Since I fell in love with Jesus, I have a newfound celebration and passion for life. I can say I have been to hell and back because of my passion for Christ—but it has been worth it all. God knows best how to position you, provide for you, and propel you into your God-given destiny through connecting you with the right people. It doesn't matter what you do in life, choose to do it with passion and purpose to leave a legacy.

I also know that being in ministry doesn't make you immune to adversity, attacks, challenges, and problems. As a matter of fact, I have learned that you may experience more attacks to prevent you from moving forward and to ultimately stop you. The divine shift to living with eternity in mind changes your perspective for all of life. You begin to see the why behind the what and understand that every person has value to God. What matters to God will matter to you as well.

While repentance and faith in God are requirements for salvation (being born-again), I am forever grateful to God for the life lessons and blessing of obedience He has taught me that I shared in my first book *GOD'S PRICELESS TREASURE (How To Overcome Challenges, Be Transformed, and Know Your Purpose)*. In the book, I share real life stories and truths about moving from drama to destiny. The Lord gave me an acronym for drama—the **d**evil **r**acing **a**fter **m**y **a**ssignment. He is after your assignment, too.

You are created to live with passion and purpose. Whatever you elevate becomes bigger in your life. Choose to elevate God over all. Shift from pain to purpose—from living under your circumstances to knowing you are seated with Jesus Christ in heavenly places. He desires for you to tap into the power of God through living by faith and finish your course here on earth.

PRIDE AND MONEY

BY SHAYLA BOYD-GILL

"Think like a queen. A queen is not afraid to fail. Failure is another steppingstone to greatness."

–Oprah Winfrey

I grew up watching my mother run the show; she knew exactly how to get things done, no matter what. I became accustomed to that lifestyle, as Malcolm X would say, "...by any means necessary." I grew up with that being my normal. I was expected to make things happen. It often equated to crying later, meaning handle it, "Olivia Pope it" and once you're done, you can cry. This was the strong, black woman I was raised to be.

Now hear me out, it's not a terrible thing to be a strong, black woman but there's a gap. There were some missing pieces. For example, I did not have a clear model of what it looked like to allow yourself to be supported. I saw a lot of things with a different lens than most. I never knew who my true blood father was. Although I had a father figure in the household, I always felt like I had experienced a loss. Who would not want to know their baby girl? The fatherless experience taught me to become independent.

I watched my mother work long hours and making great money in the 1980s. I equated hard work to big money. That became normal for me. We never really had a true conversation

229

about what it took to make the money, nor did I know the back-story of the bills or debt occurring. As a matter of fact, my mother worked as an accountant, so she showed me the skills she used on the job to track money coming in for the company and how to pay the bills. She even let me check out our small household bills every once in a while. She taught me how to write a check and balance the checkbook.

I understood the paper I wrote the check on pointed to some form of money but still there was nothing tangible that could show me where the money went. I didn't understand the management of credit cards along with your household bills. I didn't see any of that; I only caught a glimpse of what she made happen in our household.

One summer during my high school break I went to Syracuse University to study in their communications program. And with one lousy experience I decided maybe I should go for what the world was telling me I should do. In my head, the communications program was just an English class and I was not only bored, but also not thrilled about the possibilities of what I could do with studying English. My family did not know how to guide my decision making process and I did not fully use the resources available at my high school to work through the issue. I sold myself short on that journey. When senior year came around and everyone asked what I wanted to be, I said what everyone expected, "I want to be an engineer—I want to be an aerospace engineer." It sounded great and I could make a lot of money straight out of college.

I was feeling myself, coming from a magnet high school, which was supposed to be for those students a bit more studious. I went to college feeling proud of my achievements. I was the first in my immediate family to attend a four-year university and receive a bachelor's degree. Everyone had high expectations of me and my family was proud. I started hearing the world telling me that I should be an engineer or someone that studied math because I was good at those subjects. Secretly, I wanted to be someone that would speak around the world. I had something to say so I wanted to be an anchorwoman.

My mother and I made the journey to Florida A&M University. I was excited about being an aerospace engineering student. What I did not know was that I would really be entering into their mechanical engineering program. I was going to the college with the highest of Tallahassee's seven hills. Let me be the first to tell you, I felt betrayed and bamboozled. I arrived at the school as a spoiled, only child, not in love with the experience of sharing a room with someone. The first night in the dorm I experienced flying cockroaches that had invaded the room. When I got in the bed and looked up at the ceiling I saw that there were bugs hanging out above my head. My college life could not possibly be starting out looking like this. I survived the night.

The absolute highlight of being away from home for the first time was when I received my first credit card. Can you say "FREEDOM?" I was able to manage the card because it was being paid for by my mother. This means that I was mindful of my purchases and amount that I spent each month. Eventually the circumstances shifted. My mother had to leave her "good-paying" job as an accountant while I was in school. This is where things got "real" in my world.

Money had always been available—never once did I have to question if money existed. Now money was only available when it was *really* available. I had to start taking responsibility for my debt.

Things became challenging pretty fast as I started stressing about my engineering classes, and doubting my capabilities. There was no way I was going to tell my mother I was failing anything. I took it upon myself to get credit cards, loans, and grants to pay for repeat classes because I couldn't dare reveal I had wasted her money she had set aside for my education. She had no idea what was really going on with me and I was too independent to ask for help.

I also didn't step up and ask for the support from the teachers because I felt inadequate about learning for the first time in my life. I completely knocked myself out of the game once again by not asking for support beyond what was being said in the classroom. I made every effort to understand enough just to pass classes, but it was looking bleak.

Eventually I moved over to the college of technology and engineering and signed up for the construction engineering technology program. All I know is if someone had told me about this program when I first entered into the university, I probably would have graduated within 2-3 years. I absolutely loved it because I could apply it to the real world. It was as tangible as I saw buildings created from the ground up all over the city where I was raised. I understood processes. I learned that I had the ability to bring teams together. I learned I was good at project management. I had no idea that I could take a sparse plan and figure out the right people to make it work. It took me too many years and too much money to graduate and make it a reality.

In the midst of figuring out my life as an engineering student, I met and married my husband, and by the time I graduated I was pregnant with my second baby. I actually walked across the stage pregnant, hours before going into labor. This woman was determined to finish out her degree work because the process had been so long. I took breaks, got married, had a baby, worked odd jobs, and other thing before I became focused again. Most people graduated in four years, for me it was an eight year journey.

Upon graduating, I secured a job as a project manager with a construction company and I thrived for three years. Eventually I left, after having baby number three, and decided I wanted to be a stay-at-home mom. I also needed to replace my income so I chose to homeschool my children and sell natural baby products. It made sense to do what I already knew how to do—having had awesome birth experiences and using amazing cloth diapers and baby carriers. As I referred customers to these alternative items, I started to share what worked for my births and became a certified childbirth educator. That led to me becoming a certified Doula through two different organizations.

I had a thriving birthing practice. The money was coming through with ease once I got into a rhythm. The classes were sometimes filled to capacity and other times only two to three couples. When we had a lull in registrations, I would supplement the business expenses with my credit cards. This started a vicious cycle of accumulating a lot of credit card debt that I would only make the minimum payment on. Life experiences were showing up. Money needed to be invested in different places and the more we needed to invest, the more it became a struggle. I needed to feed our babies, take care of the household, get certifications, pay business expenses, and more.

The growth of my online baby products store did not happen fast enough and I had to carry a lot of inventory in my home. I spent my time constantly going out and finding places to market my goods and paying for different online platforms that added up quickly. I purchased ads in magazines that did not convert as hoped. It became more than I could handle without the knowledge and support to make the right moves. I started picking and choosing which bills I would pay and I was avoiding the phone calls and hiding out of fear and embarrassment.

My children would get sick or someone would get hurt and I knew that would be another debt that would take away from my household. My husband trusted me to pay the family household bills from the family account and make sure that everything was on time. I did the best I could to keep the family finances straight as my business bills were piling up while some of my personal bills were falling apart. My husband and I had some joint cards and everything was impacted by my independence. I started telling my husband that money was tight and he knew that he could not produce more so the only option for producing more would be me. I never told him how tight it was, this meant that there were many nights I set up in the bed looking up at the ceiling in fear and feeling disgust and stress. I had so much lingering over my head and no way to possibly pay it off in a reasonable amount of time.

When I realized the mortgage was rising, utilities were increasing and children were costing us more, I knew that things were too far gone. I was limiting activities for the children to participate in, living way below our means, trying every money-saving strategy that I could come across. It made me angry that I had nothing to show for all of my hard work.

After one of those sleepless nights, I woke up at 5 A.M. to go to my office and reflect on my next moves. My husband and I both were stressed. One of the biggest reasons that marriages fail is money and our communications were impacted at this point. As I was sitting in the office, I saw bright lights stopping right at my driveway. I knew something was about to go down. My protective instincts made me leap out of my chair and run out the door. As I'm running, all I think about were the rainbow envelopes that had been filling our mailbox. I hadn't been opening the mail because I couldn't do anything about it. If you know anything about the rainbow envelopes, you know that they are usually warning signs from your utility companies letting you know that your bill is late or has a termination pending.

I got used to getting these notifications and somehow I would always figure out a last minute solution. This was normal until the truck showed up in my driveway. I went outside completely distressed and discombobulated as I ran towards the truck. The driver put his hand up and he said, "Ma'am, we're not here to turn off your lights. Your neighbor said that your street light was out and they didn't want you to be in the dark." I took a deep breath and thanked him. It was really embarrassing as this man had probably seen this scenario before. I wasn't the first person that ever came running out of the house pleading for their lights not to be turned off. This was the ultimate moment of truth.

I had to come clean with myself because debt had finally won. Not only had it won, it had taken a dangerous turn because I was in a place where I was willing to do anything to make sure that my husband didn't go to work embarrassed that his family was sitting home in the dark.

I could no longer cover my tracks. I was being exposed and in that moment I knew I only had one choice. The choice was to make a decision. My husband and I had started a debt consolidation program and the more we tried to consolidate the more the company would call back and request more money on behalf of the credit card companies. I remember arguing with them and reminding them that they were supposed to help me consolidate the bills. The agreement was to make the payments more reasonable. However I learned that they were advocating for some of the credit card companies.

A gentleman on the phone told me that I had two choices, pay the credit cards off with their plan (even if all the card companies did not agree to reduce payments) or file for bankruptcy. I could not believe that he would even suggest that I file for bankruptcy. I was mortified—completely humiliated. I didn't know what to even think. The second moment of truth hit me when I realized I would never catch up with the debt. We were almost $100,000 in debt. We needed to lawyer up and file for bankruptcy.

My husband was humiliated, confused, and absolutely stressed about the amount of debt that really existed. How could this possibly happen? I found a lawyer and booked our consultation. The third moment of truth was when the lawyer tallied up the revenue and debt. He looked at me and said, "You don't have any money left after paying your bills, so I don't understand how you're feeding your babies." Tears started streaming from my eyes because my now five babies were everything to me. I felt irresponsible as I questioned everything about myself. We had been serving them oatmeal, pasta, canned beans, and rice—a lot of starch. I worried about their health all of the time. They were humble children and I did not want them to grow up with a negative relationship with money. The one blessing was that my babies learned how to cook everything from scratch.

The bankruptcy could have been avoided had I not been so independent but it opened up the doors for more communications between my husband and me. It was a fresh but humble start. If I would have told my husband sooner instead of trying to figure it out myself, we may have been able to come up with a better solution earlier. If I hadn't been so independent I may have requested my extended family to assist, but I had too much pride to ask for help. We may have taken up my mother's offer on moving into her house which would have allowed us to have half the bills that we had, but I had too much pride. If I hadn't been so independent, I would have hired a coach or mentor sooner instead of waiting until after the bankruptcy. If I hadn't been so independent, I would have let my friends in, instead of hiding out. I would have told the truth and allowed myself to be supported earlier. I recognize my role in this journey, and it resulted in me becoming exactly what I didn't want. I had a history indicating that I was not fiscally responsible so I carried the weight of the bankruptcy guilt.

In 2012 I decided that I would no longer be defined by my financial mistakes. This was a game-changer for me. I learned to make friends with my money. I could no longer blame my mistakes on money but instead I took a good look at my role in my money circumstances so that the lesson could be learned. When I took ownership for my role and practiced forgiving myself for the mistakes that I made, my money relationship was enhanced. I was no longer a victim of money; I was a partner. Money was a tool that I have learned to use responsibly. I attracted it with ease because I had a new respect for my money relationship.

I was able to get on the other side of my bankruptcy by asking for help in my business. I knew how to make money but I did not understand being a true business owner. I invested in people that were doing what I wanted to do so that I could make sound decisions. I also looked at my birthing business and online store and determined that they were not sustainable with my lifestyle. I let go of my pride, closed shop, and started a new business that would allow me to spend time with my family, have the freedom to do things that I desired, and make money all at the same time. I coached women entrepreneurs through their money trauma and taught them how to not only make friends with their money but take responsibility for their bottom line.

I took small steps to nurture my money relationship and learned to be patient with my walk. The entire experience helped me to grow a thriving business that teaches the lessons I needed in the beginning of my entrepreneurial journey. The greatest lesson learned was the importance of not doing business alone. Independence is not a badge of honor. It can make life extremely challenging if you take it too literally.

I have opened up to the gift of being supported. It is normal to allow people to take care of you. I really had to release the need to be in charge of everything because there was no way that I was going to know it all. I practiced the art of being vulnerable and allowing my circle of friends and family to see my weaknesses. It helped me to expose my human side. People will not offer to help you when you look like you have it all together. My friends were absolutely shocked when I started sharing my story of debt. They had no idea that I lived a double life—smiles on the outside and tears on the inside. If you have made financial mistakes or you see yourself on the path of destruction, take a step back and ask these questions:

- What is my role in this situation?
- What can I do to turn this around?
- Who can I ask for help?
- Have I been here before? If yes, why am I here again?

It takes brutal honesty to get to the source of the problem. If you are not willing to face your truth, it will consume you. If you are on the other side of major debt, answer these questions:

- What was my role in the situation?
- What can I do differently?
- What is my relationship with money?
- How can I make friends with my money?

Money does not have to be hard. We set the tone for the relationship. If you don't respect money, it has no reason to stick around. If you don't take time to track your money, it will get away from you. If you are reluctant about paying your bills or you complain when you have to spend money, it will not be available to you.

You have a direct line to money freedom. It takes nurturing and being congruent with what you say you want and what you do with it. If your words and actions do not align, your money relationship will be flawed. You get to decide your journey.

NOT ON MY WATCH

BY TRACI HENDERSON SMITH

"Don't ask yourself what the world needs. Ask yourself what makes you come alive and then go do that. Because what the world needs is people who have come alive."
                              –Dr. Howard Washington Thurman

I am often amazed when I recall my capacity, at such a young age, to discern. For instance, what I thought was stupid at four, was still stupid at forty-four. Whether spiritual or natural, this degree of acumen equally applied to what was unfair, sad, or evil—all the bad stuff; and there has been lots of bad stuff. And how does a child, unable to care for itself, form the propensity to right the ills of the world, avow resistance, and assert change now and indelibly?

It was the summer of 1980 at the height of the Atlanta child murders. My younger sister, who was six at the time, my cousins, two and nine, and I were at a playground in Perry Homes, a now demolished housing project on the west side. My sister, oldest cousin, and I visited my aunt there a few summers. Going during this particular time though seemed a little tricky [the precise description from a thinking child]. Odd. Disconcerting. I mean, *I would not have sent my children to a place where they were killing children,* I recall thinking. Nonetheless, barring the horror of

239

abduction never to be heard of again, ATL did not disappoint. We had the best time ever, as always.

The park was clean, really nice as parks in the projects go. Open and surrounded by trees. Dense wooded areas with unattended children, however, just didn't sit well with me at the time. So, they played. I stood watch. No one told me to. I just did. I sat on a great boulder at the best vantage point, fixed in a curve of the hill just a few feet away, with a fairly healthy oak branch in my hand. I didn't know if anything was going to go down. What I did know was that I was ready and we were all coming out alive—all of us. I was the oldest. I was eleven; and I was ready. Where did this come from? The proclivity to protect. Where exactly did it come from? And don't think I haven't thought it in my older age. I have. *What precisely did I think an oak branch would accomplish?* But at the time, in my mind, I would not be taken down. Neither would anyone who was with me.

Likewise, when the time seizures were explained to me. I was eight years old. I sat on the side of my parent's bed with my dad watching television. It had to have been a Saturday. I was in my normal Saturday regalia—tank and undies. And Saturday would have been the only reason my sister and I were so carefree. Suddenly I heard this peculiar noise come from my father. Approximating muffled tones of someone struggling to speak but could not. I turned to find him blinking intensely. Initially, I dismissed it as jesting, and I laughed. The guilt from that split moment of amusement took more than a decade to dissipate. He began to lean toward me. It didn't take long to realize he was falling over. For a second I froze. Then I braced up and called out to him. He didn't answer. I called to him again. No answer. He kept falling. By the time he was between the bed and dresser, I had already sprung into action. I went to our room where my sister, nearly four years old at the time, was playing. I didn't say anything to her. I got dressed first. It must have been cold outside. Or maybe not. I don't remember if I was dressing her for the weather, or if I was being "adult" and overly efficient. I covered her from head to toe, dressing her quickly and rather roughly. Tights, coat, hat. She asked repeatedly what was I doing and where were we going in between the occasional "OUCH!" I would only reply, "We have to go."

I called my grandfather and told him quite frankly to come get us now. Logically, he asked, "Where is your mother?"

"At the hairdresser," I replied. She had left my father on daddy duty, except, in that moment, he wasn't. So, activate big sister duty. "We're ready and on the porch. Come now."

Then, there it was. The question that would lead to future murmurs and sidelong glances accompanied by the occasional curiosity, uncertainty, and periodic censure for my "peculiarity".

"Where is your father?"

"He's dead."

I hung up the phone, grabbed my sister by the hand, marched her to the front porch, closing the door tightly behind us, where we stood and waited. Shortly after, a friend of my father's came up the walkway, dirty hands, like that of a mechanic, and dusty, ruddy complexioned. He asked if my father was home. "He's not available," I said.

"What do you mean he's not available?"

I didn't want to lie, but I didn't like his tone. I didn't like him. I hadn't seen him often, but I recognized him. I think he was one of the men that used to come up to our car and speak to my dad whenever he'd take us riding through the old neighborhood where he grew up. The neighborhood was filled with affluent Black families when my dad was coming up. Not anymore. He peered at me and took a step closer. I felt uneasy. I went into protective mode. Squeezing my sister's hand and pulling her closer to me, "He's not here."

"He's not here, or he's not available?"

"I'll tell him you came by."

"Do you know where he is?"

"I'll tell him you came by."

"Do you know my name?"

By this time my eyes are roaming for something, a brick, a stick, anything to hit him in the head with if he came any closer.

Our only option was to the left of us through the under stairs alcove, with him now standing just a few feet from the bottom of our stoop. I looked for the easiest out for my sister to allow her to run while I fought him off, if it came to that. He told me his name and asked for a glass of water. I just wanted him to leave. I went back into the apartment, sister in tow, quickly closing and bolting the door behind us. I waited, hoping he'd leave, but I was stuck. I couldn't let my sister stumble upon my dad. I told her to stay put and I went to the kitchen. The apartment was small, so I was just a few feet away, but made sure to talk to her while preparing the glass of water. That way I could gauge where she was in the room by her voice. A trick I had learned. I grabbed a Tupperware tumbler, filled it with water, and my sister and I resumed our post.

"There's something in this water," he grimaced. "See, look."

I hesitated. I didn't want to be near him. He definitely wasn't getting anywhere near my sister, but the only way to prevent that was to come off the stoop and go to him so he didn't come closer to her.

"See, come look," he insisted. "See. What is this? What did you give me?" I stepped down to look into the cup. He put it really close to my face. I remember thinking he was going to either shove my face in it or throw the water on me. Either way, I could not have been more ill at ease. I looked into the cup. He was right. It looked like cayenne pepper swirling around the bottom. And with a feeling I could not articulate then, but can better put into words now, what had to have been an eight-year-old's version of, *this simply cannot be my life,* washed over me. With his next cup of water, I encouraged him to leave.

"We can't talk anymore. My grandfather is pulling up in a second. You can take the cup with you." It was one of my mom's favorite tumblers. The green ribbed one with the white rim. She may be upset, but it was the lesser of two evils in my mind. I'd "deal" with that later. Besides, it seemed she threw a Tupperware party every other week. She could get another one. I needed this man away from my sister.

Unexpectedly, the next face coming up the walk was not my grandfather's, but my mother's. I remember the relief so vividly from seeing her. She took us inside and sat us on the couch. I held my sister closely. I could hear her on the other side of the wall talking. Who was she talking to? She called out to me to bring her some water. There was no way I was going into that room. I didn't move.

"Traci. Did you hear me?"

"Yes, ma'am."

"Go get me some water."

I could hear stirring, but I was still slow to move. She stepped out of the bedroom and on her way to the bathroom medicine cabinet we made eye contact.

"It's okay," she assured.

Seeing my father up and talking, I didn't understand. My sister was none the wiser, but I didn't want to go near him. I had seen him lifeless on the floor. After a few reassuring words and an eventual embrace, things were semi back to normal. I had apprehensions though, and I couldn't stop staring. My parents sat me down and explained what a seizure was and why some people have them. In my dad's case, he had gotten hit in the head with a golf ball as a kid out on the golf course across the street from where he lived. He had them from that point on. They went on to tell me the seizures would sometimes happen when my dad overexerted himself. My mother sprinkling in how stubborn my father was and how he not only sometimes did too much, but also didn't always take his medicine. They were attempting to comfort me, but all I could hear was everything he should and should not do in order to avoid scarring his children for life. I've always been a deductive thinker. Do this. Don't do that. All sounded pretty simple to me.

For me, this information shifted the parent/child dynamic between my father and me. I became his shadow. I watched his every move. I took an otherwise strong, healthy, hard-working, active, full-grown man into my personal, middle childhood care— asking him daily if he had taken his medicine, or reminding him to do so. If I thought he blinked too long, I'd ask him if he were okay. I set up vigil during every extracurricular project or strenuous activity. Watching. Waiting. Thanks to my disquiet: *Do you need anything? Can I bring you something? Do you want something to drink? Should you rest?* were all questions he heard more frequently. The other children played on our street while I watched my dad work on the car. I'd bring him a sandwich just the way he liked it if I thought he needed to eat something, or a tall Tupperware cup of lemonade to keep him cool in the scorching sun that I was certain he wasn't supposed to be in. This newfound knowledge changed family day at the beach forever. While my mother talked and laughed with family or friends or was busy setting up lunch, and the children built sandcastles, I attended to my father's noncompliance. Roughhousing and horseplay, football, tossing the Frisbee; all had me with watchful eye. But nothing put my soul on edge like the venture into the deep blue sea. I was a reader and that was the only way I knew to describe it at the time. He loved to swim and he'd always go out too far. I grew to depend upon the lifeguard's whistle and beckon. No lifeguard on duty signs was the worst. I sat, or stood on the shoreline, depending on how high the waves were. I'd watch for his arm on the stroke. He was too far out to make out anything else. Back and forth, parallel to the horizon, he'd swim what seemed like miles both ways. At times, I'd lose sight of him. I hated it. I could not breathe easily until he was safely on shore. I was always so upset with him for doing that, though I never mentioned a word. I never said anything. Not even about my self-appointed duties as the watchful eye. I did my job quietly, so I thought. I learned his triggers. He'd always say he was fine and most times he was, until he wasn't. In those times I was glad I was there and able to call my mom in to catch him before hitting his head.

This attentive and shielding nature was ever present during my childhood. It got stronger, some may say worse, as it sustained into my adult years. Once, I refused under direct order, to take my potty-training sister to the bathroom because I sensed the ceiling was going to give way. I was accused of being defiant and I fearlessly stood my ground, only to have the ceiling collapse mid scold. One cousin, an upstanding officer of the law, who now towers over me and I'd trust with my life, tells stories of how I handled his neighborhood fights at home in Jacksonville, Florida and during those summers in Atlanta. Then there's the time I made the manager at the cookie stand of my younger cousin's first job, pay her cash out of the register. She needed her check. He coldly asserted not having it and offered no word on when he would. I could offer a word on it; and I did.

They all transitioned from enjoying the benefits of my protection, remedy, or sacrifice during our early years, to comments like, *"You think you're everyone's mother,"* when they felt old enough to do for themselves. Or my sister's favorite, *"The last time I checked my driver's license, I was grown."* My brother, however, never once criticized or protested. He is ten years my junior and was mine from the day he came into the world. He did, however, require redirection as a toddler when he started calling me mama. My mother made sure of it.

I built quite a reputation. Difficult, fighter, and back talker were a few of the negative names. Protector, nurturer, and motherly were attempts at a more positive approach. Either way, the descriptions were assigned inaccurately. What I was, was invisible. It was like I was screaming and no one could hear me. No one noticed I very seldom fought for myself. The amount of hurt and pain I internalized was unspeakable. I was immobilized when it pertained to me. As evidenced by my broken spirit, effortless shut downs, and the unquestionably sadistic bully who lived above us, bossed me around, and beat me up at will. I couldn't lift a hand to help myself mentally, emotionally, and yes, even physically at times, but I would put myself in harms way for those I loved in a heartbeat.

This role I had taken on, over the years, morphed into something else. Something deeper. Putting others' protection before mine, twisted into putting others' significance and aspirations before mine. This warped existence reached beyond family and I ultimately put so many people's dreams, goals, and projects before my own that my authentic self ceased to exist. I became each of them, working relentlessly in their vision while leaving mine by the wayside. Pouring everything I had into their plan while what and who I am, what I wanted got pushed to the back again and again. They called me anointed, superwoman, the clutch, the go to, the one to have on your team, the one to call, the fixer, the one to get it done, a builder, a creator, and all the while I was dying. Invisible.

The SHIFT happened in a moment of realization. This is unhealthy and I cannot do this anymore. I'm tired. I have no balance. Fact is, there was never any balance. Things that transpired over my life caused me to create a life that worked until it didn't. Yes, it is perfectly fine to care for the needs of others. Most do out of compassion, but what I created was unhealthy. I had worn a cape since the age of eight. That was nearly forty years of a fragmented identity. What I created began in pain, anger, fear, and self-righteousness and grew into something crippling and exhausting. My core pattern of behaviors, emotions, and perceptions were based on compulsive heroism. My need to save everyone in their dilemma or head off any potential dilemma; the need to make everyone's world right, had ruled me for decades and many times made me easily susceptible to manipulation, misuse, discouragement, and disappointment, and I was tired. My self-worth was wrapped up in what good I could make happen for others. That looks great on the outside, but it often came at the expense of my own personal life enhancement and/or enjoyment. I decided I was done. I had to do something for myself. This was clearer to me than anything had ever been. The problem was, now that I've had this revelation, why was it so difficult to actually worry about myself? Why was the decision to do what I wanted—what I needed—such a struggle? I was mentally bombarded with thoughts of what it would mean to walk away from certain people, situations, and responsibilities. What would it mean for others? How would they feel? What would they think? How would they respond? How were certain visions and projects I was involved in going to continue? Who was going to make it work, and would it work *right* without my [controlling] thoughts, touch, and action? What was going to happen? Would certain people be okay? Would certain programs I was heading continue to thrive? I was tormented and rendered immobile *and* subsequently miserable for two additional years after the SHIFT had begun to take root in my spirit. Then it hit me. Traci, you're doing it again. This is what you do so well. Everyone and everything comes before you. You are incapable of caring for someone else, and yourself simultaneously. Someone has to go without, and that someone always ends up being you. At that unveiling, I began a journey of self-discovery. I set out to find myself. I began with a simple question: Why do I do this?

The journey took me back to my childhood—to the protector, the watchman, the fighter, the avenger for others, who was also incredibly unsure of her place in the world. I started peeling back the layers, reliving these instances. Truth is, I had tucked the real me away a long, long time ago; right around the time I started being molested in daycare. Being laughed at by family and neighborhood kids because a drunken uncle visiting from Palm Beach "liked" me more didn't help either. He'd pull me away from the group and send everyone else off to play. It's hard to remember all of what or who I was before any of this because I was so young, but I have a belief. Those who never come into the knowledge of the truth, those who are without a witness or bearer of the truth, still have what is right and wrong written on the tablets of their heart. I can only imagine that I was happy and felt loved and safe prior to these ordeals, but what I know that I know in my heart of hearts, without a witness or bearer, is how I was created. I was created to thrive. I was reading at three, writing at four, in love with books, eager to learn, creative, gifted, and advanced. I had a voice that needed nurturing. Though that voice was buried, I have felt this all my life. After the incidences of molestation started, I felt like the people responsible for my preservation didn't see me. My original creation needed safeguarding and ample opportunity to cultivate but I was invisible. I was blamed for changes in my behavior like pushing back where I had been silent before, or nonconformity; mood swings—happy yesterday and sad today, being withdrawn, isolated, and quiet. No one saw the changes in progression, they were only irritated those changes were present. I felt they were incapable of taking care of me. So I formulated very early, my view of what it must look like to care for someone—because this wasn't it.

When my sister started attending the same daycare, I grilled her daily when she came home. She didn't understand, but I needed to know. Did anyone bother you? Did anyone touch you? Did anyone say anything to you? At the time, she's four and I'm nine, but I'm there for her. I needed her to know, you are not invisible. I see you and I'm watching out for you. She didn't comprehend why, but I was asking her all the questions someone should have asked me. I looked for changes in her personality, behavior, and attitude. I believed I could identify them because even at a young age, I could recognize them in myself. I was in and out of uncertainty and anxiousness. I was suspicious and sad. I felt oppressed and paralyzed, unable to say or do anything when I felt hurt, disturbed, or taken advantage of. Powerless. The same disgusting powerlessness that was present while I lie on the nursery cot at naptime anticipating my abuser's arrival and waiting for it to be over. So for me, something as simple as *if she was happy yesterday and not happy today*, meant there must be something wrong. Thankfully, there was nothing wrong. When she was moody and didn't want to be bothered, she just really did not want to be bothered on those days. My point was, someone should have been in my face trying to figure out what was going on with me on the days I wasn't happy, or did not fit the mold of what a child should be doing.

I built the house of, *I am your protector and nothing is going to happen to you,* out of feeling no one did it for me. I was vigilant. I scrutinized everything. If it was going down, it wasn't going down on my watch. Anyone connected to me, anyone I cared about, was going to be cared for if I thought they needed protecting in some way. The origin of the hero complex was beginning to take shape, but there was more. As I continued to peel back the layers, another question was now on the horizon. Why do I stifle myself? I am my biggest hold up. Why? And how was the need to protect and the practice of holding myself down connected? We hit a rough spot and didn't have a whole lot as I got older. I stopped receiving gifts for birthdays, and Christmas. I don't remember the age, as I labored to block it out. I know I was still in school. Maybe Sr. High. The reason was, my sister and brother were younger and I was expected to understand. I'd get told, "Let us do this for them and we will take care of you later." Sometimes, later never came. After a while, I grew accustomed to waiting when it came to me. I made it okay. Eventually, I stopped expecting all together. I did not complain about that. I was a giver. I found ways to ease my parents' guilt, assuming they felt guilty. What I didn't realize was how I was being affected, how I carried it. I was training myself to be last. Somewhere between not being protected, the insistence to protect, and acceptance of no expectation, I built a life of putting everyone before me. After doing that for a long enough period of time, it became the norm, a part of me, and a part of how I viewed myself. It became expected for me to wait. And you wait and wait, and then you're 45.

WAIT! What happened to all the years? What happened to the writer, the poet, the speaker? What happened to the girl that was going to change lives with her words? Getting back to who I was authentically was now proving painful. Why? People make decisions to go another route, and move forward. You want something? Go for it. But it hasn't been that simple. I had to first undo a history of wrong thinking, break up fallow ground, and push through this hard place. I was telling myself yes, where I had trained myself to hear no all my life. It has not been easy. Knowing I needed to do something was not enough. I had to get to the core of the issue. Making the discovery about Christmases and birthdays and going back to the start of the "caregiver" behaviors really helped me see, putting myself last was woven into my fabric. I had to change the idea that, *everyone else gets taken care of but me.* Somewhere I had moved beyond being invisible to others and had become invisible to myself—battling between the authentic me, and the person I was turned into.

249

I knew at four what I wanted. Books brought me life. I remember the door-to-door salesman who spoke the words, "Books take you on a journey to wherever you want to go." I'll never forget staring at the hot air balloon logo in the corner of the cover, believing exactly what he said, and the total elation I felt when my mother made the purchase. By seven I wrote my own, complete with poems, prayers, short stories, and illustrations. I cut the pages and glued them into a cover I created with cardboard I wrapped in fabric from my mother's sewing scraps. By nine I was up speaking before large audiences and continued to do so for years.

My four-year-old self came to visit me on this journey back to my authenticity. That little girl has always known. I got off somewhere, but she never did. She politely took me by the hand and led me back to my authentic self. She fought for me. She was protecting and preserving the deepest, truest parts of me when no one else could see it. She reminded me of how good it felt to imagine and helped me move in a completely different direction. It's new in the sense that I am finally saying yes. It is not new in the sense it has always been a part of me.

"And the day came when the risk to remain tight in a bud was more painful than the risk it took to blossom"—Anaïs Nin

This hasn't been a story about healing. I'm not hurting nor am I angry with anyone. This was a story about causation. I was GREAT for everyone EXCEPT me and I needed to know WHY. These type discoveries can't be made until we get gut raw honest with ourselves and peel back all the layers. It's no longer enough to say, *Oh, that's just the way I am.* No. Why? It's the only road to true authenticity.

Being authentic means going beyond the surface and getting to the core of who we were before it all went awry. Many of us have become masters at erecting beautiful edifices atop chaos. We can be successful *and* unresolved. I'm proof. Being authentic, for me, was getting back to the beginning, to my original intent and examining myself at the point I was changed into something else. I had to go there and course correct. Here are a few lessons I learned on my journey:

- Don't tether yourself to others, worrying about what they need and want while sending what you need and want someplace to die.

- Don't be afraid to use your 'super powers' for you. Pour as much into yourself as you do into others. And if you are afraid still, then do it scared. *"When I dare to be POWERFUL, to use my strength in the service of MY vision, then it becomes less and less important whether I am afraid." - Audre Lorde*

- Be devotedly self-aware. Don't squirm around in a life that's not yours. It doesn't matter how beautiful you've made it, if it was never the one you were intended to live. Do what YOU want [in positivity and righteousness] with your life. Do what YOU love.

I was in Atlanta for a week trying to unearth this chapter. I wanted to get a headshot done with a photographer friend while there. She asked me to meet her in West Highlands at Herman Perry Park. Just like that. It was really real. A photo shoot for a book. I was a bit emotional as unbeknown to her I was catapulted back in time. So much had changed. It was now a diverse mixed-income community, but I remembered those hills and there were still plenty of trees. There was a lake now that wasn't there before. I got teary as I recalled all the youthfulness that was lost, here and in Jacksonville, because I gave those years to the person I was turned into. But now I stood on the same hills, where Perry Homes used to stand. This time it was all about me. I wasn't protecting anyone but me. Protecting the commitment I made to myself to be completely authentic without fear or compromise, and to kick the habit of waiting and take the occasion to realize all my dreams. Protecting the promise I made to myself to come alive and to speak my truth. Perry Homes was brand new, stronger and beautiful, with a hint of the character that made being in that place a rich experience. So was I. Brand new, stronger, and beautiful, with that same hint of character. The road to this point has been tortuous, but here I am. Finally. An author, a speaker, and a coach. It has taken me more than forty years to get back to the thing I knew when I was four, to who I've always been. I won't be taken down. Not on my watch.

PURPOSE FULFILLED

BY MICHELLE DAWSON

"God grant me the serenity to accept the things I cannot change, the courage to change the things I can, and the wisdom to know the difference."

—Reinhold Niebuhr

When your mother was Superwoman, people automatically assumed that you would become Superwoman Junior. As a child, one thing that I always wondered about my mom, was how she did it. How can she be everything to everyone and not become frustrated in the process? She was a single parent, had rheumatoid arthritis, cared for her elderly parents, was active in the church, active in the community, and managed to juggle two jobs to make ends meet. I don't remember her praying for God to give her insight on how to be all things to all people, I just know that she always said that He would make a way.

My mother raised me to be an independent, confident, Christian woman. She stressed and ensured that I was educated and that I could take care of myself. She taught me the power of prayer and the importance of always keeping God at the center of my life. She told me to never walk around with my head down because I had nothing to be ashamed of. Most importantly, she taught me to love myself, no matter what. When I reflect back on my upbringing, I would say my mother made sure that I had all of the necessary knowledge, skills, and abilities to handle anything life brought my way!

As I got older, however, I learned the true meaning of, "When I was a child, I spoke and thought and reasoned as a child. But when I grew up, I put away childish things" (1 Corinthians 13:11 NLT). It's one thing to believe strongly in your faith and strength as a youth, but as an adult, when it was time for me to put on my Superwoman cape and handle real life situations, I had to really take a look within and determine if I was ready to take on the world. Life's challenges will sometimes make you question all of the things you know to be true. Yes, my mom did a great job ensuring I had the resources to survive, but she never told me there would be days like this.

The highs and the lows of life can either make you or break you. Overall, I can honestly say that I've had a pretty good life. But like most people, I had to learn to appreciate all that it has brought my way, both good and bad. I often tell people that I'm grateful for it all. I am equally happy with canned tuna fish, just as I am with enjoying freshly caught Chilean sea bass. I like getting dressed up in fancy suits, just as much as I enjoy wearing jogging pants and t-shirts. Fun for me can include traveling to a foreign country or attending a backyard barbecue to fellowship with family and friends. When you've grown up having all types of experiences, you learn to appreciate every moment and take it for what it's worth.

As an adult, I've been blessed with opportunities and experiences that I could have never imagined would happen in my life. I have completed several degrees. I have a great job that I've been at for 15 years. I have purchased several homes independently. My love for traveling has allowed me to visit places such as Japan, Korea, Jamaica, and numerous states within the United States. I trained and became an Iron Girl triathlete. I have a great relationship with both my mom and my dad. I have an amazing circle of friends, who I couldn't imagine not being in my life. And most importantly, my relationship with God has helped me towards my efforts in becoming the woman He has called me to be. Although it sounds like my life has been pretty simple, I have definitely had my share of tests and trials.

In comparison to others, I used to feel that the experiences I've had weren't worth sharing because, in my mind, there was always someone else in the world that was worse off than me. For most of my life, I've remained humble and quiet about both my accomplishments and my struggles. In the past, I would say my prayers and hope for the best outcome. But as I matured, I realized that I'm allowed to have a voice. I have a lot to be grateful for and although I continue to maintain my humility, I know that my experiences represent my story. Everything that I've been through, good and bad, has helped to shape the woman I am today. I am proud of who I am because my life experiences have not only impacted my perspective, but they afforded me the opportunity to help others. You can't help anyone if you haven't been through anything. My life is not perfect, my moral code may not always be 100 percent by the Good Book, but I have learned and experienced so much. I freely share what I know because I believe it can help someone else on his or her journey.

One of the most challenging aspects of my life growing up was trying to understand the ways of God. Okay, for all of the older people who are reading this story, I'm sure your first thought was, *You shouldn't question God.* Please understand, in no way am I trying to disrespect the Most High and His ability to do what only He can do. But I believe that He and I share a relationship. Because of our relationship, we talk candidly about life, liberty, and my pursuits of happiness. I have had so many conversations with God about my life and my frustrations of not understanding the plan. I remember the many days I watched my mom meet one obstacle after another, but she never seemed to be overwhelmed with all of the other things she had on her plate. Me on the other hand, I have struggled with understanding why things happen the way they do. I know that He has a plan for my life and I don't believe that He puts things in my heart that will never become a reality. But when

I pray for those things and I don't see how they will come to fruition, it frustrates me. I pout! Yes, I pout like a five-year-old and I get upset. It's one thing to have never seen God move in your life, but when you have already witnessed amazing things happen, you wonder why certain prayer requests remain unanswered.

In 2008, God orchestrated events in my life that allowed me to relocate from Maryland back to Tidewater, Virginia, my hometown. I had no idea why I needed to move back home, but He made the path so easy, I literally just changed my address. I had a job and family in the area so I didn't think the transition would be challenging. Once I returned home and began to assess why I was there, I realized that it was not about me. Unbeknownst to me, my mom was really sick and needed me during a trying time in her life. She has rheumatoid arthritis and it had begun to affect her mobility. Originally, during my relocation, I moved back in with my mom. I stayed with her until I was able to secure my own place and sell the house I still owned in Maryland. I eventually moved into my own place, not knowing if I would need to reside in Virginia for the duration or if my relocation was temporary. Although I was in my hometown, Maryland was my happy place.

I lived back in my hometown for about three years. During that time, my mom had knee replacement surgery on both of her knees and she had back surgery. I wondered if she would ever return to having full mobility. It can be very stressful watching your parents age. To watch my mother, who was always a busy body, now have to rely on others for help was a very tough season in both of our lives. One thing about my mom though, she is a fighter. After every surgery, I would see her get stronger and she was returning back to her old self.

Around 2011, I remember sharing with God that I wasn't happy with my current circumstances. I was very unhappy at work and just living in the area. The environment I worked in was negative and I didn't see any opportunity for advancement. I had two managers that were degrading and if I didn't know any better, I felt that their daily mission was to find ways to frustrate me. I knew I needed to leave, but I had no idea what was in store for me. I made it a daily requirement to apply for multiple jobs back in the Washington, DC area, but for whatever reason, I would have first and second rounds of interviews, but no job. It was disheartening and I often wondered why God would bring me to a place and leave me miserable. Although I realized I was there for my mom, she was getting better and I was becoming an emotional wreck. I was just unhappy. Then one day, God told me to put my house on the market. I literally asked God, "For what?!?! Why do I need to put my house up for sale? No one has offered me a job and I am not interested in moving back in with my mother." God didn't answer, He was just persistent. Daily I would hear, "It's time to put your house on the market." So, the words just stayed with me until one day, I was playing on Facebook and my realtor's name popped up on the screen. As I chatted with her, I mentioned how I had been thinking about reaching out to her regarding my house. She said, "Whenever you are ready, let me know." Maybe a week later, I called her and told her that I wanted to sell my house. If you remember anything about the housing market back then, you know that trying to sell a house during that time was next to impossible. Not to mention, the house next door to me had been vacant and on the market for almost four years. When I shared with my mom that God had told me to sell my house, she looked at me like I was crazy. I honestly had no clue what was going to happen in my future, I just decided to finally be obedient. I completed all of the necessary paperwork with the realtor and she put a sign in the front of my house. It sold in 30 days! I had movers to pick up and store my household goods for an unknown duration, and I moved back in with my mother.

Surprisingly, I ended up having surgery on my knee about two weeks later and it was perfect that I was living with my mom because she was able to help me recuperate. It was approximately one month after my surgery that I received a telephone call from Human Resources asking me to accept a job back in Washington, DC. I had no clue what was in store for my life once I sold my house, but I knew that God had told me to do something that sounded ridiculous. He already had a plan that I wasn't privy to. In the end, everything worked out.

This lesson helped me to learn to be at peace with the unknown. When I can look back on answered prayers and see how everything came together in my life over the years, I am much less consumed with the intricate details of how things will work out. I will not lie and say that I don't get anxious, but I am at peace knowing that He has already worked everything out and in due time, it will all be revealed. My passion, for as long as I can remember, has been motivating others to not lose hope, but to stay encouraged regardless of their circumstances. Knowing that my gift is exhortation has helped me to accept life's experiences as opportunities for growth and that they allow me to help others. I have always been interested in being a life coach, where I could have a platform to help others walk in their destiny. I have also wanted to conduct speaking engagements and become an author to share my knowledge about life. Today, my prayer request is not how will all of these things become a reality, but trusting that He has already worked it out. I have no idea what plan He has already crafted, but what I do know is that my steps are already ordered. It's up to me to not only have faith, but to be obedient and to work towards my goals. I know that if I take one step, He will take the next step with me to continue opening doors towards my future.

I find that there are so many people who are afraid or ashamed of their truth, which in turn causes them to misrepresent themselves. People only disclose what they want you to know. Everything else is a private struggle. I find myself wondering, *Is it taboo to be honest about your highs and your lows?* Growing up, my mother would tell me, "What goes on in this house stays in this house." I'm sure everyone has heard some version of this statement from his or her parents. If you had negative things going on at home, it was considered a sin for you to share those experiences. But as I've gotten older, I have a hard time with that theory. It basically says, suffer in silence versus reaching out to someone for help. Don't get me wrong, it is not wise to tell all of your business to the world, but God brings all types of people in our lives to help us along life's journey. It's not good for anyone to go through life alone. There are so many hidden secrets that happen at home because we have been taught to keep things to ourselves. The saying, "You never know who is watching", is a very true statement. We all make an impression on those around us, whether intentionally or unintentionally. When people look up to you and seek your counsel for personal or professional matters, I think it's important that you remain honest and true about the things you've experienced. There is nothing wrong with sharing, not only the good days, but some of your struggles in life as well. Sharing how I am able to overcome hardships helps encourage others to not give up when they feel overwhelmed. I'm a firm believer that every day is not going to be easy. God never promised us a stress free life, but He did promise not to leave us nor forsake us. He gives us the strength and the resources that we need to get through every test and trial. When we are weak, God is made strong.

For most of my life, I've always maintained a positive attitude and I've tried to be a ray of sunlight to those around me. I even adopted a personal mantra, "Find the positive in the negative." I am a very analytical person, so I usually try to figure out what I'm supposed to learn from the highs and lows of life. Don't get me wrong, I definitely have "woe is me" moments, especially when I'm beyond frustrated. But I've concluded that not only have I grown and matured into a better woman as a result of my life experiences, but they have helped me to identify my purpose. What I've learned is that what I experience in life is not only for me, but put in place for me to share and help others. It's for those who suffer in silence, don't think that others could relate to what they are going through, or for those who just need some encouragement that they too will overcome whatever challenges they may face.

Once I realized what my purpose was in life, I was anxious to find out how God would use me and what direction my life would take. I remember saying a prayer, asking God to reveal to me what was in store for my life by showing me a glimpse of my future.

He indeed answered my prayer by giving me a vision of what was to come. I was beyond excited and slightly overwhelmed, because what I saw for my life was all of the things that I enjoy doing, but I had no clue how any of it would ever come to fruition. A few things that were revealed to me was that one day I would be speaking on large platforms and I saw myself as an author. When you know that something greater is in store for you, it can cause you to become anxious for change. For the longest time, I couldn't understand why God had not opened the door for those things to become a reality. I attended conferences, I networked and developed relationships with the best of them. I prayed, and prayed, and prayed, but I couldn't see how I would ever walk into my destiny. I was waiting for God to move and what I realized was that, He was waiting on me. I had to be willing to work for what I prayed for. He had given me the vision, He had equipped me with everything I needed to be successful, but in the end, it was left up to me to do the work. Faith without works is dead. In order for you to see the fruits of your labor, you actually have to put forth the work. It was absolutely absurd for me to sit around and hope that some magical door would open for my personal aspirations to become reality. It didn't matter how many conferences I attended, how many people I met already walking in a similar calling or how many times I said the same exact prayer. If I didn't put forth the work, then my desires would continue to go unfulfilled. Walking in your purpose means just that...walking and working towards the direction of what you believe to be. I had to begin to put my faith into action. Becoming a writer requires you to write. Becoming a speaker requires you to speak. Becoming a coach/motivator requires you to practice each of the areas. God has given each of us a gift, and He has already prepared us to succeed in that gift, but you actually have to put forth work in order for it to manifest.

In 2012, I started *Michelle's Motivation*. It's a motivational blog that shares motivation, encouragement, and some of my life lessons. My blog was my effort to be transparent with my followers and show others that they are not alone in life. There's always someone else going through the same exact experience, but they don't disclose their struggles. For me, I decided that being transparent would in some way act as a support system for others. Whether I share stories of emotional struggles, the single and dating life, weight loss efforts, or just lessons learned along my journey, I always wanted people to see the real me. I wanted people to witness the imperfect but perfect enough version of Michelle Dawson. Living this life and walking this walk is no easy task. It's something that comes with taking a hard look in the mirror, acknowledging my flaws, making strides towards areas of improvement, and still realizing that I'm not your average chick and GOD's best is the only thing I will accept. Don't get me wrong, I don't share every detail of my life, but if I experience something that may help someone else along the way, I'm happy to share my story.

When I first started my blog, I was a diligent writer. I knew that one of the things that God had revealed to me was that I would someday be an author. Therefore, I made writing a daily priority. I would also solicit for guest bloggers to give other people an opportunity to share their stories. My reach to the masses was my way of not only helping others, but putting myself out there for others to become familiar with my story and my writing. I loved everything about being a blogger. Often times, I would have people reach out to me to share how something I said in a blog post or motivation I posted on social media was exactly what they needed to help them in their personal lives. Those types of validations served as reassurance that I was doing what God had called for my life. But somewhere along the way, I lost my excitement. I had a hard time coming up with topics. I realized that because I wasn't motivated in my personal life, I had a hard time motivating others. Often times, when I'm having a bad day or even a bad season, exercising and spending time with friends and family are the perfect remedy to get me back into happy mode. But I was going through my own challenges and I honestly just didn't want to be bothered. The same excitement that was used to share the ups and downs of my life, had now became a burden.

They say, "when it rains it pours". When the sun is out and all things are right in the world, it's easy to stay happy, stress free, and maintain joy. But it's those rainy days that bring dark clouds and storms into our lives. Although I know that the sun will shine again, it's so easy to become overwhelmed with the clouds. During that cloudy season of my life, I was furloughed from my job. I had no idea how long the furlough would last and there were no guarantees that my pay would be retroactive. I used to get up every day and go to the gym, but even that didn't give me the rejuvenation that I needed to return to happy.

Right after the furlough ended, I injured my foot. In case you've never been injured before, it can be extremely depressing. In my mind, I thought, *Lord, how can this happen to me?* Me, Miss Independent, the person that usually prefers to help others versus receiving help, was now in need. I remember driving myself to the hospital that night immediately following my injury and being overwhelmed with my thoughts. As the doctor was assessing my injuries and asking me to describe the pain, I remember crying uncontrollably. She asked if I was crying due to the pain. I ignored her question, because the reality was I had no idea how I was going to take care of myself. I had never felt so alone in all my life. I ultimately had to solicit for food, help, and figure out how to get around. Not to mention, I had injured my driving foot. I was beyond frustrated. I remember hopping to the front door of the emergency room, only to walk out using crutches. It felt like an eternity before the doctor released me to stop wearing a boot. I couldn't exercise, I could barely drive, I began to gain weight, and I was in a very bad mood most days. I began to wonder why I was going through this season. What had I done to have this experience? I remember saying my prayers and asking God, *Why has this happened, knowing that I don't have any help?* The events definitely interrupted what I thought were my efforts to begin walking into my destiny. It's funny that I can laugh about this experience today, because this season just served as a reminder that God has prepared me for greater, but it's a journey, not just something that magically happens.

In order for me to continue to move forward, I had to and will continue to experience growing pains that serve as an opportunity for me to learn, grow, and to help someone else along the way. I learned several lessons as a result of the furlough and my foot injury.

- The furlough lasted for 17 days. Not one time during that time period did I go without food, water, and the necessities of life. All of my bills were paid on time and God took care of me, even though I was not receiving a paycheck. In the end, our paychecks were retroactive and we received back pay. "I have never seen the righteous forsaken or their children begging bread" (Psalm 37:25 NIV).

- I realized that God was taking me out of the mind-set of being independent and I was forced to learn to depend on others. It was indeed one of the most humbling experiences I've had to endure. I don't think the lesson was for me to stop being independent, but I learned that there would always be times in my life that I would need someone else. It gave me a greater appreciation for both old and new relationships. We help each other. "Let each of you look out not only for his own interests, but also for the interests of others" (Philippians 2:4 NKJV). "A man who has friends must himself be friendly" (Proverbs 18:24 NKJV).

- Although I felt lonely, I was never alone. It was a struggle sometimes to get around, but God gave me the strength and endurance I needed to make it through. "Be strong and of good courage, do not fear nor be afraid of them; for the Lord your God, He is the One who goes with you. He will not leave you nor forsake you" (Deuteronomy 31:6 NKJV).

Since then, I have returned back to writing on a regular basis and I am actively fulfilling my purpose. I am continuing to grow my brand, to ensure that *Michelle's Motivation* can be all that it is intended to be. God's blessings over my life continue to shine and they allow me to walk in my purpose. As I reflect on my 'lessons learned' and the many experiences I've had over the years, one thing that has remained constant was the morals my mother instilled in me as a child. The Bible says, "Train up a child in the way he should go and when he is old, he will not depart from it" (Proverbs 22:6 NKJV). Not only did my mother teach me to stand strong in the light of darkness, but she set the perfect example. She never told me there would be days like this because she had no idea about what I would experience along my journey. Instead she gave me survival skills; she taught me to pray and most importantly, she continues to encourage me to never give up. Everything you go through in life contributes to your journey. We are constantly evolving into the individuals God has called us to be. In order for me to be the woman I am today, I have had to re-evaluate my thought process. I have had to change my perspective on how I handle life's challenges. Instead of completely shutting down by not writing or continuing to work in my purpose in spite of my feelings and emotions, I had to recognize that life must go on. I've also had to remember that God has not failed me. When I don't see Him or hear Him, it doesn't mean that He isn't working in the background on my behalf. It doesn't mean that I should lose hope. I have learned to reflect on past blessings and remember that if He brought me through the last experience, He will bring me out of the next one. If He did it before, He will do it again. The purpose of my past was to prepare me for my future. Finally, I've had to learn to be thankful for it all! In the words of Robert Shuller, "Tough times never last, but tough people do."

There are five takeaways that I believe everyone should remember regarding their journey:

- Don't let anyone make you feel ashamed of your story.
- Everything you go through grows you.
- Forgiveness is a necessary part of your peace.
- Own your feelings.
- All things are working together for your greater good.

BATTERED BUT NOT BROKEN

BY DENISE POLOTE-KELLY

"For I know the plans I have for you declares the Lord plans to prosper you and not to harm you plans to give you hope and a future."

Jeremiah 29:11 (NIV)

In life we all have a date of birth and a date of death. The most important part is the dash that lies in the middle of those dates. When I look back over my dash, I've lived and grown through some serious issues.

I knew God but we didn't have the right relationship, so I was a young woman wasting and missing blessings and opportunities that were just for me. I had the opportunity to go to college even after having my first son. In hindsight God had set up a wonderful relationship for me. Instead of receiving those blessing, I left college and pushed that part of my life deep down in a box to seek what I thought could be right for me. I was running from God. I met a man, we got married a few years later, and although we were married we were not God designed. I stayed through the loneliness and emotional abandonment issues. Initially I thought our marriage would be forever and I wanted our sons to have a stable two-parent home. My forever came to an end after seven years, and I was left raising my sons as a single mother. Devastated and hurt,

267

I spent months fighting the feelings of failure. I was embarrassed that my children were now a statistic. I was a statistic; at least by society standards. Still determined to make a better life for my children, I continued to pray in spite of my hurt. God spoke to me in a dream and said so clearly, "You are purposed to pour into the lives of women."

With all the storms I had come through, I was the flicker of light for a woman trying to make it through the dark places in her life. In everything I'd gone through I could always trust God to never leave me but I was running and following my own plan. The light doesn't always come on in our heads immediately. Years had passed; I've had financial issues, another failed relationship, and spiritual setbacks.

Working as a realtor, I moved to Covington, Georgia as a sitting agent in a new subdivision and also had a home in that subdivision. It was so convenient to walk across the street to work every day. I made a lot of connections, even received an invitation from one of my clients to visit her church. At the time, not only was I selling homes, I was promoting a gospel artist and a gospel cruise and was invited to meet with their pastor. During our meeting, a very distinguished looking gentleman was there for a separate meeting with the deacons. He saw me and backed up to say hello.

I had to be cool because I was in God's house, so I smiled and said, "Hello." In my head I was screaming, *Oh, My God!* This was a good looking man. Standing six feet, three inches, he had a slender but muscular build and the most peaceful eyes. They were soothing and I could see God in him—all over him. He had a patch of gray hair in the front which made him look even more distinguished and sophisticated. I started to sweat and my pulse was racing. As I caught my breath, my mind reeled at how sexy he was. Pastor introduced us and we shook hands. This was a man of character who loved the Lord, and there was a light showing about him— within him—and I could feel it when our hands touched.

Meeting someone and getting involved in a relationship was not on my to do list. I'd already gone through a divorce and wasn't ready to go down that road again. Still, I remember thinking, *This man is supposed to be in my life.* Something about him was uniquely different. Our meeting was brief but his presence lingered.

Around this time God spoke to me again in a dream and once again revealed his purpose for me, and I was clear about what I was destined to do. That's when I decided to totally trust Him to be in charge of my life. I began talking to other women about their struggles, counseling and mentoring them through a young adult group. Finally, I was walking in my purpose, no longer weighed down with the burden of failed marriages and spiritual, emotional, financial struggles. I saw life from a different and new perspective.

Shortly after the meeting, I seized an opportunity to work on a contract in New York for 15 months. When the project ended, I was excited to return home and become active in the church. I loved singing so I joined the choir. As divine order would have it, the distinguished gentleman was a member and loved singing as much as I did. After rehearsal one Saturday he asked if he could talk to me for a minute.

Absolutely.

My mind raced. He told me he liked me and my reply was, "I like you." Seems a little childish thinking back but he and I were like teenagers experiencing new love. His name was Winston and we connected instantly. We started dating, spending time laughing and talking for hours. We'd let the top down on the car and ride for hours on end. We barbecued and spent time watching whatever game was on—or sometimes the game watched us. We were in a good place together; both previously married and divorced, we decided to take our time and get to know one another well before making family introductions.

We both loved the Lord, family, music, and our church. We both had dreams to grow in ministry, to sing, travel, enjoy our sons, grands, and family. Everything was going to be wonderful. We planned to enjoy life, our true pure love, and grow old together. We were in love and absolutely sure what we had was real and destined. The way he looked at me, I knew I was safe and he was never going to let me down. He was all I had hoped and prayed for and God blessed me despite my past.

As time passed, we talked about marriage and soon started wedding plans. We were excited to experience the real love of God and how He blessed us to share this space and time of our lives together. Planning in the evenings every aspect of our wedding ceremony had a meaning that reflected us as a couple. We researched songs to make sure they reflected our love though the lyrics and melodies.

My family loved Winston and it was impossible to be happier knowing soon I'd be his wife. My angel surprised me at my bridal shower, bringing me beautiful tulips—one of my favorite flowers. He apologized for the interruption and asked the ladies to indulge him as he pulled out what looked to be a Hallmark greeting card. He read the beautiful words and ended with, "Because I care to share the very best." Tears streamed down my face as I realized he had written the card himself.

March 6, 2010, in a beautiful, spiritual, candle light ceremony, Winston came down the aisle as I stood in the door of the sanctuary waiting with my daddy to escort me. As he walked, Winston placed royal blue rose pedals on the isle runner lining my path. I remember our Pastor, with a big smile on his face, asking, "Who gives this woman?"

My daddy responded, "Her Godparents, her mother, my wife, and I." Daddy was so proud saying those words and I saw the love and peace in his eyes. It spoke volumes about Winston for my daddy to release me to him with no regrets. He loved Winston— we all did.

On our wedding night, we sat on the floor of our bedroom as husband and wife. Winston said to me I was the beautiful blessing God created just for him and we were here this night together. We talked into the wee hours of the morning before falling asleep. It was funny because it was not what you might call your typical wedding night but we weren't your typical couple. When I woke Sunday morning it was to the gentle touch of my husband saying, "You are mine forever and I love you completely. I love the air you breathe…" To hear those words from a man and know without a doubt that he meant every word was amazing. We planned to leave for our honeymoon on Monday but due to a family emergency, we had to postpone the trip.

The following Monday, we were back in work mode and made plans to honeymoon in October 2011. We settled into our lives, living and loving together. I loved this man and made sure he knew it. He left home every morning with his lunch for the day and a little love note tucked inside his bag just to remind him of how special he was and how grateful I was to God for blessing me with him. We prayed together and after closing the prayer our next words were, "I love you," and in unison we'd say, "So much" and then off to work we'd go.

For almost three years before we married, I suffered with migraines. Some days all I could do was go to work, get through the day, come home, take meds, and close my eyes. Three months into our marriage the migraines were so bad I found relief only by sleeping in the closet on the floor because it was dark, cold, and quiet. My precious Winston made a pallet on the floor in the closet for me and he would lay right there beside me in the dark until I fell asleep. There was nothing normal about grown folks lying on the floor in the closet but we did. He promised to protect me and this was just one of the ways he helped me.

After visiting a specialist it was determined the migraines were menstrual related and I was scheduled for hysterectomy surgery—my husband with me every step of the way. The surgery was scheduled a few days before Winston's birthday, so knowing I would not be able to celebrate with him, I decided to surprise him and take him to the Motown festival in the square.

When we arrived, the square was already crowded. Winston was a popular man in town and loved by many. He stepped back and asked if all of this was for him. The crowd burst into laughter and the party began. It was difficult planning a surprise for him but my sister/friends helped me pull off a special evening of food, drinks, and close friends. God was in all of this because it was no coincidence that a Motown review band was live in Covington Square, in Covington, Georgia during my husband's birthday week.

On the day of the surgery, my parents and sister/friend Pat came over to wait with Winston. We prayed and said our 'I love yous'. I told him, "When I wake up, your face is the first one I want to see." You better know he got to my room before I did and when I awoke it was to him smiling at me. He said he was watching me breathe. I smiled and fell back to sleep. At home, Winston made sure I was cared for while he was at work. I had breakfast so I could take medication every morning before he left. I couldn't prepare his lunch for a few weeks but I made sure he had a note in his bag and he told me it was the highlight to his lunch period.

The Dark Season

Winston began experiencing fullness whenever he ate and was only able to eat small portions. That seemed weird because he loved to eat and had a healthy appetite. He was health conscious, didn't sprinkle salt after a meal was prepared, took vitamins, exercised daily, and had his yearly physical. We scheduled an appointment for a checkup and discovered he had a hernia. He was scheduled for surgery on Thursday, December 30, 2010. He intended to go back to work the following Tuesday but due to a terrible snowstorm, school was cancelled the entire week. That was a blessing as it gave him time to recover.

Several months after surgery, he still had that full feeling so we scheduled an appointment with blood work, and he was scheduled for a colonoscopy and endoscopy; both tests showed nothing. It was August and the full feeling is still there but now Winston's appetite is fluctuating so off again to the doctor, and the routine exam was complete. This time a CT scan is ordered for August 22. The day started normally. Winston left work for his appointment and I met him at the hospital. As they called him back, I sat waiting as other patients went in and came out; it felt like an eternity. I began to pray, "God, please fix it." After what felt like an eternity, the door opened and the nurse asked me back. Suddenly I felt flushed and struggled for air. Once I reached my precious husband, he took my hand and smiled. The nurse said the doctor saw something in his reports from the visit on the 14th and the CT scan gave him cause for alarm. They admitted Winston through the emergency ward; he was in renal failure and needed more testing. I was falling apart on the inside but I had to be strong so I put on my mask to hide the ugliness that was consuming me.

The test results revealed my Winston had stomach cancer. I couldn't process what I had just heard. Neither of us had ever heard of stomach cancer. I was thinking this was a nightmare and I would wake up in a minute. My mind was racing. I stepped out and called my daddy, but having to say those words hurt to my core. In the waiting area, I sat alone and cried, but Winston needed me and I had to go into supporting wife mode. We had been married 17 months and we had the fight of our lives ahead. I asked God, "Why did Winston have cancer?" This couldn't be happening to us. Not now. Not to him; he loved God too much for this to happen.

I became a medical researcher and care provider, searching out the best care for my blessing. We had an appointment for Cancer Treatment Centers of America (CTCA) and spoke with an oncologist who was an area local. Winston wanted to be close to home and what was best for him was all that mattered to me. Winston was not giving up nor giving in; he said, "We are going to fight and win." We would later be able to share this victory as a couple and in time others would be helped.

I had to locate treatment specific to his cancer. It was not easy for him to see me planning and working overtime to manage our home, work, and his care. We didn't discuss plans if he passed, so I suffered in silence to protect him and his feelings. He would not talk about anything negative and stood firmly on: whose report will you believe? I stood with him but kept trying to make sure we spoke with experienced doctors and surgeons so he would receive the absolute best care.

It was September 2011 and the surgeon came after 45 minutes of what should have been a two-hour surgery to remove Winston's stomach. The surgeon said his abdomen looked as if it had been sprinkled with salt, the cancer had spread so quickly and there was nothing they could do.

How could this be happening, and why? How are we going to beat this? Whose report will we believe? I'd moved into overdrive in order to help my precious husband. He must be healed. We have to fight. *Okay, God, what are we supposed to learn in this? What do You want us to do in this situation? We believe in You and know that You are a healer, so please heal Winston.*

We did everything the doctor recommended, yet this rare cancer was aggressive and spreading, even with powerful chemo treatments. My precious husband never complained nor lost his positive outlook. He trusted God and continued to read the word. We'd have church at home. He could not be in large crowds because his immune system was compromised. This life was new and he was adapting to not working, going to church, nor driving himself around.

October 2011

We were preparing to travel to CTCA. I was thinking, *Okay, we get there and they'll help him.* We prayed. Other people prayed and we believed he was going to beat this cancer. God blessed us with one another so we will be able to testify that he was healed. Through our testimony others would be educated about stomach cancer.

Our plans are not always God's plan. I was led to take leave from my job for a few weeks to nurture and care for Winston. Fall break for the school system came and I had three days off so we planned to spend some time together. Wednesday, we laughed and talked about everything except cancer. Thursday we were at the doctor and things were not good at all, everything quickly changed for the worse. For the first time on Friday morning Winston admitted this battle was difficult. Friday we were at the ER when he was admitted into intensive care. I prayed and asked God to heal him, deliver him, and remove the pain. God had His plan and I was not in control.

The hours passed and I stood at the bedside, talking to Winston. He was in a coma and on the ventilator. I put my hands on my husband and whispered to him. "If God is calling you to rest, please do so in peace. Thank you for making me your wife. Be free and rest. I will be okay. I love you." I stood as he slipped away. On Saturday, October 22, 2011 at 6:24 P.M. my precious husband, Winston, was gone.

I couldn't feel anything—I was so numb. I was told I had no color and I stood with an empty stare on my face. I could hear people talking but I couldn't understand what they were saying. I was empty and lost; my head and my heart hurt. The pain was so deep it was piercing my soul.

The doctor asked if the funeral home had been called. I'm thinking, *Who is he talking to? What? He can't be talking to me.* I couldn't think clearly. I couldn't breathe. This was not good. *What am I going to do? How am I going to do all that needs to be done? Where do I begin?* My heart has been crushed into a million pieces and I will have to exist in the rubble. Oh God, how could you allow this to happen?

Home

My Winston was not with me and he never would be again. This nightmare would end shortly but it didn't. It was dark and I couldn't see through the tears; I couldn't breathe. The depth of the pain made me feel nauseous and like the blood was leaving my body.

His Funeral

I could not stand the thought of watching people view Winston's body, so I waited in the car until that part was over. I went in to the church with my daddy just as we did on our wedding day. As I stood in the doorway of the sanctuary my heart started to race. It was beautiful and the service for a dignitary. The choir wore black and red, his favorite colors. The music ministry, the ministers, the sanctuary was full with people showing love and respect for my

SHIFT HAPPENS

precious Winston on a Saturday morning. He would have been pleased and that was important to me. I had to be the last hands on his body—I needed that moment for myself.

I had no plan. I was so mad at God, I was screaming, "Where are you, God? Why is my husband gone? What is the purpose for all of this pain?"

"One day at a time," is what people said to me.

"Don't You know I'm struggling to make it one second at a time?" I answered. The sadness was so deep and my heart was totally shattered. How could God have done this to me? Why my precious husband?

People tried to comfort me but they said all the wrong things.

"I know how you feel." *You can't know how I feel because I don't know.*

"God knows best." *Best was being here with me.*

"He's in a better place." *Being here with me was the best place.*

"God makes no mistakes." *This was a huge one.*

I found myself in a deep, dark pit and the walls were closing in on me. I saw no light; I lost my smile, happiness, joy, and peace. I was existing in turmoil and felt God had turned His back on me. I was furious with God and he knew it because He knows me.

Living Through

God didn't turn His back on me. He had been right there with me every step of the way. I was blinded in grief but eventually could see clearly. All that I had accomplished in and through that entire season was because God was holding my hand. When I felt I couldn't walk, He carried me. I poured my heart out and asked God for forgiveness but He had already forgiven me. I encourage others who found themselves in this situation to know that God is God and He is the ultimate planner. I knelt down before the Lord, fasted, and prayed to God, and asked for protection of my fragile heart, for peace in this storm, and the understanding that some secrets were God's alone and we may never know the answer.

November is Stomach Cancer awareness month so I decided to organize a walk in Winston's memory. The Winston H. Kelly, Sr. Memorial Foundation was established, and we are a 501(c)3 registered Foundation. We give stomach cancer a voice, educate people, and support families affected by this terrible disease.

It was March and my family was with me when Winston's headstone was unveiled. It would have been our second wedding anniversary. Initially I felt God robbed me and I was struggling badly. The next month I was speaking at workshops, seminars, and symposiums. Working with men, women, and families through Winston H. Kelly Sr. Memorial Foundation and Phenomenal Women Purpose Driven where I continue to counsel and mentor.

God helped me through my grief by sending others for me to draw on the strength I didn't realize I had until I was faced with losing my angel. If you experience similar grief with losing a loved one, go deep inside yourself and give God back your hand. He will guide you, help you, and move you from the battered state of existence to living a life of victory. Here's what I want you to remember:

- God has not failed or turned away from you because of your dark struggle. The key is to keep pressing through it. Live through it not in it.
- You matter. You are important. Take care of yourself.
- Your struggle makes you stronger. Hold to your faith.

In the midst of my tsunami I gained strength and courage to face each new day; and now five years later on October 22, 2016, I rejoice knowing that my precious Winston lived, loved, and was loved. I see now God trusted me to be with Winston so he didn't have to be alone. I loved him and only God could love him more. I'm so grateful to God for continuing to take care of my fragile heart. God blessed me with an extraordinary man, and the storm that was sent to break me is the storm God is using to make me.

I encourage you to grieve and heal, recommit yourself to God so you don't lose your covering and trust that He will not turn away from you and keep you in the middle. The life we live—our dash between our birthdate and death date—is what really matters the most. I had to get music back into my heart; it is what helped me through that dark pit experience.

I was battered but not broken.

SHOW UP AND LEAD

BY NATASHA GAYDEN

"I'm unfinished. I'm unfixed. And the reality is that's where God meets me is in the mess of my life, in the unfixedness, in the brokenness. I thought he did the opposite, he got rid of all that stuff. But if you read the Bible, if you look at it at all, constantly he was showing up in people's lives at the worst possible time of their life."
–Mike Yaconelli

I think I'm having a heart attack. My head is hurting and I'm sweating everywhere. We are three points down in the last quarter of my son's basketball game with three seconds to go. The cheers and screams of the crowd on both sides is deafening and my heart is about to beat out of my chest.

See, this was my son's school rival and the last game of the year. Up to this point, they were tied in terms of wins and tonight they were playing for the championship. My son, who was the starting point guard for his team, took the ball up the court and yelled out final instructions to his team regarding the play. Then, he dished the ball to his teammate who was setup to shoot a 3-point basket. He shot the ball and missed. With 1.7 seconds on the clock, the game was over as far as we all were concerned and we were in motion to leave. Then it happened; my son stole the ball from his opponent and ran up to the basket to dunk on their 7-foot,

250-pound center. When he went up to dunk the ball, due to the enormous size of the center and my son being 6-foot-tall weighing 185 pounds, my son never made it past the other player's chest area before the impact knocked him to the floor. We were all stunned! Why would he go up against this goliath for a 2-point shot with the game already over?

Then the coach helped him up from the floor, gave him a big smile and a high five. Meanwhile, I couldn't wait to ask this kid what he was thinking. Not long after, my son came out of the locker room limping but with a big smile on his face. I immediately dug into him and attacked him with questions. "What is wrong with you? Why did you do that? What were you thinking?"

He looked at me so confidently and said, "Mom, why would I suit up if I'm not going to show up? I'm the leader of this team. I have to still show up when things are bad." That day I learned a valuable lesson from my son which would become a foundational life principle. Always show up!

My childhood could only be described as a mix between "Boyz in the Hood", "The Color Purple", and "Akeelah and the Bee". I was born Natasha Pitts in Helena, Arkansas to a 15-year-old mother and 17-year-old father. My parents married about a year later, and then my father joined the Marines and fought in the Vietnam War. I am the eldest of three girls and grew up in Flint, MI from the age of six. We moved to Flint after living in Arkansas, Nebraska, North Carolina, and Wisconsin. Because my dad was a Marine, we moved around a lot until we settled in Flint. My childhood was filled with lots of family around. We celebrated everything. However, my childhood was also riddled with pain, sorrow, loneliness, fear, and shame.

My father suffered negative effects from the war and became a severe drug abuser. Crack eventually became his primary drug of choice. Many in my family were also drug and alcohol abusers. Growing up, I remember seeing all types of drug and alcohol use. My grandmother, Elsie, was the saving grace, my rock when things became really unstable. The instability in my life showed up in the form of extreme poverty, psychological issues, teenage rebellion, and an overall lack of direction. The ability to keep the bills paid became increasingly hard since my mother was a stay-at-home mom and my dad was the sole provider.

Around the time I was 16, my mother went back to school to learn a skill to get a job. She wanted to create a more stable environment for her children. However, this did not prevent me from becoming extremely rebellious and angry, which caused me to frequently fight. I was angry with my parents because my life was not like that of my friends. While my friends were concerned with dances, grades, and prom, I was concerned with whether we would have to move again or if one of the guys on the block sold someone in my family drugs.

As General Motors began closing plants, there were many people out of work and the city became drug-ridden and full of crime. It was a worry for me. I was embarrassed that we didn't have money for basic items at times. I wanted the normal family; and normal and perfect we were not. I had fond memories of my father prior to the heavy drug use. I remember him taking me to and from school every day. He taught me how to read, write, and tell time. He was patient with me and I thought he was the smartest, best dad. I was mad with my father because he was always around in my memories of old, and then one day, he just wasn't. I felt alone, in a life filled with addiction and violence, and I was barely surviving.

As I grew up, I rationalized that I had to fight to establish a reputation of "don't mess with her or you'll get eaten alive." I was never a bully, but I was quick tempered and did not shy away from a battle, of which there were many. To fit in with my environment, I began smoking weed and drinking alcohol to cope. I literally had my first alcoholic beverage at age 11 and smoked marijuana at age 9. This on and off use of weed and sometimes alcohol continued until I turned 19. I was self-medicating. I was hiding.

In the midst of all of the turmoil in my life, I was victimized on several occasions by men who were supposed to be my protectors. I was often molested by a so called godfather around the age of 10.

He was a corrupt police officer whose wife was viciously murdered in their home. Her murderer was never found. I fully believed he was capable of having done it and through whispers of the adults around me, some of them believed it as well. To me, this man was dangerous, and I was deathly afraid of him. He frequently fondled my private areas in public places and threatened me not to tell.

Over the next few years, I endured the same type of abuse with men who were considered family friends. I often think of the line Sophia delivered in "The Color Purple" when she said, "A girl child ain't safe in a family full of men." Nothing could be truer in my case.

If all the chaos wasn't enough to drive me insane, I was raped at the age of 15 by my best friend's boyfriend. "Come over to my house and get your girl right now or I will kill her," is what he yelled through the phone. He was my best friend's boyfriend and they had a violent relationship. I was scared for her and rushed to his house a few blocks away to retrieve my friend. Imagine my surprise when I was led to the basement to find her nowhere in sight. I was raped that day and would never be the same again. I had been dating a guy for two years who at first appeared to rescue me from all of the drama. I clung to him for dear life and became sexually active with him. At this point in my life, I had no direction and he was my North Star. We remained in an on again, off again relationship for 17 years before we finally went our separate ways. I had two children by him at ages 17 and 19. After becoming a mother, I knew my life had to change.

Once I had children, I started college and worked two waitress jobs while raising my children. Since I was such a hard worker, my employers rewarded me with promotions. I was eventually promoted into management and from there to a trainer position within corporate. This was the beginning of my career climb up the corporate ranks. I worked hard and cultivated relationships because I was determined that nothing would stop me from having a good life. More importantly, my children would never grow up the way I had. However, my ambition came at a cost. I was often away from them due to work. Everything became about work and achieving the next level of success. Even though I was there with my kids, I wasn't always present. Instead of going to college straight through, I had to take breaks between semesters so pursuing my degree became a long process. I missed out on a lot in my pursuit of what I considered to be a better life.

I was making myself over, leaving the past behind. I became such a different person that people from my old neighborhood didn't recognize me. I began going to church and learned about God. My new church family taught and helped me with forgiveness. In those days, I was in church just about every day. I learned to pray. I mean—I really learned to pray and understand God's love for me. I had a new family so I took my hurts, pains, and sorrows and wrapped them all together and tucked them somewhere down deep inside. I forgave my parents, and as I grew older I realized they had been victims just like I had. They had babies too young and had issues that kept them from being better parents. I went through hell growing up, but I never doubted my parent's love. I knew they loved me. So I forgave them and we started fresh. And just like that, poof, the past was gone.

"From the ends of the Earth I will cry out to you, and when my heart is overwhelmed, lead me to the rock that is higher than I."

Psalms 61:2

After all I'd gone through and overcame—the struggles of my childhood—I thought I was invincible. I also thought the past wasn't relevant, so why even bring it up? It was a chapter in my life that was long closed, so why reopen it? I was 39 years old and married to my husband of one year. I was enjoying a wonderful, new life and successful career.

Life had thrown its worse at me and I still survived—or so I thought. Then it happened. Life hit me with three punches. Sucker punches at that. And all while I was going through an Intensive Executive Development Program at work that would seal my next promotion. My grandson, Jordan, passed away suddenly at 13 months old. My oldest son went to prison for a year, not even six months after his son died, and I developed an incurable chronic pain syndrome called Fibromyalgia.

The heartache from my grandson's death was piercing. The hurt and shame from my son's imprisonment rendered me unable to breathe, and the pain from the fibromyalgia was shocking to say the least. Then in the midst of all of this, I began thinking about my past—all day, every day. I didn't understand why all the memories were resurfacing. It was overwhelming and every terrible thing I went through continued to replay in my mind. That's when something which never happened to me before manifested—depression and a lack of will to live. I thought I was done with the past, but here it sat in my face taunting me.

Three sucker punches forced me to deal with my past, but I also learned how to still show up when all hell was breaking loose. Even though my life was in turmoil, I couldn't just lay down and die. I was needed. I had a purpose, and I had my wonderful husband and God on my side prompting me daily to wake up. I needed to show up because my promotion was on the line and I needed to successfully complete the Executive Program. I asked for help from friends and family so I could focus and graduate successfully. I also built a better team around me at work, so everything didn't just depend on me. I learned we all need to have a team of folks in our life who will help take on the load so we can do what's important.

I had to show up for my son, and the mother of his son, because they were so distraught at the loss of Jordan, they couldn't breathe. I had to show up to breathe for them. I was their life support. In order to do this, I had to put on my whole armor of God and pray unceasingly. This allowed me to plan the funeral and help my son through his grief, while experiencing the peace that surpasses all understanding. I had to show up for myself and get active with my health and wellbeing because the pain and symptoms from the fibromyalgia would never go away. This was my wake up call. It was time for me to start taking care of myself and it was this painful condition that helped me to get my priorities together. I was in effect working myself to death... literally.

Learning there was no cure for the pain crushed my spirit. The pain and other symptoms from my condition made it almost impossible to get out of bed most days. However, every day, I made a decision to get up and beat this condition. I showed up by continuing to work my corporate job for another five years with 80 percent travel away from home. Yoga and meditation helped me cope because I refused to take pain medicine. I am in pain EVERY—SINGLE—DAY. But, I get up and show up anyway.

Finally, I had to show up for all the single mothers, molestation and rape victims, and anyone else who had led a tough life and this required me to tell the truth about my story. While suppressing my past and not dealing with the pain, I realized I had not healed. As much as I wanted to help others, I couldn't until I had helped myself. I began seeing a therapist to help me resolve my issues with the past and finally, I was really able to let go.

Once I was healed, I helped single mothers by teaching career skills and providing mentorship in an effort to level the playing ground for them in the workplace. My husband and I devoted ourselves to being small group leaders in our church as well as taking a mission trip to Haiti. We believed if we modeled what serving looked like, we could motivate others to get involved. I became active in my community and I started a women's organization which focuses on visioneering and personal development. We celebrated our five-year anniversary in 2016. And my greatest achievement is supporting my family as they achieve their dreams and goals. I learned that showing up doesn't always mean leading from the front. Showing up also means serving and supporting those you love.

Yes, my life had been mired with trial after trial and yes it sucked, but I still had to show up. I became a leader at work, in my community, and amongst my peers. I became a wife, stepmother, and grandmother. God delivered me from so much and I had faith. I learned what it means to have a resilient spirit. I was a leader and as my son said, "I still have to show up when things are bad. Why suit up if you aren't going to show up?" What does this mean to me? It means that God has a special calling over my life and has positioned me to lead in spite of my past and because of my past pains. So I cannot lead from the bench and I cannot allow momentary hardships to prevent me from showing up and showing out. My decision then to show up was rooted in my faith in God, the promises in His Word, and the knowing of just how much He loved me. I will show up because He always shows up.

> *"See, I am doing a new thing! Now it springs up; do you not perceive it? I am making a way in the wilderness and streams in the wasteland."*
>
> Isaiah 43:19

I make it my mission to show up in life every single day. And it is a daily choice. Oftentimes because I am happy and lead a successful life, people try to discount my struggles as if, oh that was back then, or you don't understand. Or my favorite—and someone actually told me this—your rape was not as bad as my rape. I understand now that people who try to discount another person's struggle do so because it frees them from having to act and they can maintain their victimhood in life. But I make the decision every day to live a life of showing up. When I wake up in the morning fatigued and racked with indescribable pain, I have a decision to make. Do I lay in bed and let life pass me by? Most days I decide to get out of the bed and show up. Sometimes it's an hour to hour or minute to minute decision. The point is, I didn't make one decision and then my life miraculously shifted. No, it's through daily prayer and faith that my decision is to "go on and see what the end is going to be" as the elders would say.

> *"But they that wait upon the LORD shall renew [their] strength; they shall mount up with wings as eagles; they shall run, and not be weary; [and] they shall walk, and not faint."*
>
> Isaiah 40:31

My family has since healed in a mighty way. We still have room for improvement. In fact, we probably would have the highest watched family reality show ever. But we love God and we love each other. The love was always there even when individuals were facing their personal demons. My parents are still together after 43 years and more in love than ever. My father is 25 years clean and the Godly Patriarch every family needs. My children and grandchildren are thriving. I am close to my sisters, In-laws, nieces, and nephews. I adore all my cousins. We are family—good, bad, and ugly—and we still celebrate everything. With God's help, we are healing.

I often wonder: Do they know how many generational curses we have broken? How many strongholds we have torn down? I wonder: Do they notice how often they showed up and led during tough times? I notice.

And me, well I'm more at peace than ever. I quit my corporate job that no longer served me and started my own Life Coaching and Consulting Practice. I woke up one day and realized what I had to do because I was a single mother, I didn't have to do anymore. I spent all those years doing what I had to do to survive and I just wanted the last half of my life to be about what I wanted to do and what God wanted me to do. God has given me specific gifts and talents and it became time for me to give them back to edify the body of Christ. It required me leaving a successful six-figure career to starting my own business. Talk about having to show up every day. If I don't show up to my own business, I don't eat and people are not helped.

I get to use my deepest hurts and greatest shames to help other people deal with life. So I show up every day because there is a lot on the line. And call me crazy, but I love it. These days I experience peace, joy, laughter, and the feeling of making a difference. I can handle anything which comes my way with God on my side. I've shifted from being defeated to showing up. By making the decision to show up daily, I have become the leader God intended me to be.

My shift took place when I changed my mentality about the troubles in my life. The bible tells us to be transformed by the renewing of our minds. It also tells us in 1 Peter 4:12, "Dear friends, do not be surprised at the fiery ordeal that has come on you to test you, as though something strange were happening to you." What this means is as a Christ follower, I understand that as long as I am here on this earth troubles will come. How I look at those troubles... my perspective on those troubles determines if and how I show up in life. So after years of showing up intentionally and changing my perspective about my troubles, I have developed a method to help me show up:

- Wake Up

  Ring! Ring! This is your wake up call. Your wake up call may come during a terrible point in your life. It could be that rebellious child, a divorce, disease diagnosis, lost job, or unexpected death. Either way, you will at some point experience a time when you will receive a wake up call. A wake up call means you have been sleepwalking and it is time to fully realize your current situation. Waking up means you become intentional about your life, you set priorities, and you are fully aware of the things, circumstances, and people that may be holding you back. Even if that person is you.

- Fess Up

  Fessing up requires you verbally acknowledging to God or those people close to you, your mistakes, your intentions, and your plans. This is the beginning of accountability. By fessing up, you commit to having a better life and you make yourself accountable to others.

- Suit Up

  So now you are at the point when you have become aware of what's going on in your life and you also have committed yourself to accountability by fessing up. It's time to suit up. Suiting up means putting on the Whole Armor of God and being ready to do battle. Life will hit you. It's not a matter of if, but, when. And when it does, will you be ready to stand and deal, or fall back into defeat?

- Team Up

  It is essential you have a tribe around you to push you, encourage you, lift you up, and hold you accountable. Your team should be comprised of people who have your ultimate well-being in mind. They should be like-minded and hold your same values. No one in this world can make it on their own. We were made to commune with each other. So pick a great team who can help you win in the game of life.

- Show Up

  Finally, understand you must show up. It's your job to. God has fashioned you for a purpose and that purpose must be fulfilled. There are people counting on you. You are needed. You matter. More importantly, God will always show up for you if you call on Him. So just show up!

SINGLE AND SATISFIED

BY SANDRA JOLLA

"The will of God is not something you add to your life. It's a course you choose. You either line yourself up with the Son of God...or you capitulate to the principle which governs the rest of the world."

–Elisabeth Elliot

Single and Satisfied? What an oxymoron to me. What woman who desires marriage and family is ever satisfied with singleness and the emotions of loneliness, longing, and long suffering that it brings?

Life has many "things" and possessions to fill this obvious void of companionship. For many, we climb the ladders of our careers looking for excellence; we seek popularity in our clubs, sororities, and other venues; we strive for perfection in our dress, filling the shopping malls and restaurants, realizing none of these material things can fill this emptiness—this void. We realize eventually that all these pleasures, these things, are temporal and temporary. The next day, the next hour, the next week, the thrill is gone.

These earthly possessions and provisions are only a temporary fix. It's not until we are obedient to the scripture in Matthew 6:33, which clearly sets our paths: "But seek ye first the kingdom of God and His righteousness, then all things will be added unto you." I learned this lesson, and what a lesson it was for me.

I remember my mother, a single but strong woman who worked three jobs and went to school to provide and raise four children. I heard her cry out to God many nights. Little did I know how her Christian faith would have a lasting impact on me. After high school, my friends prepared to go off to prestigious Historically Black Colleges and Universities (HBCUs), the likes of Tuskegee University, Howard University, and some to Spelman College. I recall my mother sitting across from me at our dining room table firm, but compassionate, saying to me through tear-filled eyes, "I just cannot afford it. You'll have to stay here and go to Alabama State." I couldn't fault her, because I knew if she could, she would.

Alabama State is a progressive HBCU in Montgomery, Alabama and was certainly equipped to educate a young and tender mind such as mine. So, I knew God had His hand on me even then. As a single mother, doing the best she could, my mother helped me learn one of life's best lessons—make the best of what you have. She had always demonstrated a strong faith and shown that when driven from within, God could take your desire and set forth a path far beyond your imagination.

After four years of college, here I was, a young, unexposed, and highly protected African American girl from Montgomery, Alabama off to the big city. I'd begun a thrilling career at one of the largest technology companies in the world. After four short years with this company, I was promoted to a position in Dallas to work in a newly formed group. They selected ONLY the best to be a part of this startup. I worked on the team that sold a major office system to the State of Alabama which opened the big, bright door for my 32-year career. I was on top of the world. For the first time in my life, I was away from home on my own. I was ready to climb Mount Everest! The sky was truly the limit for me. I'd just finished reading Zig Ziglar's book, "See You at the Top."

Another principle my mother taught me was to persevere. She would often say, "You've got to push yourself; take an obstacle, one obstacle at a time and before you know it, you've tackled them all." The old saying, "When life gives you lemons, make lemonade," was certainly one of my mother's theories she so deeply implanted into me, even to this day.

Here I was in Dallas, Texas. Professionally, I was on the move. I looked good on the outside, having it all together. Physically, I was a mover and a shaker, but as beautiful as I looked on the outside, having it all together, something was missing in my life and I was out to find it.

Naturally, I did what any young person would do—I tried the club and party scene. I'd fallen into the age-old routine—Friday night happy hours, shopping on Saturdays, church on Sunday. That's right, I was raised that whatever you do through the week, you always go to church on Sunday. That routine was as engraved in me as the newly engraved plaque I received for "outstanding sales support" on my job. But something was strange; something was missing.

I met Michael, this smooth, debonair, business oriented, and intelligent engineer who treated me first-class. He had two clothing stores, and what a gentleman he was. He would bring me flowers, candy, and an entertaining life. Shoot, I even went home and told my mother, "If I could find a man like Michael, but a Christian man, that's all I could ask for." You see, we had fun, but there was no future. We had pleasures, but no plan. He would not even go to church with me. I knew something was still missing. Some nights when he wasn't there, I would have feelings of loneliness and wanting commitment. My time clock was really ticking as I approached 30 years of age.

Like many single women, I wanted to be married. After all, by this time most of my friends were starting their families. I was tired of nightclubs, monetarily broke from shopping, but enjoyed my sorority involvement; however, I was not being fulfilled. There was a void. Sunday after Sunday at this very dear and traditional church I attended, I sat and watched young married couples as they would come in, excited and loaded down with baby carriers, diaper bags, and bottles.

At age 29, I thought surely I deserved that, too. I pondered, what's wrong with me? Why do I have to be single? I'm young, level-headed, and pretty good looking. My desire to be married swelled within me. I felt the signs of singleness that you may be feeling if you are a single woman. You know the "lies" we ponder in our minds and sometimes believe:

- **L**oneliness – I need someone of the opposite sex to be fulfilled; to be whole.

- **I**dentity – I cannot be happy and be single. I have no purpose. Do I need to change something? Career? Image? Looks?

- **E**mptiness – How do I fill this void? This emptiness I feel of being alone?

- **S**elf-Worth – I am not worthy of marriage and family happiness. Why not me?

One day a dear friend convinced me to host a Bible Study in my home. She was so excited about the purposeful fulfillment she was getting from the Bible Study, so I thought, *Sure, why not?* This particular time, the evangelist broached the subject of "presenting your body as a living sacrifice, holy and acceptable unto God." Romans 12:1. And then on to I John 3:6, "No one who lives in Him keeps on sinning; whosoever sins has not seen Him, neither knows Him. Fornication is sin!" No one had ever really broken it down to me like this. These words rang so loud in my ears it was like sounding brass and crashing cymbals. I thought to myself, *You are striving to satisfy you.* That is why I could never be satisfied and the reason for the emptiness.

I felt so convicted in living a life of sinful pleasure but a change was coming. The spirit talked directly to me that day. It was at that moment that I realized that despite all my worldly accomplishments, my void was my lack of walking in obedience with God's

Word. Not just the motion of going to church on Sunday. I realized that He wanted a personal relationship with me. I realized that I could not have a wholesome relationship with a man until I had a wholesome relationship with God. The truth crashed into me like lightning during a spring storm.

The nightclubs were a smoke screen I had pushed through. The shopping was a mask Satan had used to blind me, to rob me, to plant these worldly temptations and deepen my debt to bring temporary joy. It was a trap to keep me in bondage, to take control of my mind. The real battle is in the mind. "For we wrestle not against flesh and blood, but against principalities, against powers, against rulers of the darkness of this world, against spiritual wickedness in high places" (Ephesians 6:12).

Single women, hear me out: I went to church every Sunday. I shouted out as the reverend was preaching, sang in the choir, and attended Singles Sunday School. I was even at Baptist Training Union (BTU) in the evenings. I went through the mechanics and motions of church, but Christ was not the LORD of my life, materialistic and worldly things were, climbing the corporate ladder was, and I still did what I wanted to do to get a glimpse of life's cheap pleasures.

This breakthrough was a "taste and see that the Lord is good" invitation for me. I was traveling down the worldly road to success as the driver. I realized I needed a different driver. I needed to move over and let Him be the driver. God wanted to be Lord; He wanted to fill my void. I was so excited.

I knew I had a decision to make, so through no strength of my own, but only trusting and relying on God, I parted from my worldly desires and broke up with that fine, debonair engineer. Partially because I knew he was not ready to walk in obedience to God and I did not want to play with God any longer. I became ready and eager to do whatever God wanted me to do, and I knew that fornication and self-seeking pleasures were not in His order. I wanted more and I finally knew Who could give me more. This time His way; not my way! No thirst for more worldly goods, possessions, or fame could keep me from building my relationship with my Heavenly Father. Being a "distinguished performer" on my job or winning the "risk-taker" award was no longer the primary driver for me. The fact that I drove a bright shiny new Mercedes Benz or even my floor length Black Glama mink coat with crystal fox sleeves could make me waiver on my new walk with Christ. These things were not so important to me anymore. The vanity of all vanities, I realized were merely smoke screens. Pleasure-seeking worldly antics to pull me off course. I craved eternal love, eternal salvation, and eternal life. I desired a real relationship; I desired a relationship with Christ.

My SHIFT had come! For the first time I was okay with being single. I was single and satisfied.

> *"The most important thing in life is* <u>knowing</u> *the most important things in life."*
>
> –David F. Jakielo

You see, when I found Him, I found me. The real me! I wanted to be the best single woman for Christ I could be. The void I had felt for so many days and lonely nights as I longed to have real companionship had finally come. I had renewed life. I was all right with being single—it was a state of mind.

I used my time in ministry versus miserable pity parties. Mark states it clearly when he says, "seek ye first the kingdom of God, and let him add to you as he sees fit. He will give us the desires of our hearts."

I am so grateful to God for this Shift in my life because it plunged me into the whole new world of trust and belief. I learned story after story of how God rescued His people. I read stories about the strength of women in the Bible. By the way, if you don't have a woman in the bible to study, I encourage you to find one. There are many of them. I totally admired the Proverbs 31 woman, with all her strength, wisdom, and work, but the woman I clung to during this particular time was Hannah, I Samuel 1. I admired Hannah's strength, her faith, and her determination. I reflected upon my own mother's teachings and admonition of perseverance. Regardless as to how she was tormented, ridiculed, and oppressed, God found favor and had His hand on Hannah; and all she wanted, more than anything, was to have a relationship with Him. Hannah's model became my model. As a single woman, I grew totally satisfied in my singleness, starting to put Christ first in everything I did, making Him head and Lord of my life. Instead of happy hours, I now found myself at the hour of power—prayer meeting. Like Hannah one day I prayed so intensely to God that He would hear my prayer and if He desired would one day bless me with a husband and two daughters. To me it seemed a minor request, but I wanted to make sure that whatever I did was pleasing to Him first.

From that point on, Hannah became the woman for me to study. I found strength in many of Women in the Bible. I encourage all of my single women to find a woman in the Bible to gain strength from. Here are a few to study:

- **Ruth** – a woman of dedication and faith; she didn't look for Boaz, the king and her new husband. She did what was right and Boaz found her. **Ruth 1-4.**

- **Lydia** – She was a super-successful single business woman, but spiritually, she felt lost until she heard the truth of God. **Acts 16:14**

- **The Widow of Zarephath** – She was a desperate single mother who couldn't feed her child. But when God sent her help in an unlikely way, she was willing to trust Him enough to take it. **I Kings 17:9**

- **Esther** – a woman willing to take a risk for a cause. Because of her, her entire race was spared. **Esther 2:7**

At age 31, I was confidently single and satisfied. But the plan God had for me wasn't over yet. I needed foot surgery, and being the overachiever that I am, I decided to have both feet done at the same time. Now I know what you are thinking, a single woman, many miles away from home, both feet at the same time, come on, really? I never considered how I would get to my doctor appointments; I just assumed that my friends would come to my rescue. One lesson I learned was not to put your trust in friends because they will let you down, just when you need them most.

It was so interesting to me that, just when I needed someone to drive me, whom would I call? You got it, Michael. So here I was, a woman with a newfound, enriching relationship with Christ. Little did I know, the same man whom I left to grow in my renewed relationship with Christ, God was in the midst of beginning a transformation in his life, too! His transformation was underway during our time of break up. God began to draw him into His love.

Now that I was growing in my relationship with Christ, Christ was drawing us back into a relationship together with Him. But Momma didn't raise no fool. I was not going to be tricked. You know men will tell you what you want to hear to draw you back in and go right back to their normal operations. While I was appreciative, I hesitated to enter into a relationship. I'd been there and done that. But none-the-less, who would show up on Friday nights with fish and on Sundays with yogurt? My favorite foods on those days. Still, I held steadfast to my conviction of not restarting our relationship. One day he asked if he could go to church with me. *Hmm*, I thought, yet I still did not bend.

Then our conversations changed. He was now quoting scriptures, no longer drinking and going out to night clubs. I thought, *Maybe he really is seeking a life with Christ.* After about three months, I finally let him go to church with me. At first, just one Sunday; that one Sunday led to another. Suddenly, I realized… a change. A shift was taking place within him, too. Much like Hannah again, I chose to make another vow to the Lord. "Lord, I will know it's You when he gives his life to You."

At age 33, Michael had never been baptized and he wouldn't go to church because he didn't believe in playing with God. He never felt it, so he never played with it. However, this particular Sunday, I noticed his knees shaking and he was sweating profusely. I didn't know what was going on with him. Before I knew it, he plunged forward like a strike of lightning had hit him, too. This was the Sunday that he committed his life to Christ. Three Sundays later, that handsome and debonair engineer, humble in his spirit, went into the water with an old pair of overalls, a t-shirt, and tear filled eyes. It was his time. His change—his shift had come, and God confirmed that He had transformed the same man that I'd proclaimed to my mother about two years earlier. Look at what God had done. Once I surrendered my life to Him, that Matthew 6:33 scripture came into fruition and God fulfilled this desire of my heart. Michael is now my Pastor, husband, and the father of my two daughters, whom I'd prayed so fervently for.

God will take care of you and is ready to give you the desires of your heart, but you *MUST* put Him first in all that you do. Because I was willing to put my trust in Him, He chose to put His love in me. When I made that promise to God, that if He did this for me, I would serve Him the rest of my days, and that is exactly what I have spent my days doing. Because I stood on God's promises, my husband now stands each Sunday, proclaiming God's Word to a lost world. He sold his stores, went to seminary, earned his Master of Divinity, and a Doctorate in Ministry. God more than fulfilled His promise to me. I got the two girls I prayed for and I thank God daily for His true and abiding love. It gives me chills sometimes when I think back 27 years ago. What if I continued to do it my way? What if I continued to live a life of sin and fornication? What if I never let go and let God? You may be today where I was 29 years ago. Softly and tenderly, Jesus is calling. He wants to be Lord of your life, too. He wants you to have the desires of your heart, but you have to do it His way.

I say this to you today singles, you can be *Single and Satisfied.* "Draw near to Him and he will draw near to you." but not until you truly surrender your way to God's way, and **shift** to Him, will you find satisfaction. We are no longer our drivers and Christ is fully the guide in our lives, our great commission to "go ye therefore" is finally being fulfilled.

To the married ladies, don't think the emptiness is oblivious to marital status. I just happened to be single. If you too, are feeling a void, if emptiness or loneliness has crept into your home and you are looking for a remedy, try Jesus. If what used to be a happy and good place in marriage has now morphed into a pit of pity and misery, try Jesus. If deception and corruption have snuck in and stolen your joy, try Jesus. He can and will restore your marriage, your brokenness, your void.

God is a rewarder of those who diligently seek Him. Seek Him today and unveil the JOY that He has for you. If single, be satisfied in singleness. If married, let Jesus be the guide that mends your misery and your marriage.

Only God's metamorphosis can change hairy, wormy caterpillars into beautiful, soaring butterflies. Let Him change you today.

God's Promises as taken from the GospelCentre.com:

God's Word is full of promises just for you and me. Here are just 10 of them for us to remember each and every day, that when things aren't the way they should be we can count on God to bring us through stronger, wiser, and with a great JOY!

- **I WILL** GIVE YOU REST – *Matthew 11:28*
- **I WILL** STRENGTHEN YOU – *Philippians 4:13*
- **I WILL** ANSWER YOU – *Jeremiah 33:3*
- **I BELIEVE** IN YOU – *Ephesians 3:17-19*

- **I WILL** BLESS YOU – *Jeremiah 17:7-8*
- **I AM** FOR YOU – *Isaiah 41:10*
- **I WILL** NOT FAIL YOU – *Deuteronomy 31:6*
- **I WILL** PROVIDE FOR YOU – *Philippians 4:19*
- **I WILL** BE WITH YOU – *Deuteronomy 31:8*
- **I LOVE YOU** – *Jeremiah 31:3*

Whatever your state of being, God wants to have a relationship with you. Become a woman of faith and not a woman of fear. God never fails. Keep your head up. God gives His hardest battles to His strongest soldiers. This is how you can be **SINGLE AND SATISFIED!**

STRONG AND COURAGEOUS, NOT AFRAID AND DISCOURAGED

BY RUSSELL M. WILLIAMSON SR.

"Children born to a young man are like arrows in a warrior's hands."

Psalms 127:4 NLT

I am the arrow and my mother, Elizabeth Williamson, is the young woman. I am who I am because she was a strong woman and her tension, tenacity, and aim helped launch me in the right direction. I felt this was an appropriate time to share my humble story as I am right in the middle of redefining myself and executing a *Shift* in my life. I'm recovering from having the largest rug you can imagine pulled right from under my feet. Six years ago, I lost my mentor, my voice of reason, my angel, and the woman who poured herself into raising me. She was truly a warrior in her own right that would succumb to the insidious disease of cancer. I left a job that I thought would be my career until what seemed to be the most significant schism in leadership philosophy, I had ever experienced, would drive me to make the decision to resign sooner than later. The next blow came within a few months when my routine doctor visit became a diagnosis of cancer. Talk about a plot twist. *What else could happen?* is a question you should try to avoid asking because even when you think it's bad it most definitely could be worse.

As I would soon learn within months I felt the sting of betrayal from friends, family, and even myself in my business and personal matters. This series of rugs had been snatched from beneath me suddenly and what seemed repeatedly over a multi-year period.

In 2010, I was just getting settled in and really feeling more positive about some of the most recent corporate restructuring that had taken place within the company I was working. More importantly, my family and I had just returned from what I considered a hardship tour of residing in the northeast—living in New Jersey and commuting into midtown Manhattan, New York for work. Our time in New Jersey was an unfortunate change we had to bear in order for me to reach senior leadership responsibility in the company and achieve a goal my wife and I established when I started in the business some fifteen years earlier. Often times, we establish goals for our lives; however, we don't always realize the level of sacrifice we will have to make. Moving to New Jersey was a huge sacrifice that cost our family in more ways than one. We moved four previous times for positions with this company, but they were all going further south or to the west. My wife is a southern belle and moving back north was not something she was overly excited about doing. She attempted to play along and tried to make it a positive for herself and our children but it didn't go over well and no one was buying it. Our goal of me being a Vice President, running a division and my wife being considered the "First Lady" of my division went very well when we were on stage for corporate, but at home you might say there was no joy in Mudville. What a glorious day when I came home and said to her, "We are moving back to Texas!" Momma couldn't put the house on the market fast enough. The next day I had my typical 12-14 hour work day and when I got home the movers had been to our house, packed, loaded, and were pulling away with our goods. It wouldn't be until about nine months later, after we returned, that I had my team in place and I was kicking off the new year now in Texas.

In late January, I received a call that my mother was not doing well and she really wanted me to be with her. I worked the past 18 years in the healthcare industry and learned a number of things along the way, so Mother often relied on me to talk with her about her health and to engage with her healthcare providers asking questions. She shared with me her issues and I quickly synthesized that she was deeply concerned. I have always known her as a lady that was tough as nails; however, this was different and I knew I had to travel to rural North Carolina to be with her. The local doctor was savvy enough to realize the care she needed required a higher level of expertise but wasn't sure. I looked at her and knew, by the uncertainty in her step and the dimness of light in her eye, we needed to seek more intensive care. She had to travel by ambulance from her rural town to the city of Charlotte to be seen by an oncologist. This was scary and very concerning for me as I could only pray for the best but prepared my mind for the worse. Unfortunately, I received the worse news I could imagine; that my mom was diagnosed with stage four cancer. The oncologist's prognosis was 4-6 weeks to live. Devastating news for her and news I didn't want to accept.

The company extended to me something I didn't expect given my responsibility; however, I was extremely grateful to be able to be by her side for everyday she had left. It was the most precious time I had with her since leaving home at seventeen years old. You could define me as a momma's boy and so much of who she was impacted who I am and much of what I carry today. Clearly, my life is an amalgamation of my experiences yet I know my approach to each day is filled with the lessons and sage wisdom of a very influential mother. She passed almost four weeks to the day we received the news of her diagnosis. In her final moments, I saw and felt one of the most incredible things I believe an individual can experience. As her body was shutting down, she called an end to all life support assistance by the nurses and asked them to move away and summoned me to come closer to her. She asked me who is going to take care of me, and I said, "God has me, Ma." I began to cry. She slowly stopped breathing and I held her head in my arms. As she passed, I literally felt her spirit leave her, pass through me and around me with such a presence and force that I could feel my body temperature double. It was as though an electrical current went through my body. I cried harder wishing she would come back, but I knew she was headed to be present with the Lord.

I'm an only child and now I really felt alone. My wife was with me, my children were in Texas, and I was floored, physically exhausted, and feeling a rush of emotions. Mom was gone. What was I going to do? How would I make this transition into a world that would forever be different from the one I knew? However this was no time for me to get sucked into a place of sadness. I worked with my family to make memorial arrangements and to hold a burial service. I traveled to get my children and to communicate the bad news of their grandma's passing. They took it hard and that hurt me because I wanted them to have another chance to see her alive. I compartmentalized and packed away all my feelings, emotions, and grief as we handled all the business that comes after you lose a loved one, and I didn't go back to that packed box.

I did what I thought was a good way to refocus my energy and jumped right back into my work. My boss had just given me thirty days to be with my mother during her last days so the least I could do was come back with a renewed focus. I wasn't ready. I think my leadership team recognized it and possibly thought I would return as the leader they knew; however, that didn't happen soon enough. I had the worst year of performance I ever had and there were issues in the business that I would have usually been out in front of. I was in complete reactionary mode. Little did I know my tyrannical boss felt that I wasn't performing well as a strategy to make her look bad and trying to get her removed from her job, with me ultimately taking over her position. Given the loss of my mother, my boss and her job were so far from my thoughts she would have been wildly disappointed on how little I truly considered her from day to day. It took my team to point out to me that she was out to get me. I had spent eighteen years building my track record of leadership, people development and performance, and now this woman no one knows wants to ride rough shot over my reputation.

By years end I missed my target by one percent and she wanted to stick it to me. I didn't receive that well and an anger rose up in me that I couldn't contain. My boss never sensed it because I refused to give her the pleasure of knowing she was getting on my last nerve. However my wife knew it because of my ranting at home, and daily my team experienced the deepest intensity I could deliver on why it was important to be the number one performing business in the company. It became evident to me she wanted me to have successive bad year as grounds to remove me and another business leader. My team and I jammed it down her throat and for that matter the organization's figurative throat. I felt justified by our performance and if there was any question that I wasn't the well-deserved and well-earned leader needed to be put to bed. Candidly, she needed an executive coach and if she had one they weren't very influential with her. My boss had another trick up her sleeve.

As the year 2011 came to a close, my boss along with her peers decided it was time to usher out all the established leadership in the organization however using the typical evaluation of your most recent performance wouldn't allow them to move certain people out, namely me. The decision was made to have everyone at my level interview for their positions. Incredibly, not really as I saw it coming, I was not selected for my position which I had led to the highest performance and generated the greatest amount of revenue for the organization. I was also ranked in the top ten percent of leaders in the company for employee engagement. I was offered another position in the company but it was at a lower level and would geographically require my relocation. I declined and left the company with twenty years of service under my belt. The nasty little heifer that I used to work for had the nerve to say to me, "You are handling this a lot better than I expected."

I responded, "I will be fine because I am a child of the King." She looked so puzzled at my statement as though she wondered, *Is he related to Martin Luther King or Elvis?*

As I left my office with a few of my items in a box, I called my wife. She asked, "So what's your new role?"

"I am the CEO of my sports management company," was my response. I had my own sports management company and for the foreseeable future that was going to be my employer. When I finally arrived home, I completely erupted. I was furious, embarrassed, humiliated, aggravated, and downright breathing fire. That went on for hours until I finally went to bed and as I looked at my wife I just broke down in tears. Everything I felt like we had worked for had been taken away from us by a jealous, ungrateful, ignorant, bitter woman that couldn't lead a fish to water. There were days full of that fury, sadness, and a feeling of depression that followed. The last time I had to transition between jobs had been twenty years earlier and my fiancé and mom helped me through that change. Mom wasn't available this time and that made the pain of this change even worse. What was I going to do?

I began to spend time on my athlete representation business but it was tough because it wasn't generating any revenue. I knew I would be taking a big risk; however, I was battle worn and fatigue from wrestling with corporate giants. That fatigue brought fear along with it so I was reluctant to jump in with both feet and found myself back at work and this time leading a non-profit organization that had been around for twenty-five years with a well established reputation among regional businesses. It was a nice job that didn't pay as well as my previous job. I tried to mask my disappointment and displeasure of losing my mother and now my career by throwing myself into the role and by trying to get my sports agency up and going. But I was sinking into despair. I physically felt bad but I really couldn't see anything wrong with me. Luckily, I was scheduled for my annual checkup and there really was no more appropriate time to see the doctor given the way I was feeling. She gave me the full examination and everything seemed okay so she sent me on my way and gave me the customary closing statement that she would call me with the results of my blood work.

I had been gone from my corporate career job all of two months when my doctor called to give me the results from my physical exam. She told me she wanted to run more test however all initial screenings indicated I had an early stage cancer. I freaked out. This can't be happening as every possible negative outcome I could think about flooded my head. I knew my mother had cancer and what happened to her. I had to call my dad only to learn that he too had had cancer and survived because of early detection. Now with this information I obtained from my father and what I had witnessed with my mom, I needed to choose a path. Clearly my cancer had been detected early so surgical treatment made the most sense. It was still frightening proposition to have surgery. The Lord knew I needed Him and finally I turned to Him in prayer. I spoke to God and asked Him, "Is this how it's going to end, with me dying from cancer?" His message was clear, "Do not be afraid or discouraged. For I am with you wherever you go" (Joshua 1:9 NLT).

I could hear and see God's promises but I was also trying to stand up straight after the solid gut punch I sustained. This was another blow to me to be diagnosed with cancer and even harder when it was clear that I had to have surgery. I seemed to sink lower and lower.

When we are tired or exhausted we will most likely cower and take the path of least resistance. Surgery was the best path and it was a good chance should I emerge from the other side of it that I would be cancer free. The surgery was a success. My recovery took almost a year and I was filled with questions about my chances of remaining cancer free and regaining life the way I knew it. While I was recovering I tried to piece things together and wondered what happened to me. I could not get myself together. I resigned from the non-profit organization and didn't work for months. Some time was spent developing my agency and I gained a pretty signif-icant client. That gave me a burst of energy as it was just that—a burst. I had gotten my past clients exposure into professional teams so they could win a spot on the club's roster, however this client was a sure fire, or about as sure as they come, to be drafted by a professional football club. I had put in eighteen months cultivat-ing a relationship with him and his handlers, and finally won his business. I mentored, counseled, and loved this young man like he was my own son and he became friends with my wife and children. The kids maintained contact with him on social media and my wife became well acquainted with his girlfriend. Unfortunately, he and his handlers were using me as leverage "to get payola" from another agency and when that was all exposed we had to part ways.

I was shattered when we reached this juncture. I had invested my money, myself, and my time only to be betrayed by someone that clearly deceived me about who he really was and the types of people he chose to surround himself. The money was gone; however, I believed I could make more money, but the time was lost and I couldn't get that back. It seemed like everything I was touching was not moving in the direction I expected. I had doubled down my efforts to secure this young man as a client and now with him gone I was in effect out of work again. I threw my hands up and said, "Lord what must I do!"

> *"Such love has no fear, because perfect love expels all fear. If we are afraid, it is for fear of punishment, and this shows that we have not fully experienced his perfect love."*
>
> 1 John 4:18 NLT

Life had been happening to me and I had allowed myself to fall into a place of fear because everything I thought I knew to be true had now become false. Crazy for me to think Mom would always be with me and the family, and that death does not come as a thief in the night. Even sillier for me to have the wild notion that I could work for one company until I chose to retire. It's absolute madness that a ravenous disease like cancer could only be a disease for everyone else but invincible me. Or that I would become the super sports agent overnight and retain any and every client that signed with me. It was time for me to make a change, an about-face, seize a new direction and *Shift*.

God had to grab me by the collar and snatch me out of despair, disappointment, and some form of depression. Satan was closing in on me and I couldn't see the way out that God had left for me. So He rescued me from myself. When I lost my only client, it was like everything came crashing down on me. Who had I become? I had lived my life by a code of integrity, excellence, and results. That was something that had been consistent in my life since I was a child and the way I was raised. The key was I hadn't been honest with myself. I hadn't truly grieved the loss of my mom. There is a multi-step process you go through when you lose someone that significant in your life and I hadn't completed that sufficiently. Making matters worse, I had experienced multiple key losses over the past few years such as my career, my health, and my own entrepreneurial dream. Each one carrying huge implications on how I defined myself personally and professionally. I was down to nothing and clearly God was up to something.

This was a time of earnest reflection on my life up to this point. I had defined myself in large part by my professional achievements and that was for me, my family, and Mom. Mom had always wanted me to do well and I always wanted her to be proud to call me her son. I had been a no nonsense competitor and loved to keep score which sometime meant I was laser focused on winning and missed the opportunity to enjoy the journey. I wouldn't do that going forward. I repented to the Lord for being so sinful and ungrateful in so many ways. I had to ask the Lord for guidance and be willing to wait on God's timing. I want to be in His will. The Lord began to show me just how faithful He is by opening a door that I didn't even expect to open. The Lord blessed me with employment in a job that exceeded my previous level of responsibility, compensation, and influence over the business. He did this while I experienced His redemption. I still had challenges with my other businesses so I was sure to remain in constant communication with my savior. I owned five franchise businesses and we worked as a family to get them off the ground to break even and slightly beyond yet I recognized after a lot of back and forth in prayer and conversation with the Holy Spirit the season for those businesses has now passed. I sold four of them and planned to sell the remaining franchise. God was guiding me to clear a path so I could better view His plan for me.

My *Shift* would allow me to more clearly define the standard in which I lived of integrity, excellence, and results. Integrity would be defined by living the same life publicly that I live privately. It's great to be authentically me at home and at the office. Plus it enhances my ability to recognize and acknowledge the genuineness of others. Excellence would be about working for an audience of one—Jesus Christ. I want to live a life that reflects the one true Christ that lives in me. Jesus Christ always delivers excellence. Results are required. When God pours out blessings to you it's not just for you but for you to also bless someone else. The more we seek to know of God and His word it should result in good judgment. Most importantly, I don't ever want to portray myself as being perfect. I make mistakes and I have struggles; that's why I need Jesus. Every day is a day of surrender.

I have experienced some of the most trying times over the last six years yet when I look back I know God has allowed them to shake me at my core, to break me so He can begin to build me into the man He desires me to be. I believe He wants that for all His children. It's up to us to determine if we want to accept His process for taking us from fallen to redeemed. If we all live long enough, we will experience transitions throughout our lives and I want to encourage you to embrace the ambiguity and uncertainty of change. See it as an opportunity to reinvent yourself and to grow and develop yourself as a contributor to society. When you feel like you have hit rock bottom, I have found that Jesus is the rock at the bottom. Place your trust in Him and not man to be your foundation from which you can build and transform yourself.

> *"This is my command - to be strong and courageous! Do not be afraid or discouraged. For the Lord your God is with you wherever you go."*
>
> Joshua 1:9 NLT

My major keys that I carry as life lessons from my *Shift* experience:

- Fair exchange is no robbery. Be prepared to compensate those whom you request support, counsel, and/or labor. In that same spirit, know your personal worth and establish an agreeable amount of compensation for the support, counsel, and/or labor you provide. This is unless you are feeling philanthropic.

- Nothing beats a failure but a try. If you have a goal, write it down so it can be seen. Be determined and perseverant about achieving it. If you aren't successful the first time don't give up. You will never reap the reward of achievement if you quit.

- You can remain in the same place spiritually, mentally, and physically so the experience will never change; however, you should plan for a transition every ninety days by growing and developing yourself spiritually, mentally, and physically. As you evolve in these areas you'll gain numerous new experiences. If you aren't growing, you are dying.

- Mental toughness is critical. You won't succeed if you don't have it. This means bouncing back after you weren't successful in your initial attempts. You'll face rejection, disappointments, and discouraging situations. Speak words of affirmation and encouragement to yourself and surround yourself with wise and encouraging people.

- Love and care for yourself. Exhaustion leads to giving up.

- You are responsible for your own path. Go with God and through prayer allow Him to map it out. Now, own it.

- Time is a nonrenewable resource. Use it wisely.

- Always make the maximum effort. This is about delivering excellence and achieving results. Work as though you are working for the Lord.

- Your giving and service does not have to be weighed and measured. Give from your heart and it will not be in vain.

THE COURAGE TO BE ME

BY LESHAWNDA LARKIN

"We can't become what we need to be, by remaining what we are."

–Oprah Winfrey

Have you ever felt like a hamster in a cage on a spinning wheel? You are moving in complete circles, but not progressing forward. Every step on the wheel seems to expend so much of your spirit's force. What about a caterpillar in a cocoon? You think you are ready to transform into a butterfly but you cannot break the shell. Something is holding you back. Maybe you don't know how to make the change. Maybe it is fear, self-doubt, or procrastination. Regardless, the end result is the same. You are stuck and there is no progress.

That was my reality four years ago. From the exterior, everything looked great. I was living "the dream life" for a college educated, African American woman. I was employed at a top Fortune 500 company, and receiving the blessings that my ancestors prayed for their future generations by working the plan that I had envisioned for myself—a successful marketing leader in the consumer packaged goods industry. However, I had a secret that I did not want to recognize or admit to others. I was smiling on the outside but had a disconsolate spirit. I was unhappy with the direction of my life. Even though I had a great job, I was not fulfilled. I felt like a fraud. I didn't want to appear ungrateful for the things that I have achieved and received in my life. I was also concerned with what my family and friends would think if I started to shift in a radical direction from a career perspective. In the back of my mind, I would hear these constant thoughts, *You are almost 40. You should be stable with your career at the executive level. You need to continue to climb the corporate ladder.* However, this feeling deep inside would not go away. I have a strong connection and interest with the entertainment industry. I was destined to do something greater that would impact many people in a profound way, but I was headed in the wrong direction. How do I course correct and start heading in the right direction?

In the book, *Risk/Reward*, Author Anne Kreamer stated that more than half of Americans are contemplating changing not just their jobs but their careers. However, 46 percent of those interested in making the change did not know how to make it happen. So, it was good to know I was not the only one who felt this way. I didn't realize it at the time but the conflict that I was feeling was my destiny starting to pull me in a different direction.

Spinning Wheel

> *"I most fear God showing me all of the things I could have done but chose not to do."*
>
> *—T.D. Jakes*

My interest in arts and entertainment started when I was a young child. My mother placed me in piano lessons when I was seven years old. When I was in the 3rd grade, I auditioned for the Cleveland School of the Arts and I attended from 4th-12th grade as a music major. I thank God for allowing me to attend that school. It was a place where I felt comfortable to cultivate my talents but also escape the troubles of growing up in inner-city Cleveland. I had amazing experiences at the school, such as traveling to Japan for a jazz festival and performing with James Galway and the Cleveland Orchestra. I loved reading entertainment publications, remembering random entertainment industry facts, and learning details related to production—whether it was a movie or a song. I wanted to know who the writers, directors, and producers were behind the creation.

Even though my parents were supportive of my artistic endeavors, they stressed the importance of going to college and obtaining a solid, financial job. My parents had great intentions and did not want their children to struggle in life. So, I listened to them and chose a profession that was the furthest away from entertainment—chemical engineering. Before my senior year of high school, I interned at the NASA Glenn Research Center at Lewis Field and thought that engineering would provide a respectful career with job security. I also felt that my interest in entertainment was superficial. After graduating from Howard University with a degree in chemical engineering, I worked as an engineer at a soap plant in Kansas City, Kansas. One day, I was assigned to work with the marketing team on new product innovation. The marketing team would fly down from New York City and we would discuss new product innovation for soap and dishwashing gel. I was so in awe of the marketing team and their role that I said, "This is what I want to do next. Take consumer insights and develop and market consumer products." I thought that this would be a great way to tap into my creative side again. It was like the heavens opened up for me. I thought I saw the light. I quit my job and went back to school full-time to enter the field of marketing. I also felt that marketing would provide some exposure to entertainment because brands used entertainment properties and celebrities to endorse their products.

During this time, I was able to work on some amazing branded entertainment programs for the Snapple brand, such as *The Celebrity Apprentice* partnership. Snapple is a nationally distributed tea and juice beverage brand. *The Celebrity Apprentice* is a TV network show that has celebrities paired on teams participating in challenges to win money for their respective charities. I was able to lead one of the most successful branded entertainment retail/consumer programs for Snapple at that time. The Snapple brand was part of the show finale where the two finalists, Bret Michaels (lead singer of the rock band, Poison) and Holly Robinson Peete (Hollywood actress), developed new Snapple flavors. The flavors they developed were among the top ten newly branded tea products in 2010. I was able to lead a cross functional team to develop the appropriate level of consumer and retail activation to support the program (TV commercials, Public Relations, Promotions, Retail Programs, etc.). I also had to ensure that the new products were in stores when the finale show aired on TV. The promotional program was a finalist for InnoBev's Best Marketing Program. The tea developed by Bret Michaels (Diet Trop-A-Rocka) is still available in retail today.

Before I started work on *The Celebrity Apprentice* program, I had a conversation with an agency partner over dinner. She asked, "If you could do anything that you wanted, what would you do?" Quietly, I told her that I wished to work in entertainment marketing. Shortly after finishing work on *The Celebrity Apprentice*, that agency partner came back to me and said, "You actually just worked your first job in entertainment marketing with that program." I really enjoyed the synergy of combining entertainment programming with the science of marketing (understanding insights, data analysis, etc.).

After gaining more than ten years of diverse marketing experience working at great Fortune 500 companies, the vision for my life started to evolve. Deep down, my interest in pursuing projects in the entertainment industry was stronger. However, I wanted to be more faith-based/inspirational focused. For example, I would love to work on programming for networks like the Oprah Winfrey Network (OWN) or the Hallmark Channel. Even though I had this interest, I pushed my "entertainment" feelings away and took another consumer packaged goods job at a top tier company. Looking back, I was frightened and had a lot of doubt. I was discounting my talent. In T.D. Jakes' book, *Instinct*, he stated that the fear of failure could compel us to hide our talent rather than risk exposing it for risk of failure.

By the end of 2012, I was totally burnt out from work. I was in a position that I didn't enjoy and was overloaded with work. I had gained weight, my face broke out with acne, and my hair fell out. I was not feeling great physically, spiritually, or mentally. To sum it up in simple terms, I was a "hot mess." So, I decided to take a quick weekend trip to Los Angeles to visit one of my sorority sisters, Adia May, from college and escape the troubles in the world. We were meeting for dinner and before I knew it, I broke down and cried in the restaurant…in Beverly Hills! I was so embarrassed that I was crying in front of people but at the same time, I didn't care. I had to let it out. I confessed that I wasn't happy with my life's direction and that I had this strong feeling to pursue entertainment.

My friend, Adia, provided some "real-time" feedback for me. She said, "Leshawnda, you have talked about working in a different career field for a long time but you have not moved forward in that direction. You have great experience in this field and you are discounting it. You led some amazing branded entertainment programs in the past; however, it is time for you to put up or shut up about this."

At first, I was appalled to hear that message. Talk about having a "mic drop moment." But, mine was more like a "mouth drop moment." I thought Adia would say, "Girl, it will be okay." However, the sign of a true friend is being honest with you at every stage. It is so important to surround yourself with a supportive network of family and friends. You need a group of individuals who want you to succeed and win in life but will also provide that critical feedback to help you grow and become a better person. After I got over the initial sting of her words, I realized that she was right. The first part of the battle is admitting that something requires change. For years, I tried pushing my true feelings aside because I didn't want to appear that I didn't have it together and I wanted to please my family and friends. The second part was recognizing that

I didn't know how to make the change and was scared to death. That is when my SHIFT started to occur.

Then, something remarkable occurred that sparked hope within me. I recently learned that my sorority sister, Medina Collie, who was in engineering with me at Howard and was also a Harvard trained lawyer, made a huge jump. She quit her job to pursue a career in theatre and enrolled into The Juilliard School in New York. I thought, *This is one of the bravest things that I have ever seen.* She had the courage to be herself and I was seeking the courage to be me.

Surrender the Wheel

"You must learn a new way to think before you can master a new way to be."

—*Marianne Williamson*

> Over the next year, I prayed fervently to God. I meditated on the following scripture: *"For I know the plans I have for you, declares the Lord, plans to prosper you and not to harm you, plans to give you hope and a future"* (Jeremiah 29:11 NIV). If I was going to make a change, I had to put together a plan and start moving forward. Following are the steps I took to begin achieving my goals:
>
> • **Develop a clear vision for my life.** I attended Oprah's, "Live Your Best Life Tour" and those sessions helped me to formulate my life's vision: To be a God-centered, fearless, consistent, and authentic woman who lives with intention, purpose, and embraces life to the fullest while encouraging/inspiring others to do the same.
>
> • **Give up control and surrender to God.** I allowed God to become the Director/Orchestrator of my life.

- **Become comfortable with being uncomfortable.** I was stepping out of my comfort zone by learning a new industry and building a new network. I was placed in many situations that were unfamiliar to me. It is very easy to let fear turn you around. The key is to stay steady and progress forward even as you feel uncomfortable.

- **Become more knowledgeable about the entertainment industry.** I subscribed to reputable entertainment publications such as *The Hollywood Reporter* and *Variety Magazine*. This allowed me to broaden my knowledge base of the industry.

- **Arrange informational interviews with people in the entertainment industry.** I was able to ask a lot of questions—questions about their day to day tasks, why they worked in entertainment, etc.

- **Attend entertainment conferences to network and learn.** I started attending different entertainment conferences like "The Merge Summit" and "The Variety Purpose Conference" in Los Angeles. My friends were shocked that I flew from Texas to California by myself to attend the conferences. However, it was inspiring to surround myself with individuals who exhibited such strong faith. They received multiple rejections every day but they kept their eyes on the goal. I felt that if these people could have this type of faith and follow their dreams, so could I. One of the most moving discussions I heard was an impromptu speech by James Lopez at "The Merge Conference". At the time, he was a movie studio executive at Sony. He discussed how he made a major jump, changing his career at the age of 39 (going into the movie industry). After one of the panel discussions at that conference, I approached a movie executive for advice. That encounter turned into me gaining a mentor in the industry. I speak with this executive from time to time to ask for advice as well as provide updates on my projects. As I went through this process of inching closer and closer to shifting, God was starting to surround me with people and situations that allowed me to further move toward my area of passion.

During this time, I started to become very close to one of my coworkers, Seckeita Lewis. Every day, we'd meet to discuss various tasks at work. Over time, our discussions shifted to our dreams and aspirations. One day, Seckeita shared with me that it was her dream to direct a full feature film. Seckeita and her husband, Brandon Lewis, had worked on short features for the past couple of years and gained recognition at various film festivals. They decided to make the jump and start the process of making a comedic film called, *Jerico*, written by Brandon. We began discussing the film every day at work. All odds had been against them for this project coming to fruition. It was their first time making a full length movie. However, they trusted the vision that God placed in their life.

Jerico is about the dramatic events that make up the history of African Americans, but most of the story unfolds on the morning after the signing of the Civil Rights Act of 1964 in Mississippi. I thought the concept was unique, clever, and refreshing with a great message. Seckeita invited me out to the filming of the original trailer for the movie. I decided to join them after church one Sunday and visit the set. I was so impressed with the set-up. I actually felt like I was on a movie set. From that point on, I knew that Seckeita and Brandon were serious about this endeavor.

Little by little, I was being pulled into this movie. I really felt like *Jerico* was a magnet. I was able to leverage my network to connect them with different resources and assist with film production. For example, I introduced them to my sorority sister, Adia May, who eventually joined the team as the entertainment lawyer. I also made a donation to their Indiegogo campaign, an online fundraising site. But deep down, I wanted to do more. Eventually, Seckeita and Brandon asked if I would come on as an executive producer. The role of an executive producer is to help enable the making of a commercial entertainment product such as a movie. The executive producer also helps to finance the movie. I was very excited about joining the film but was scared to make that type of financial commitment. I was on the brink of quitting my job and knew that I would need my "nest egg" to assist with living expenses. Oh ye of little faith.

Produced by Faith

"Be still in the presence of the Lord, and wait patiently for him to act."

Psalms 37:7 (NLT)

In his book, *Produced by Faith*, Devon Franklin wrote, "Have you ever experienced a moment when you knew God has just put his hand on your life? If you have, then you know it's unforgettable. No matter how deep your faith, seeing God intervene directly and transparently in your life sends a chill up the spine." I experienced this moment at the beginning of 2015. At this point, I was closer than ever to quitting my job. I also shifted focus from myself to helping others at the job, spending time encouraging the young marketers on the team as well as assisting on a big diversity program. Every night, I was up late working on all of the marketing creative and signage for the program. I continued to pray every day, asking God for a change, a sign, anything. During this time, a family friend, Debbie Johnson, was in town for the College Football Playoff National Championship Game for Ohio State and spent time with me at my home. She ministered to me for an entire week as I shared my aspirations and dreams with her. During her departure, Debbie said to me, "God is calling you into His presence. Trust God and He will guide you."

The next day, I was contacted by a headhunter regarding a position at a technology company in the area of virtual reality. I was so shocked that they would reach out to me based on my background. I prayed to God for guidance and a sign to help me know that I was on the right path. As I prepped for the interview, I learned that this company had recently announced a partnership with producer David Alpert and Skybound Entertainment (the team behind the show, *The Walking Dead*) to develop virtual reality programming. I was eventually awarded the position, getting the opportunity to learn about a new "buzz" industry in Hollywood—virtual reality. When I received the offer to come on as a consultant, I was laid off from my existing job. Instead of being upset about it, I was finally able to exhale. I was hearing the song "Break Every Chain" by Tasha Cobbs in the background. I knew that God was closing one door and opening another one.

As a result of the change, I officially signed on as an executive producer for the film, *Jerico,* which featured the following great talent: George Wallace (Comedian), Irma P. Hall (*Soul Food*), Gregg Daniel (HBO's *True Blood*), Jo Marie Payton (ABC's *Family Matters*), and Numa Perrier (Black and Sexy TV). One of my friends, Grammy-nominated jazz singer, Nnenna Freelon, signed on to develop original music for the film and I assisted the team with obtaining music licensing approvals from record companies for the various songs being featured. It has been such a pleasure to work on this project because I was able to see the impossible become possible. This film was developed outside of the Hollywood system and network. We experienced many obstacles such as bad weather, delays, etc. However, the team persevered and created a wonderful work of art. The film has inspired so many lives.

The full circle moment occurred when the film *Jerico* world premiered in April 2016 at the Cannes Pan African Film Festival in Cannes, France. To premiere this film in another country was such a surreal moment. When the film won two awards—Best Actor and Best Supporting Actor—I knew that all of this was orchestrated by God. This was totally out of my control.

The Process of Progress

"I want us all to fulfill our greatest potential. To find our calling and summon the courage to live it."
                                            –Oprah Winfrey

I am still a work in progress and in the midst of my SHIFT. I am not at the finish line. However, I am no longer afraid to step out and make the jump. Is fear still present? YES, and I still feel very uncomfortable. The key is to be ready and open to experiencing the shifts. Life Coach and motivational speaker, Valorie Burton, said, "Everyone feels fear, but the courageous ones make a choice to do what feels hard despite their fears." I have received some comments about my new ventures—some positive and some not so positive. However, I am keeping my eyes on the prize. I want to be a renaissance woman like Maya Angelou. Maya Angelou was a myriad of many things—poet, writer, educator, civil rights activist, actor, director, producer. I don't want to be limited or defined by one thing. "Why stop for crumbs on the way to the banquet?" jazz singer Nnenna Freelon once asked me. That's when I recognized that I was created for more than what I could access in my previous environments. I was able to start the process of moving beyond the ordinary into where I belong. I finally had the courage to be me. I don't know where God is taking me but I know that I am committed to the process.

I will continue to work on marketing projects as well as find new projects that spark inspiration. However, I have now started my own production company, Larkin Productions, and my goal is to develop and support positive content across all creative mediums that sparks change and inspiration in people's lives. So, now it is your turn to fulfill your greatest potential. Seek the courage today to find it, but most importantly, live it!

THE LONG JOURNEY HOME—ONE BABY BOOMER'S JOURNEY TO HER ENTREPRENEURIAL DREAMS

BY CHERYL J. KETCHENS

"Strength comes from struggle. When you learn to see your struggles as opportunities to become stronger, better, wiser, then your thinking shifts from 'I can't do this' to 'I must do this."
–Toni Sorenson

As a child of the fifties, I am a proud baby boomer and a late bloomer. My journey into entrepreneurship has been long in coming and late compared too many. At this stage of life I'm not the least bit intimidated by a late start or my age. I know my value, I know my worth, and I believe in me. I am much, much more than a date stamp on a birth certificate, a few facial lines, or a couple of digits obsessed over by an age focused world.

The seeds of entrepreneurship were planted into the soil of my spirit at a very early age by my father, who was an entrepreneur himself. He owned a small diner in the South and Momma was an elementary school teacher. My father abandoned his one-man enterprise when he learned the automotive industry was booming in the North and good paying jobs were plentiful. They packed up and moved north to Michigan with three small children in tow and found a home in Jackson, Michigan where my father landed his manufacturing job.

Mom and Dad had seven more children before they stopped having babies. The increasing demands of our ever burgeoning family stifled my father's entrepreneurial dreams and postponed Momma's dreams of returning to her teaching career. Dad no longer had the option to pursue his small business ventures full-time.

Even though Dad was not able to pursue his dreams of working for himself full-time, I was fortunate enough to watch him start numerous small, but successful business ventures while working his full-time job in the automotive industry. Even though he did not amass great wealth, our large family of eleven lived very comfortably with one wage earner. The on-going demands of a large family delayed his entrepreneurial plans until after his retirement from his manufacturing job. He became a slave to a full-time job and a regular paycheck.

Dad held steadfast to his dreams and never gave up on the idea of someday owning a small business of his own to support our large family. He often said, "One day I'll be working for myself again and not for some company that tells you what you can and cannot do, when you can work, and how much you can earn." This became my father's mantra. I saw how much it killed his spirit and vowed that this would never happen to me. I never imagined that many years later it would become my mantra, too, and that I would have to survive many shifts in my own life before I would finally be able to pursue my entrepreneurial dreams. I also never imagined that they would be delayed by nearly 40 years.

My own entrepreneurial dreams started very early. I was seven years old when I set up a Kool-Aid stand and sold my first cup on the sidewalk in front of my family home. I did not make much money selling at ten cents a cup, but I was so proud of my accomplishments. You would have thought I made a million dollars. After the success of my Kool-Aid stand I told myself that I was on my way to owning my own enterprise someday.

By age twelve my dreams were bigger and I had abandoned the Kool-Aid stand. Now I was dreaming of owning an interior design business after discovering a hidden passion for decorating when I started re-arranging furniture, pillows, knick-knacks, and rugs in my parents' home. I loved the idea of creating new looks, and Momma liked it, too. She did not hide her excitement about the newly re-arranged rooms. "I don't have a creative eye like you do," she often said.

I was extremely shy so I think her compliments were intended to boost my self-esteem as well as bait me to create a new design look for her. As it worked out we were both happy.

I told myself that if I wanted to become a real interior designer I would have to learn the trade. I found the perfect place to learn and I could do it for free. I found all the resources I needed at my local library. I remember sitting in the library for hours perusing through the books until I found the right ones.

As I grew older, the dream was still alive so I enrolled in an interior design program. Sadly I would never finish my design program, because life happened. I was no longer that shy, naive little twelve-year-old with big dreams. I was married with a husband, children, a job, family obligations, a home to maintain, extracurricular activities for the kids… My priorities were forced to shift. My entrepreneurial dreams would have to be deferred until a later time.

After reading all those interior design books and completing some of my design courses I had learned a lot about design. Even though I was unable to finish my studies I had gained a lot of knowledge, as well as skills. My time was not wasted because I was able to help one of my girlfriends finish her interior design studies and receive her certification. She moved away to a large metropolitan city and went on to have a very successful design career. I had coached her as well as other family and friends and would not realize it for a number of years.

It wasn't until I read a 1998 newspaper feature article about a local Michigan woman named Nancy who was a Life Coach. Before

Nancy's story I had no idea what a Life Coach was. I remember being so enthralled with the lengthy, two page article that I was unable to put it down until I read the entire story. Nancy's story so resonated with me, and literally leapt from the pages into my spirit. I had an epiphany as I suddenly realized that I had been life coaching for many years without realizing it. I thought I was just helping family and friends solve a problem and embrace their talents. Some of my happiest moments of my childhood and adulthood occurred when I was helping others.

I saved the newspaper article and later contacted Nancy to learn more about life coaching. She was friendly and seemed eager to share information about what she did and how I could do the same. Some of the things I queried her about were educational requirements, credentialing, available schools, tuition costs, and length of time it would take to earn my certification.

My telephone conversation with Nancy was extremely helpful and gave me a much better understanding of who a life coach is, what they do, and who they serve. She was very encouraging and helped me see that I had already been practicing coaching with my family and friends and didn't know it. "You have a good start to a successful coaching career," she said. Nancy suggested I go to the internet to learn more about what was available to me.

She cautioned me about coaching websites that make claims that aren't necessarily true and how important it is to do your homework in order to find the right school for your specific needs. In other words, she was telling me to find a legitimate and reputable coaching school. She talked about the importance of proper accreditation and to steer clear of schools that didn't have the proper credentialing.

After my conversation with Nancy, I was so excited. I was absolutely certain that coaching was now the true path I would someday follow to live my entrepreneurial dreams. I did not realize that it was already interwoven into my spirit. I finally found my true passion, if I could easily convert it into my own business.

Becoming a life coach was definitely the direction I would be heading. In the meantime, I could still use my interior design talents as a hobby to help family and friends. However coaching would be my ultimate goal and the direction I wanted to take to start a business. I still had to wait a number of years before I was able to pursue my coaching business. I had to wait until my husband and I had an empty nest and I experienced a job loss.

Through my research, here are four recommendations for individuals seriously considering a career as a Life Coach:

- Talk with someone who is already working in the industry. Preferably someone who has an established coaching business. This individual can provide you with invaluable insight, information, and resources that will steer you in the right direction, like Nancy did with me. A veteran coach will help you understand who a Life Coach is, what they do, and who they serve. This is important because coaching may or may not be the dream career for you. It definitely is not a one size fits all career. This will save you time, money, and energy. The internet is a great resource for learning more about becoming a Life Coach.

- Take an assessment test to determine whether or not a coaching career is a good fit for you. Coaching has become very popular and seems rather glamorous to many. Despite its popularity it is not for everyone. The internet is a great place to find assessment tests. You should be able to find one on the website of the school you are interested in enrolling.

- Use the internet to help find a reputable coaching school with the International Coaching Federation

(ICF) endorsement. It is also very important to pay close attention to the fine print before you sign an enrollment contract. You are investing time and money, so it's important to know whether or not the school you are considering is a good fit for your academic needs. Are on-site classes required? Tuition costs–make sure you know what is included. You need to know whether your tuition covers your books, manuals, access to your instructor as needed, audio, and other learning aids that you will need to successfully complete your certification program.

- Hire a Certified Public Accountant (CPA) or Tax Accounting Firm as soon as you establish your LLC, and definitely before you start taking clients. A reputable CPA is an essential part of creating a successful business and keeping your finances on track. You need to know what financial implications your business tax filing may have on your joint tax filing with your spouse. You absolutely have to know this long before tax time rolls around. Poor book keeping is certain death for any small business. A CPA will help protect you and your business from a serious financial entanglement with the IRS.

"Just Let Go – Let go of how you thought your life should be and embrace the life that is trying to work its way into your consciousness to become stronger, better, wiser, then your thinking shifts from "I can't do this" to "I must do this."

–Carolyn Myss

My job loss in June 2012 was the catalyst that allowed me to follow my entrepreneurial dreams. My last employers did not always treat me kindly, but I felt trapped by a regular paycheck and benefits, just like Daddy did many years earlier. How many of us can actually walk away from a good paying job? I sure didn't feel like I could, and the longer I stayed the more trapped I felt. I finally decided it would be better to view my job as a short term delay instead of a permanent one. This shift in mindset allowed me to keep going until I could do what I wanted to do. I was determined to persevere knowing one day I would pursue my entrepreneurial dreams of having my own coaching business.

After receiving an indefinite layoff notice that June from my nine year job as a youth career manager, I had one of those deep down gut feelings in the pit of my stomach that my job would not be restored. An indefinite lay-off meant I was fired, and my employer no longer needed, desired, or wanted my services. I remember holding the layoff letter in my hands and thinking how much I would miss the kids I had worked with over the past nine years and the bond that I had formed with many of them. However the realization that I was finally free and had graduated from the classroom of working for others was powerfully liberating.

June 30, 2012 was my final day of working 9–5. Funny thing is, when my last work day finally rolled around and the clock struck 5:00 P.M., I simply shut down my computer, quietly gathered my personal belongings, and said a few goodbyes. I piled my things into the rear seat of my car and smiled to myself as I pulled out of the parking lot for probably the very last time. I don't even remember looking back at the building as I drove away where I spent nine years of my life working, I simply drove out of the driveway and never shed a single tear. To this day I still haven't shed a tear or looked back. There's a saying that goes something like this: *If you look backward you'll stay there.*

After years of working for others, God was already preparing me for the next shift in my life, and it was time to embrace it. I was so certain my job was ending that I started doing research on various coaching schools until I found one that would meet my needs. After many years of experiential and educational learning it was time to appreciate the lessons learned and the knowledge I gained working for others and not myself. It was time for me to bury any perceived grudges I might still be harboring from a lifetime spent working in jobs that sucked the life from my spirit. It was time to move forward with fulfilling my entrepreneurial dreams.

Thankfully my intuitive gifts helped me prepare for what was coming before I was totally blind sighted by the loss of my job. My gut instinct gave me early warning signs that there was a shift coming my way and that I had better pay close attention to the people around me, my bosses in particular. I began listening to the language they were using whenever I was around. Things such as possible staff changes. They began ignoring me completely, and some conversations would suddenly cease anytime I came near. As far as I was concerned the handwriting was clearly on the wall and I needed to focus my energies on my next shift. If my intuition was right, this would be the shift I had waited a lifetime for.

I followed my instincts by anticipating my job loss and began planning my future while still on my job. Thankfully I was able to prepare for my next journey in life. Once I found the right school I started having serious conversations with my husband, Michael, because I knew that any decision I made would affect him as well. Initially he seemed unsure of my proposed business endeavors, but quickly got onboard. "I love you very much," he said and he assured me that he would support my decision to pursue my entrepreneurial dreams, because he knew how much this meant to me to finally have this opportunity.

After gaining Michael's support, I was ready to go. I enrolled in Coach Training Alliance, a coaching school in Boulder, Colorado. Fortunately I had enrolled several months before my final day arrived. For those last few months of my job I was so happy, excited, and giddy. I felt like a kid in a candy store, because I had a plan already in motion, and I knew the direction I would be headed when I was finally free to follow my dreams. It felt so liberating!

My coaching classes were scheduled to begin one week after my last work day. I was so excited for the new opportunities God had in store for me, and I was finally free of the 9–5 drudgery that keeps many aspiring entrepreneurs from following their dreams. I call it "paycheck imprisonment."

"Do what you have to do until you can do what you want to do."
—Oprah Winfrey

After talking with Life Coach Nancy years earlier I already knew that getting my life coaching certification was essential if I wanted to be successful in my coaching career.

In July 2012, just one week after being laid off from my job, I started my educational coaching certification program. I was over the moon with excitement that I was finally able to begin my long journey home to my entrepreneurial dreams. The transition from work to school was a relatively smooth one. My advance planning had paid off.

I was both confident and prepared and had several things working in my favor. Two of the biggest barriers standing between me and my entrepreneurial dreams were now gone. One of them was the most incredible thing that can ever happen to any human being. I'm talking about parenting a child or children. It was one of the most indescribable, significant, and life changing experiences of my entire life. For me personally there is no greater gift in life than parenting a child. Thankfully I was not a single parent and had my loving husband by my side. We were a team. Our children are grown now. They are independent, self-sufficient, and living on their own.

As much as I loved each of them with every fiber of my being, with every beat of my heart, mind, body, and soul, raising them was no longer a barrier to moving forward with my personal dreams. Yes! My dreams of owning my own business were delayed by nearly 40 years. However I have no regrets because regret reeks of self-pity, and that's not a place I want to reside. I absolutely loved every moment of being a parent. I even enjoyed the teen years that most parents seem to dread.

The second barrier that contributed to the delay of my entrepreneurial dreams was working a full-time job. Now that barrier was gone, too. After losing my job I secretly decided that I would not seriously engage in seeking a replacement job until I was absolutely certain of the direction I was headed. It did not take long for me to realize that it was my time and when the stars align and God has a plan for your life, nothing and no one will stand between you and the plan that He has for you.

None of it mattered now because I was truly free and I would be able to devote my time, attention, and energies to my coaching studies. I already had an undergraduate degree, three national certifications in workforce development, and other certifications, so doing well academically was not a worry for me as long as I stayed focused and applied myself to my schooling. This was my job now, and it was all about me for a change.

My coach training was both challenging and comprehensive. I learned how to get clients, how to create a business plan, how to coach, set up an LLC, goal setting—commonly referred to as Specific, Measurable, Attainable, Realistic, Timely (S.M.A.R.T.)— goals for myself and my clients, social media, networking, and the value of having a coach for yourself. I was determined not to waste a moment of my educational training, and took full advantage of it by setting up my business before graduating.

Coach training and certification requirements were no cakewalk and required a great deal of self-study, pre-class prep work, and pursuing clients while studying. Students were required to have a minimum of three clients, and successfully complete all final exams before a coaching certification was awarded.

I established my Limited License Company (LLC) in September 2012. I searched the internet for hours, days, and weeks before finding a corporation to set up my LLC. I finally settled on Corp-Net, a California based company. I wanted to have my business in place and operational before my studies ended in January 2013. I found a tax accounting company first, then found a Certified Public Accountant (CPA) in my home state of Michigan. Everything was falling into place.

In January 2013, I successfully earned and received my life coaching certification from Coach Training Alliance and was ready to start my coaching business. I officially launched my coaching business in February 2013. Like any new adventure in life the beginning was a bit rough because I didn't have a firm plan of action in place. In the absence of a plan you flounder.

"Death Is Not the Greatest Loss In Life. The Greatest Loss Is What Dies Inside While Still Alive. Never Surrender."
–Tupac Shakur

Even though it's taken me longer than many, and I have a few frown lines and a couple of grey hairs, I have no regrets for the many shifts in my life that delayed my entrepreneurial re-birthing. It would be very easy for me to feel sorry for myself and wallow in self-pity, or hang on to the idea that this was all supposed to happen 40 years earlier. That would be counter-productive to the doors that God is now opening for me. How selfish would I be to waste these new opportunities on events and circumstances that I cannot change? Neither can you.

If your dream is still alive and tucked deep down in your soul, don't leave it there to rot and decay or wilt like a beautiful flower beaten down by the sun. Your age is truly just a number that our society may deem as old. Sometimes it's as though some members of our society were clutching a medal of honor tightly in their hands, inscribed with the words, *I'm younger than you are.* The perception is that the younger you are the more valuable you are. This is total and complete B.S., because the only barrier standing between you and living the life of your dreams is you. If you listen to the white noise coming from society that says you're too old, too grey, too fat, or too wrinkled, or any other label that choice is yours alone. Don't bother blaming others if you decide to take the merchandise off the shelf and buy it.

This is one proud Boomer who is embracing her age, her God given talents, innately unique gift's, and decades of life lessons learned from an early marriage, raising a family, surviving postpartum depression, working mediocre jobs, earning a degree, being marginalized, undervalued, passed over for promotions, meno-pause, betrayal, rejection by friends, and a paralyzing shyness.

Today I challenge you to take a self-inventory of where you are in your life and what you still want to do, see, or accomplish before leaving this earth in a beautifully decorated steel box or urn. Don't waste another minute, another hour, another day, or another year, depressed, mad, sad, or angry, while blaming others for things that only you can control. Why waste another beautiful day living with regret? You truly are worthy and deserving of doing and being any-thing you want to be. You've earned it.

For me it was reviving the dreams of a naive twelve year old girl who wanted to someday own her own business and work for herself like my daddy wanted too. Today, I'm living my dreams and I am free of the shackles that I chained myself with. My eyes are wide open to the long fought after journey that God has given me. I am happier than I have ever been in my entire life. I know how good it feels, and I want the same for you.

Don't allow your dreams to shrivel up and die like an over-rip-ened grape hanging from its vine because of a date stamp on your birth certificate or a few grey hairs. Why would you selfishly want to deny yourself and the rest of the world of your unique inner gifts and talents? God has already endorsed them and the blood has already been sacrificed for you. Somewhere in the world there are throngs of fans waiting for the very gifts you carry inside of you. Stop using your age as a crutch. It really doesn't matter if you're, 50, 60, 70, or 100 years of age if your dreams are still alive. The only thing that is standing between you and fulfilling your life's dreams is you. Remember always that a Dream Delayed Is Not a Dream Denied!

TIED TO OUR SOUL

BY TINA TYUS-SHAW

"We wish we could see and touch you just for a minute. Like shattered glass gone so fast, but in our lives forever."
                                                        –Tina and James Shaw

"How very softly you entered our world silently. Our hello was goodbye. Your little footprints left an imprint in every pocket of our hearts. We will forever love you. Rest on, sweet angels. We will see you again." Closing my eyes, I see images of what life would be like if only...

In 1998, I had a promising career as a television News Anchor/ Reporter in Savannah, Georgia. My visions, hopes, and dreams were like clockwork. My desire for true love came that November. A tall, handsome, fine Army man stole my heart and later proposed to me at a famous Savannah Jazz Club–Hard-Hearted Hannah's. We won the lottery...each other. We had the perfect chemistry! Our engagement stood the test of distance, time, and trust. While I was in Savannah, James (Jimi) was at Fort Jackson, in Columbia, S.C. and later transferred to Fort Gordon in Atlanta where he retired. Our relationship accelerated to marriage on August 26, 2000.

December 5, 2000 marked another special moment for us. At age 36, I was pregnant and we got a double blessing. Twin boys would change our lives. My husband and I were overcome with emotion. Twins run in his family, and by all accounts it was time for a new set. I immediately started thinking about how to take care of the double—outfits, schools, and names. We settled for Julius and James. I was surprised I would carry two babies because I have always been a small framed person. Even with morning sickness and a lot of back pain, I did not worry because I had the best Gynecologist, Dr. James Carr.

One day I started having back pain, and I remember Dr. Carr gave me an elastic belt to wear around my waist. It was supposed to ease the pain. By now my ankles were swollen and my complexion was a shade darker. Being in the public's eye I still felt beautiful. I even got calls from my television viewers about how I was glowing and pregnancy looked good on me. My appearance was on point every day.

On April 4, 2001, eight days after my birthday, my life's shift started and I didn't realize a ferocious storm was coming. It was an exhausting day. I had a special Eye Care project to present in a live report during the six o'clock News on WSAV-TV. I showed up and I shinned.

Moments later, my high step into the live truck triggered a painful pulling feeling. Seconds passed the discomfort. I made it back to work and started preparing for the 11 P.M. newscast.

My life was shifting without my knowledge. When my Co-Anchor, Jim Carswell, and I went on the air at 11 p.m., I read well and got through the first block of news. Holding on for dear life, in the first commercial break I felt something was wrong. Suddenly I was in excruciating pain for three minutes. On air again, I was reading the news again with no problem. Wouldn't you know the pain started again at the next break? This time I told Jim I did not feel good. He offered to finish the news without me, but being strong willed, I decided to stay. Looking back that was not a wise decision because that same pain happened in every commercial break. After the newscast I called my husband and told him I did not feel good. He offered to bring me home, but I said, "I'm okay. I can make it."

He said, "I hope you're not..." and then he got quiet. I did not leave WSAV that night until I taped morning news for a radio station. My Director, Tim Thomas, offered to have someone else to tape it, but here I was again insisting to complete my daily tasks. I finally left the station at midnight. Home by 12:10 A.M., a new day, April 5th, and the pain was back. My husband said, "I'm taking you to the hospital."

I said, "No. Once I take a shower and put this belt around my stomach to relieve the pain I will be okay." After my shower I felt better and decided to get in bed. I knew whatever was going on God would handle it. I tossed and turned for an hour and a half. At 2:00 A.M., I felt my husband's toes touch my leg. Worry and confusion covered his face, and he took me to Candler Hospital. That three minute drive felt like an eternity. Once there the nurses called Dr. Carr to alert him. Dr. Carr told the nurses to have me transferred to Memorial Hospital since I was high risk because of my age (37). Before the transfer the nurse checked me and said, "We hear two heartbeats." What a blessing! Relief!

We were still hanging on edge hoping our babies would survive the trauma. By 3:30 A.M., I was in a hospital bed at Memorial. I knew Dr. Carr had arrived when I heard the fast walking, hard knocking sound of his shoes. Visibly worried, he said, "Tina, how are you? I told you to call me if you feel any pain."

I replied, "I know, but I thought I was okay." My Storm of Life was raging and I felt like a ship being tossed out to sea. The storm didn't cease, the winds kept blowing, and the currents were fierce. All I could ask was for my God to stand by me. Dr. Carr gave me medicine and began examining me. My eyes were closed shut and my body numb. After a couple of hours, my blurry eyes peeled open to a room filled with people.

My ears heard my husband's cry.

Our Shift Arrives

I asked, "What's wrong with me? Somebody tell me what's wrong."

Dr. Carr said, "You lost the babies."

Distraught, I remember grabbing a nurse's hand saying, "Isn't there something you can do to bring my babies back?"

She said in a somber voice, "I'm sorry."

Our hearts were broken. Losing our twins was our deepest ache. I felt those waves crashing inside of me as if my life was over. I still had to deliver our precious boys. Our first baby was delivered at 3:03 P.M. weighing 1 lb 1.4 oz, 10½ inches. Ten minutes later our second baby was delivered weighing 1 lb 0.2 oz, 10½ inches. They were monochorionic twins which means identical sharing the same sac. Ultimately a tangled umbilical cord choked them to death. In an instant our hearts were changed forever.

Shortly after delivery, they were placed into my arms. Wearing crocheted light blue hats, our angels were tiny, yet fully formed but they were not developed enough to survive outside the womb. James and Julius entered our lives in a precious, powerful, and quiet way. Our hello was goodbye. We never heard their cry.

My husband and I were grateful that we had a chance to hold our boys. Our loss spun us into a dark, lonely pit. A few days later on the way to let their souls rest in the place we consider their garden, our hearts were raw like an open wound. Arriving at Lincoln Memorial Cemetery on Hunter Army Airfield, I thought in amazement how the rest of the world just keeps on going, and how our lives were changed in only a moment. Friends, family, and co-workers at the funeral for our boys gave what they could, their presence and some a gentle tear.

As the casket holding our loves was lowered into the ground, I felt a breeze and dropped my head in disbelief. I thought my heart was going to jump out of my body. Struggling to be strong for me, my husband's emptiness was evident.

Grief and exhaustion leaves little energy for anything else. We felt we had lost the battle of our lives. Understanding that every day is a gift, my husband and I often reminded each other not to lose hope. I feel like we hugged and held hands more than ever. My husband never left me home alone because the loneliness would drive me crazy. Jimi knew my mind would be consumed with the special moments we would miss. As parents we never got to hear the pitter patter of their footsteps, never signed school papers, or decorated our refrigerator with their pictures. I never got to dance with them at the Mother/Son dance. In this life being tossed through a raging storm, I knew I had an Anchor in my Lord.

In the coming weeks, agony and frustration led me to my Minister Henry R. Delaney.

Nervous, I asked if it was okay for me to ask God why...why me.

Reverend Delaney said yes.

I wept and wept. Leaving St. Paul CME church, I felt resolve. This shift in my life kept me out of work for 18 weeks. Grief counselors visited weekly. On the surface it seemed like I was getting better emotionally, but on the inside my sadness was hard to repair. There were many days where I could not think straight. This is a painful and complicated place to be. I felt guilty about trying to be Wonder Woman. I worked hard and did not call my doctor right away when I started feeling pain. I kept pushing to get through every newscast instead of having my co-workers to step in for me as they offered. Only prayer and time moved me past the guilt.

One day my sister Penny said, "I'm going to take you for a ride. You need to get out." We had a sandwich and rode around Savannah. It sure was nice to see the pretty blue sky, the sunshine, trees, and people. On the way home I asked her to take me to Kroger. The moment I stepped out the car I felt all eyes on me. Attention is the last thing I craved. I walked into the store with my head down hoping no one would notice me. When I saw someone I knew I walked fast so they would not see me, and then imagine taking the wrong turn. I ended up on the baby aisle.

Panic and fear covered my body, and I was losing my footing. I screamed, and Penny took me home. Seeing bottles, pacifiers, diapers, and bibs shattered my heart into a million pieces.

Healing Takes Time

My news viewers played a significant role in my healing process. They are like family. You see, my husband and I allowed them to follow my pregnancy. I posted updates on the internet and a pictures of our ultrasound. Learning about our loss gripped their hearts.

On my return to work, 4½ months later, touching cards of support covered my desk, and my inbox was overflowing with messages of hope.

So how would we go on? As the days passed we started to move forward in our grief.

There were moments when we had to pass the cemetery as we went to the commissary (PX) or grocery shopping on the military base. My eyes would tear and my throat tighten as I remember being in the PX and my husband decided to buy toys to put on their grave. The mini tractors he bought made me think of plans we had for all the tomorrows. Withered flowers, leaves, and twigs covered their garden. As we cleared debris there were no words, there was only tears and love. We put the toy on the grave and left. Little by little you learn to live your life again, but there's always something missing. These were the most precious months of my life.

Trying Again

It takes faith and courage to try again. We had mixed feelings because of the emotions tied to us. In our situation we looked at how we would cope realizing that having a new baby could never wipe away our grief. Our lives forever changed, we decided to move forward four months after our boys passed. Layered with joy was concern. In August 2001, we revealed to Dr. Carr that we were trying to conceive again. Three months later on November 7th I had a pregnancy test at Dr. Carr's office. We got positive confirmation that I was four weeks and six days pregnant. We were cautiously overcome with joy. The main worry was, will this baby be healthy?

Feeling good and glowing with confidence, on April 29, 2002, after a checkup I went on the Military base to have my prescription filled. As I waited, I felt water running down my legs. Thankfully the restroom was not far away. In panic mode, I stuffed my underwear with tissue and told the pharmacist, "I'm taking this roll of tissue; forget the prescription, something is wrong. I need to get back to my doctor's office." It was a packed waiting room and all eyes were on me. Military police offered to escort me, but I chose to drive myself. A calm feeling crossed my heart. Praying silently, our twin angels were guiding me off the base onto one of the busiest streets in Savannah—DeRenne Avenue. I felt time stopped for me because there was very little traffic and that's rare. Ten minutes later, I arrived at Dr. Carr's office. Imagine walking into the building with your hands covering your back end. My clothes were soaked. Turns out my water broke at 31 weeks. Once my husband arrived, I was loaded into an ambulance and taken to Memorial hospital.

Enroute to the hospital, I remembered we had arranged for someone to do work on our front door at home so I called him to reschedule. The paramedics were looking at me in disbelief like, *This lady is really concerned about her door!* When we arrived at the hospital, thankfully my room was ready. Dr. Carr was not taking any chances. The hospital was now my home for the duration of my pregnancy. I remember saying I could not be on bed rest because I was working on a special project for my job. Dr. Carr's comeback, "Let your job know you're on bed rest." As Doc left he said, "Tina, you need to stay in bed and I will check on you later." Well, I was one hardheaded patient because three hours passed and I decided to take a shower. Two minutes later there was a knock on the door. Oh no!

Dr. Carr asked, "Tina, are you okay?"

I replied, "I'm fine, I just needed to shower."

Dr. Carr said, "I told you to stay in bed. I will be back in 10 minutes."

When he came back there was no biting his tongue or mincing words. He reminded me that the life of our baby girl depended on me following orders. A nurse arrived 30 minutes later and explained I would be on a low sodium diet and gave me a few food choices for my three meals a day. The next words out of her mouth shocked me. She said, "You don't remember me, do you?"

I replied, "No, make me remember."

She said, "I was with you when you lost your twins."

Teary eyed, I hugged her. This was the same nurse whose hand I touched and said, *Isn't there anything you can do to bring my babies back?* What a moment and proof to me that God brings people in our lives for a reason. Once she left I thought about her for hours. She appeared to be my guardian angel.

During that first week on bed rest, I watched more television than normal, paid bills, and did a lot of starring outside. I had never been so bored in my life. I wanted to breathe fresh air and enjoy the sunshine. Staying focused and remaining prayerful was key to make sure that our baby girl would make it into the world without any problems. Week two started with Dr. Carr making his daily visit. I would meet other moms-to-be. They were on bed rest, too. We shared conversations about our conditions and laughed a lot together. We also had a class each day about preparing for our babies. Week three came and I've carried my baby for 34 weeks. I thought about how everyone suffers at some point in their lives, but my husband and I chose not to let it break us. I began to feel something special would happen sooner than later.

On Mother's Day morning, all of the moms met in one room, and we were given white carnation flowers. My face beamed with happiness. Around two o'clock that afternoon, sharp pains struck my stomach. I knew this was the beginning of a beautiful moment. Yes, after two weeks and three days on bed rest I was having contractions. In the delivery room every 10 minutes the experience felt worse. On a scale of 1 to 10, squeezing my husband's hands dropped the pain to a seven. Family members rushed to the hospital to be with us. After seven grueling hours in labor, our sweet baby girl was ready to see the world. She was born at 9:36 P.M. Sure was great to hold her and hear her cry. We named her Celine which means "moonlight." She was 3 lb. 8 oz. at birth. We were so happy she made it, but we could not take her home for three weeks because as a premature baby her lungs were still developing and she had jaundice, a yellowish pigmentation in her skin. Our bond was incredible; she knew me and her father. Our prayers were answered. To see this little person and to hear her cry was emotional for me and my husband. It's almost like Celine knew what we had experienced with the twins. She raised her tiny arm and wiggled her fingers as to say hello world I'm here. My husband's eyes teared and then he smiled. We were relieved. Then he leaned over, squeezed my hand, and kissed me. We considered this to be one of the best days of our lives. This ocean of life has been tough, but now the seas are much calmer.

This experience has been a Good Teacher

1. My husband and I have learned that God doesn't put any more on you than you can handle. Tough times don't last...tough people do.

Life may throw you heartbreak, but prayer and patience heals all wounds.

2. It's important to release every struggle and eventually you will gather strength from your storm. The simple truth is no one should ever give up. Don't leave a page unturned. Always have faith.

Today as a family, we have gratitude for everything that has ever occurred to bring us to this moment. We give thanks for the joys and the sufferings, the moments of peace and the flashes of anger, the compassion and the roar of my courage, and the cold sweat of our fear. The Shaw family accepts gratefully the entirety of our past and present life.

To our sweet angels, rest. We will see you in paradise.

WEATHERING LIFE'S STORMS

BY GRETA SMITH

"You can find peace amidst the storms that threaten you."
                                        –Joseph B. Wirthlin

As I sit here reflecting over my life, looking in the mirror, I discovered many things about myself. It's easy to look in the mirror and say what I like about myself while putting on my makeup and combing my hair. But it was hard to look in the mirror and say what I disliked about myself and tears began to well up in my eyes. As women we take on various roles—we are mothers, wives, grandmothers, girlfriends; we have jobs, we have to be the nurse, doctor, counselor, the list goes on and on. We make sure everyone is taken care of and with the little time that is left for ourselves, we either take a long bath or shower, read, pray, whatever it takes to relax ourselves. We go to bed in preparation for the next day. We are too busy taking care of everyone else we lose sight of who we are. While looking in the mirror, I began to see my reflection of what type of woman I used to be and the woman God was molding me into. The type of woman I used to be had no tolerance when it came to other women and their relationship; even towards friends and family. I was judgmental; my main words were, "Girl, why and how do you allow this man to treat you like that? He cheats, lies, hides his phone, and the worst of them all is he doesn't have any money. You are stupid, just plain crazy. Let him go!"

I was always quick to say that would never happen to me. Yet I did the same thing to men—cheat, lied, took their money. Even in all that, one thing I did find out was to watch how you treat people and watch what you say about people. Because what goes around, yes say it with me…"COMES BACK AROUND." True saying: you reap what you sow.

Now the woman God was molding me to be came when God gave me a vision of who I would be, but He never showed me what I would go through. All I could do is give God the praise and the glory for pushing me into my destiny. Like the woman at the well, I was searching for one thing and found so much more, like peace, love, understanding, patience, forgiveness, and faith. The woman at the well wanted to get a drink of water but God gave her living water. Sometimes God has to do a supernatural thing in your life so that nobody but God will get the glory (credit). Not the lawyer, doctor, husband, wife, friends or family. "But God chose the foolish things of the world to shame the wise; God chose the weak things of the world to shame the strong" (1 Corinthians 1:27). I am a true testimony of that.

I had no idea of the storm I was about to enter into. I'm 51 years old and born again since 1997, the single mother of three sons, also a grandmother of six. My storm began around 2009. That year started out to be the worst year of my life. Two of my three sons were sent to prison, one on my birthday and my other son followed a month after. The Sunday before, I was at my brother in-law and sisters church; my sister was doing praise and worship and began to sing the song "Go Through Your Storm". I stood up and began to praise God. It was like an out of body experience. I was actually moving. The best way to describe it is simply to say I was floating, like I was being pushed slowly the more I praised God.

Listening to my sister saying, "Go through your storm," I began to weep and cry, uncontrollably, when all of a sudden I was in a dark place and my body moved through this place that looked like some type of tunnel. I could see a lot of things coming at me but they never touched me; they would pass me on my left and right side. All I could see at the end of the tunnel was a pretty blue light, but it was so far away. Like the more I tried to get close to the blue light the wind blew harder; I was in the tunnel for a while. Then I heard a voice saying, "When you and your sons get through this, you will never worry about anything again. It is well. It is well." I opened my eyes and I'm back inside the church with my sister singing. I just began to praise God, thinking it was a sign saying my storm was just over, but only to my surprise to have learned it was just the beginning. One of my sons was sentenced to 15 years for something myself, family, and friends know that he did not do; my second son was sentenced to 25 years, to serve two years and then be on probation for 23 years upon his release from prison. I will never forget either day my sons were sentenced to prison. It felt like a death had happened. I felt like I wasn't going to live through this; it was so hard, my faith was being tested. Thank God for family and friends, but I really didn't want to hear anything at that time about anything, especially God. I felt like He had forsaken my sons and myself. I had been living all I knew how for God. I had given God my all.

For twelve years I had been abstaining from sexual activity. *Why have you allowed this to happen?* Even in all I was going through my life has to go on; I still had another son to take care of. I still had to work, some days not wanting to get out of bed, feeling ashamed, hurt, disappointed, and like a failure to my sons. Still fighting through the tears, smiling on the outside while hurting, I was broken. While my sons were doing time I was, too. It was a daily battle trying to prove my oldest son innocence, trusting man instead of God. Working two and three jobs to keep money on the phone so I could hear from them and to keep them encouraged, all the while crying on the outside. Sending money, driving to two separate prisons; I can't lie, it was hard, but something inside of me just wouldn't let me completely give up.

I had to cry, pray, cry, fast. I had to listen to encouraging songs, keep myself in church and around the saints of God. I remember this one scripture, Romans 8:28, "and we know all things work together for the good of them that love God, for them who are called according to his purpose." I had to believe that all this bad was going to work for my sons and my good. Even in my trusting God, things were still falling apart. I got hurt on my jobs, my car broke down, everything that could go wrong did.

Even in the midst of all that, I entered into a relationship with someone who I thought was the love of my life. It turned out to be the worst heartache of my life. Everything I used to tell my family, my friends, and others I found myself going through some of the same things. In your Christian walk of faith, you will go through some tough times, but remember storms never last forever. In the midst of the storm, seek the Lord and run unto Him for shelter. Don't think about the bad weather but instead seek peace through Christ. I found out one thing while weathering life's storm. I never would have made it without God. The facts were, yes my two sons were in prison, I had lost my job, car, apartment, and I had broken God's heart, lost in my relationship. The enemy wanted me to curse God and die; he was telling me to just go take out the ones that hurt your son. Now the devil will talk to you when you are at your lowest point in life. He even told me what the word said, eye for eye. If someone would have told me I would have a storm coming into my life like this, I wouldn't had believed them. Yes, all the facts were against me but my faith was saying something else, like lean not to your own understanding. My inner voice was telling me, *You have the victory.* Jesus went to the cross for me. Even while writing this, everything was coming at me. I remembered Matthew 24:12-13, "because iniquity shall abound they shall endure unto the end shall be saved."

I had to tell myself not to give up; I can't give in. I won't turn back; I am an overcomer. I had to believe His promise that He had told me that Sunday, when He had me in the eye of this storm. When my sons and I get through this storm, we would never have to worry about anything. I truly believe in all God's word. Jeremiah 29:11 says, "For I know the plans I have for you." The Lord's plan is for me to prosper and not to be harmed in life's storms, but to go through them and come out with hope in Him, and my future. Life's storm tried to get the best of me, tried to take my children, tried to take my life, but I know the giver of life personally. So I have already won. NO longer will he control me with fear and false evidence appearing real. Through my life's storm, they have left me rooted in God's word. My faith has been increased. I can do all things through Christ Jesus. I pray my testimony of how I faced my storms as a single mother, being broken in my relationship helped someone. My words to anyone going through a storm: Keep the faith, trust God, and be still because every storm has to end.

WHY I TOUCH PEOPLE

BY TONY BETHEL

"In all thy ways acknowledge him and he shall direct thy paths."

Proverbs 3:6

When I think back to when I was in the 2nd grade, Mom and I would be at the house and she would read the Gospels (bible) to me. I was so fascinated by how Jesus could change a person just by touch. I remember the story about Jesus raising the little girl from the dead—although he did not touch her. Since I was a little boy, I felt some sort of connection to the works of the hand, and it mesmerized me. When Jesus raised his own friend Lazarus from the dead, he did not touch him either. Jesus became my Superhero. I did not have any comic books at the time, so Mom read bedtime stories, but when I heard Jesus touched people and healed them, I was totally hooked. I also remember Jesus' humility and humbleness to touch people's feet. This impressed me greatly; the "King of Kings and Lord of Lords" touching people's feet. These thoughts made it so much easier to do volunteer work later with the unwashed homeless.

I remember trying to mimic Jesus' work by laying hands on my mother's friends to heal their legs after a long day of work. They stood for hours in the factory where Mom worked at a machine called the punch press. Mom shuttled three other ladies to work and two of them often complained about the pain in their legs. I put my hands on their legs and they remarked how much relief they felt. I did not recall others touching Jesus to heal him, so I wasn't affected by someone touching me as much as I enjoyed providing the touch. I wasn't pretending to be Jesus, instead I was His little helper.

My upbringing was a little unique. My mother was a single parent and finding reliable daycare was just as difficult back in the 1960's as it is now. Mom could not always depend on extended family; especially since she worked a 40-hour week. We lived in a rough neighborhood near Hyde Park in Chicago, Illinois. Enter Mrs. Robinson, a warm, big-hearted woman with a heart of gold who took me on regular walks through the neighborhood. She was late middle-aged and had no kids. I had the impression I was hers and could do no wrong. Mrs. Robinson never looked down on anyone. As a little boy I met pimps, sex-workers, people with chemical addictions, yet none of those people would harm a hair on my head. They were my protectors and confidantes, spoiled me and gave me the little money they had. They began to feel like I needed a more thriving environment because I was asking lots of questions about the world and my environment and they could not answer. My mom decided to put me in a daycare and elementary school in Evanston, Illinois, where she worked nearby. My mom grew up in segregated Arkansas, not too far from Little Rock, and she knew first hand that separate was NOT equal. She went to great lengths and sacrifice to insure my education was equal, and used the daycare address as our home address to enroll me in elementary school in Evanston.

Evanston, Illinois, a predominately white suburb north of Chicago, is where I attended grades K-2nd. Things changed when I was seven or eight years old. My parents married and we moved to Englewood, an African-American neighborhood on the Southside of Chicago. The distant travel between Englewood to Evanston became an issue so Mom stayed at home and sent me to a Catholic School less than half a block away from home. I had to toughen up. Children tested me at first because they said I talked funny. I spent K-2nd grade in Evanston, of course I would speak differently. But I did not fight differently and held my own in physical confrontations. In the third grade, there was a guy named Calvin, the biggest kid in the class, who befriended me. He was an easygoing and likable kid and it didn't matter to him that this new kid talked different. He heard what I was saying instead of focusing on how I sounded. His influence meant a lot so when other kids noticed how he treated me, they began to follow his lead. The teasing stopped and I could really focus on education, so important for me as a black male. It is my belief there are only two things that separate a black man from a prison sentence: 1) a good education, and 2) good connections. Without the education you cannot get the job. Without the connections you still cannot get the job. So we must constantly keep our credentials up and pants up, network, and work on skills like manners and dress.

Education is extremely important to me and I remember in elementary school asking my math teacher, Sister Michelina, if she could help me prepare for a high school entrance exam. She was more than happy to tutor me after school, on her own time and without charge. I got an acceptable score on the test which enabled me to attend a college prep school, which enabled me to attend the University of Illinois Champaign-Urbana. Sister Michelina started a chain reaction of confidence in me. To win awards at both places showed me the capacity to give orders, as well as take them, and to speak up as well as listen. These qualities would eventually help me immensely in listening to my clients/patient's problems as well as being able to speak up about unhealthy lifestyles they may have, when appropriate. Having a mentor or teacher is crucial in a young person's life.

My father passed away suddenly in my senior year of college. I initially had no intention of coming back to this rural community but when my father passed, he left behind not only me, but Mom and my ten-year-old brother. I attempted to stay for a few months but I was so restless with a desire to travel that I joined the Navy.

Part of the discipline of military life is personal appearance, respect, and manners; things that aren't taught as much in homes today as they were when I was growing up. These small things can make a difference between getting your foot in the door of opportunity or having it slammed in your face. There are many young men from my hood who have potential but no connections or the training. I wanted to reach back and help our youth in ways shown to me—tutoring, mentoring, financial donations, and just being a good role model because it does wonders.

During my experiences in the Navy, I was in class where a colleague began experiencing a severe headache. Another sailor, who was previously a Licensed Massage Therapist, asked if he could help and the sailor with the headache agreed. The sailor applied pressure to various areas of the scalp, neck, and base of the skull until the headache subsided. This impressed me greatly and sent my mind whirling back to memories of the power of touch Jesus displayed in the bible. Still, I concentrated on my Naval duties and put this moment in the back of my mind. I had no idea that massage therapy would eventually become my profession and remain for 20+ years.

I felt very apprehensive leaving the military and going to the other coast. At the time, I was stationed in Charleston, South Carolina and had no job prospects. I wanted to do something totally different and be in a position to physically change people's lives. I believe we change people's lives when we touch them, similar to when molecules and atoms are changed in chemical reactions. Our bodies are a chemical reaction in progress—from the time of conception through death and the decomposition process. Think of all the lives we have touched along the way—like atoms bumping into one another on this tiny microcosm of the Cosmos we call Earth.

I was 30 years old when I left the Navy and had a modest stipend. We—my wife and three small children—decided to move to the Pacific Northwest, not only for the schools and quality of life, but also for the type of healthcare that validates and recognizes the value of massage therapy.

After having such an idyllic life in the Northwest for almost two years, one day after Christmas in 1995, I received a disturbing call at work from one of my aunts. My mom was on life support at St. Bernard's Hospital in Chicago. Ironically it's where my grandmother died a few years before.

I rushed to her and held Mom's hand when they disconnected her from the life support system. I remember hugging my younger brother many years before when our father died suddenly from an acute case of pancreatitis. I felt just as confused and bewildered this time, too. I knew Mom had hypertension, but was unaware of the cardiovascular issues. She died as the result of a massive heart attack. I was now caregiver for my brother who was diagnosed with Multiple Sclerosis around age 19. His disease ultimately claimed his life around age 30. Before his passing, I helped him with his Physical Therapy and the stretches to decrease the tension in his limbs. His muscles were tight, as he experienced the spasticity, the cramping, and a series of involuntary, rhythmic, muscular contractions. The stretches alleviated his pain and range of motion, allowing him to get more out of his workouts; decreasing stress and helping him to feel better and get a more restful sleep. I would later incorporate stretching with massage and have my patients receive the five benefits of Massage Therapy:

- Control Stress
- Get better sleep
- Boost mental health and wellness
- Manage pain
- Improve physical fitness

Working with my brother inspired me to get an Associate's Degree as a Physical Therapist Assistant. Ironically, about halfway through Ashmead College (formerly known as Seattle Massage School), I experienced some severe financial challenges and thought I would not be able to finish Massage Therapy School. By the fall of 1993, I got a job as a Certified Nurse's Assistant (CNA) working nights and went to class during the day. My wife worked during the day at a daycare center and even with that, three-quarters of the way through the month, there just wasn't enough money to pay everyone. I very reluctantly asked for help from one of my retired aunts who lived in Tennessee. My aunt was more than happy to give me the money. At the most crucial times in my life I have received the money that I needed through the strong females in my life. I also got the money I needed for my brother's funeral from my sister and a girlfriend and the initial money to pay for my Doctoral studies from a colleague at one of my other jobs. Women have always been a support for my education. Not only financially, but as a source of inspiration and encouragement.

I graduated at the top of my class from Ashmead College. At first it was different touching people I didn't know. I remember practicing massage on my young children while going through massage school. I would notice how it relaxed and calmed them down before sleep, as well as improved our opportunity to bond. And I knew I had a passion for massage because the more I did it, the more comfortable I became and so did my colleagues who were my first clients. Their trust and response to my touch helped to dispel any stereotypes, which further strengthened my resolve to become a licensed massage practitioner/therapist.

Having been a Licensed Massage Therapist for over 20 years has been quite a blessing. So many people have received negative touch that it is great to be able to give them such a positive experience.

Over the years I have worked with a total of six chiropractors. It was a good experience to become familiar with different doctor's styles as well as personalities. It helped me adapt to a more clinical environment once I became a Physical Therapist Assistant. It made me feel like I was doing what I was supposed to be doing in life, like I was shifting from one level to another. It reminded me of listening to my mom when I was small and hearing the echoes of the stories of how Jesus was a miraculous healer. I remember people telling me they had never experienced body work like mine before. I was so fortunate that I had such a wide range of mentors and travel opportunities and friends that I still communicate with today. Many times I worked on clients at the Spa who had just lost a spouse, parent, or significant other, and being able to decrease that person's grief and have them leave with a smile and a more relaxed posture is a blessing. Additionally, people have noted specifically being able to rotate and move their neck more freely, which would indicate an increase in Range of Motion, since the muscle fibers have decreased in tension and are more pliable, allowing for increased movement. Another positive comment made was about the ability to move the shoulders more freely. God has been so good to me to help reduce other's pain and afflictions.

I thank God and the unknown Sailor for shifting my direction to where I needed to be.

As a therapist it was great to be a part of people's lives, to hear their stories of triumph and being sympathetic in their times of sorrow. I feel complete as a Massage Therapist. I feel the culmination of all my childhood and military experiences blended to give me the imagination and discipline to follow my dreams to fruition. Believing in God gave me the confidence to try something totally different in life without any immediate knowledge of a payoff. I had faith, prayed, and did the necessary coursework and hands on practice that made me a success.

Being a Licensed Massage Therapist and Licensed Physical Therapist Assistant has also allowed me to travel to Beijing, China to study Chinese Massage therapy, first at a hospital prominent in Traditional Chinese Medicine then at the Chinese Nationals at the National Olympic Training Center one year before the Beijing Olympics.

Having been to all seven continents and touched all seven oceans, nothing affects me more than the response to human touch. It is Universal—the response to positive touch is decreased pain, improved circulation, improved range of motion, and a more positive attitude.

What a journey it has been over the past 20 years to now. Being a confident Therapist able to alleviate others pain and suffering as Christ had alleviated my own pain and suffering throughout my life. I am thankful to God for having given me this gift of touch, and to be in a profession where I can positively and productively use my talent and skills on all God's Children. I've always wanted to touch the world and make a difference, and as a Massage Therapist I have literally owned that dream.

RISING FROM THE ASHES

BY KIM FRANCIS

"For I know the plans I have for you," declares the Lord, "plans to prosper you and not to harm you, plans to give you hope and a future."

Jeremiah 29:11

This bible verse has always held special meaning for me. It was the one my beautiful mom recited to me many times during those low or disappointing moments in my life and she would always include in the encouragement cards she sent me over the years. I'm sure many of us have had life changing events happen in our lives which shook us to our core and caused us to re-evaluate everything we have ever known or thought we knew to that point. In my life thus far, I have experienced two monumental shifts which forced me to uncover new truths about myself and have taken me on a journey of spiritual refinement. What I have discovered thus far on my journey is that the one and only thing which I can be one hundred percent sure of in life is my faith in Jesus Christ and where I will spend eternity.

My first shift in 2006 altered my physical well-being and took me on a five year emotional and spiritual rollercoaster. It was an exercise in endurance and shedding multiple layers of emotional baggage while learning that God and my faith in him, along with my mom and dad's love and encouragement were the only things I could truly count on during that period in my life. My second shift in 2015 was the most emotionally debilitating and spiritually challenging and will forever shape how I will experience the present and the future. There are many bible verses which I have drawn strength from over the years, but one I find myself repeating over and over again is Proverbs 3:5-6 since losing my beautiful and vibrant mom to esophageal cancer at the young age of 63. It gives me comfort and peace when I feel like life is becoming unbearable again and reminds me to live my life step by step and moment by moment when what lies ahead is unknown. "Trust in the Lord with all your heart and lean not on your own understanding; in all your ways submit to him, and he will make your paths straight."

In November, 2006, I experienced a rare and life altering illness leaving me in total debris. After the dust began to settle and I was cognizant enough to start picking up the pieces, I realized there were two constants which remained when it seemed that everything else in my life was gone. They were my faith and my life. And as my doctor shared with Mom and me, I was very lucky to have survived because on paper, I was not medically supposed to be here. In fact, my doctor still calls me his "Medical Miracle Kid."

My mother instilled in me the value of hard work and earning money to pay for what I want. I started working when I was 13 and if I wanted to be a cheerleader or on the drill team, I had to get a part-time job to pay for it. Over the years I realized how important those values and work ethic were in my life. I put myself through college and although it took me longer than my peers, it was one of the proudest moments in my life to be the first person in my family to graduate. I will never forget the memory of Mom taking me aside after the graduation, giddy with excitement and beaming with pride as she gave me the biggest hug and kiss and told me how proud she was of me, and then I laughed as she said, "You see, Kimberly, all of your hard work finally paid off despite all of those months living on peanut butter and jelly, Kraft Mac' n Cheese, and Ragu Spaghetti!"

A few years after college I found my dream job working for an entertainment company marketing several of their cable television networks and I loved every minute of it. After moving up the corporate ladder, I decided to purchase my first home and it truly felt like I was living the American Dream. Little did I know that within fifteen months, I would be near death and recovering from what was an unseen silent killer underneath my master shower subflooring. In the summer of 2005, four months after my home purchase, I started experiencing respiratory problems. I attributed it to allergies and remember telling my mom that my eyes would burn after I took a shower and maybe the chlorine count was just really high in my water. As the months went by, I was experiencing additional symptoms of a low grade fever, achiness, and extreme fatigue. I visited multiple doctors trying to find the cause and treatment.

In January 2006, I was diagnosed with fibromyalgia and chronic fatigue and I thought finally, there was a diagnosis and a reason I felt so poorly over the prior months. During the course of treatment, however, instead of feeling better I was getting worse. There were many times after arriving home from my travels when after just a few hours I started to feel dizzy, achy, and barely able to stay awake. Many times I laid on my couch and fell asleep for hours and went to bed only to find myself at times sleeping for almost the entire weekend, never leaving the house. I then began experiencing severe nose and abnormal vaginal bleeding. My primary doctor referred me to a few specialists who told me they couldn't find anything wrong and had no explanation for anything attributing to my symptoms. This was really frustrating because I knew my body and what I was experiencing wasn't normal. My mom and friends noticed I seemed very agitated and was unable to sit still for long periods of time without becoming increasingly irritable. I knew deep down I was having trouble remembering things and, while I kept telling others I was fine, I was scared because I didn't really know what was happening to me. After some time had passed I was having a series of disappointing experiences with my home and the HOA, so I decided to put it up for sale. Within a few weeks, I had a buyer. As we went through the inspection process, I was told there was a leak in the master shower and I needed to have it checked and repaired in order to complete the sale. I hired a plumber to jackhammer the marble tile floor in my shower to figure out what was causing the leak.

As the plumber drilled into the shower floor and began removing pieces of granite, he said, "Ms. Francis, we have a serious problem." With each piece of granite removed there was a black substance which was identified as black mold. They had uncovered almost 1½ feet in length by almost two feet in height of solid black mold beneath the subfloor. The only way to remove it was to have it professionally remediated according to Environmental Protection Agency (EPA) standards. God exposed what was in the dark and showed His faithfulness.

I called my real estate agent to let them know of the issue and Mom came to pick me up as I was unable to stay in my home until the remediation process was complete. I was in tears and distraught. I had no idea what to do or what all of this meant. As I started "Googling" black mold, I discovered my symptoms over the prior months were a result of my exposure to black mold. After obtaining a mold test of the contaminated area, the results confirmed there were three strains present of the most toxic forms of black mold. I was in stage four of five chemical poisoning; the next step was death. The good news was I finally had an answer. The bad news was I had no idea what was about to happen in my life over the next several weeks. After remediating the mold and having all repairs complete with an EPA air quality certification, I sold my home, rented a new condo, and thought I was starting over.

As the weeks went by, I started to lose a lot of weight, my skin color was growing very pale, and I went to more doctors with the mold report seeking answers to why I was still feeling badly. One of them told me exposure to the mold was an environmental illness and recommended I visit one of the best environmental doctors in the country who just happened to be in Dallas. Later I realized this was a "God Wink" in my life. Within weeks I was having an increasingly harder time breathing and found myself gasping for air one evening in the middle of the night. I called 911 and was taken to the hospital where they put me on oxygen and sent me home. After four hours of oxygen I felt better and then within 72 hours I was gasping for air and yet again I called 911. This cycle repeated itself for almost 10 days.

On a few ER trips, I could hear the medical personnel insinuating I was not mentally stable and was a hypochondriac. I knew deep down the mold exposure was the reason my health was in serious jeopardy and kept praying, "Please God, help me." Finally on the third trip to the emergency room I took a copy of the mold report along with the environmental doctor's name and asked the ER doctor to please call him to come examine me. I was told they couldn't do that and after getting yet another round of oxygen, they discharged me. I remember calling Mom that evening crying hysterically saying that if I didn't see the environmental doctor soon that I was going to die. Of course she thought I was being dramatic because she didn't understand this illness either, but I knew I was very sick and believed death was a possibility. That evening before bed I wrote out my will and a check for $1,000 to my attorney to file suit against the townhome developer and the HOA because of their faulty repair and negligence, which was the source of the mold growing. By the Grace of God I was able to see the environmental doctor the next day. I don't remember much of anything during the visit except Mom telling me later I was barely able to stand up, was incoherent, and crying uncontrollably.

After the doctor's exam, he shared with Mom that I was near death. My lungs were full of poison from the mold and with my current lung capacity I was incapable of blowing over a five on a peak flow breathe meter. From that day forward and an additional eight months, I was on disability and undergoing treatment for severe toxicity throughout my lungs and my organs. I also had severe neurotoxicity of the brain and required oxygen 24-7 for four months while the doctor and his team performed diagnostic tests to determine what internal organ damage there was, or if any other disease was present.

I spent six days a week at his outpatient clinic getting medically supervised oxygen therapy to detoxify my lungs so I could breathe on my own again. I also had to live for one month in environmentally safe campus housing because I was so chemically sensitive to almost everything in our normal day to day environment and any exposure could be a setback in my recovery. I felt like the girl in the plastic bubble. As the toxins in my body began to clear and the neurotoxicity in my brain dissipated, I began to get my sense of humor back because seeing myself in the white medical face mask I wore to and from home to the clinic felt like I was channeling my inner Michael Jackson! During my childhood and high school I used to practice singing his songs in my room in front of the mirror. *Shift 1: Learn to laugh thru the trial.*

During my months of recovery, I took my bible and a charm necklace of my grandmothers to the clinic and would spend hours alone in a treatment room reading a book called "When God Winks" by Squire Rushnell. His book is one I still give as gifts to people I meet in my life when I believe there was no coincidence in our paths crossing. Also, the story of Job became more meaningful to me during that time because I experienced so many losses at once. Among them a thriving career, physical discomforts, neurotoxicity of the brain, loss of hearing in my right ear, and the inability to care for myself without an attendant for the first three months.

I kept thinking about what happened to me and how crazy and random it was. I felt myself asking God often in those solitary moments, "Why Me? Why Did This Happen?" Another casualty of this illness was the financial impact because the majority of my treatment was not covered by health insurance and was considered alternative care. I spent all of my 401K, my savings, and disability income on treatment. I no longer had any financial savings left and had to use my credit cards to help offset the cost of my care. Having worked so hard to build for my future only to see it all disappear was very traumatic for me. I felt ostracized and very alone. Many of my peers and some members of my own family didn't understand what this environmental illness was or what I was going through.

Honestly, I didn't fully understand it either. There were many who didn't believe black mold can make someone so sick. I certainly never did. Sadly, rumors swirled that maybe I had gone crazy and other comments I later learned about which were very hurtful. Yet, I can say now after many years have passed that I found my faith was strengthened and refined as a result of my illness. *Shift 2: Cling to your faith for dear life.*

There were many hours of journaling, reading, and praying. I found myself singing a song my dear friend shared with me that she used to sing when she was having a hard time and it was God only who could truly help her. I have found it to be a source of comfort to me throughout my life especially when I was down or feeling defeated. "Lord I come to you just as I am. I can't ease this pain (sorrow, disappointment, depression, etc.) but I know you can. I need the touch of your healing hand, so I come just as I am." As the months went by I learned the true meaning of surrender—surrendering my emotions and my will to God. Yet, even though I felt like I was all alone, God was always with me and I began to feel peace in knowing if He was with me then that was enough. The verse in Psalms 27:14 became very important to me: "Don't be impatient. Wait for the Lord and he will come and save you! Be brave, stouthearted and courageous. Yes, wait and he will help you." *Shift 3: Surrender.*

I know God used this experience to bring me closer to Him. I saw everything in my world stripped away and I was left with myself, God, and my faith. Many times that is exactly what He wants, for us to know He is all we have. It took me many years to finally be able to emotionally process all the things which happened to me. When I look back and reflect on those years, I still get emotional thinking about the physical, mental, emotional, and spiritual obstacles I overcame. I am thankful that with God's grace and my mom's constant encouragement and support, I was able to rise up from the ashes like a phoenix and overcome through the grace and faithfulness of God. Over the years since my illness, I have learned so much about environmental medicine and that there are a number of people impacted across the United States by some form of chemical exposure, whether from black mold, fumes from lead paint, formaldehyde, or other environmental elements. The most common black mold symptoms and health effects are associated with a respiratory response. Chronic coughing, sneezing, irritation to the eyes, anxiety, confusion, memory loss, brain fog, rashes, chronic fatigue, or persistent headaches. If you or anyone you know are experiencing any of these symptoms, please look for an environmental doctor in your area to see and contact a certified mold inspector to conduct testing within your home. If I had known what to do early on I probably could have prevented the hell I went through. With my life being spared, I committed myself to helping others in desperate situations like mine and educating families on environmental illness. If I can prevent one person from experiencing what I did, it was all worth it. *Shift 4: Submit to your purpose.*

I felt like I was prepared for anything in life that came along and yet I was in no way prepared for what was to be the most difficult journey of my life both spiritually and emotionally. In 2014, I was thrown into my second life altering trial, silently kicking and screaming when we received the news that my beautiful and vibrant mom was diagnosed with esophageal cancer at the age of 62. She was my best friend, my supporter, and the most important person in my life. I remember praying, "No God, Not this. Not the C word. Please not her. She has already endured so many trials in her life. She deserves to live many more years and see her grandchildren grow up. I asked, "Dear God, why my mom? Why now?"

Watching her fight this vial disease and seeing the impact the chemo and the radiation had on her body was at times more than I could bear, and yet, I never wanted her to know I was in so much emotional pain watching her suffer on a daily basis. I remember telling God more than a few times during her illness how thankful I was for healing me from my near death illness so I could be there for her during her final months. I often prayed for God to take me instead so she could be with her grandkids and yet I know she would not have been able to endure losing me. Those days and weeks will always be some of the most important and most treasured memories of my entire life. Sadly, one year later, on March 29, 2015, after a valiant and courageous battle my mom, Sue Ann "The Warrior" Giles, at the young age of 63 took her last breath and went to be with the Lord, as the song "The Old Rugged Cross" played and I stood by her bedside holding her hand in disbelief. I will never forget the deep heart wrenching sorrow I felt. I don't think losing your mom is something anyone could ever prepare you for. Even if someone has been through it, it's nearly impossible to emotionally prepare for.

In the days, weeks, and months after Mom passed, I was in shock and barely able to stand due to the depths of my grief. I realized how much her death changed the dynamics of our family and that my showing unconditional love throughout the years for others isn't necessarily reciprocated. Mom raised her children with the mantra, "We may not always like one another or approve of one another's actions, but we must always forgive and love one another because we are family and we stick together no matter what." Sadly I have learned not everyone has taken her words to heart and while I pray often for reconciliation one day, I have to practice letting go and letting God while reminding myself that if it happens it will be on God's timing, not mine. In the depths of my mourning, I have spent a lot of time on my knees talking to God and asking "Why?" I told Him during those first few months and even now that it's not fair she is gone. I don't understand why He heals some from cancer and not others. And yet I hear Mom in my ear many times over the years saying, "Life isn't fair, Kimberly, and we may never know the why's of things but God does and maybe one day in heaven He will give us our answers." Her wisdom was heaven sent.

I am learning to live a different way since Mom passed. There are many things I wasn't prepared to experience and yet they cannot be escaped. Nothing can prepare you for, or explain, what it feels like late at night when you're alone in bed wanting nothing more than to call your mom. It's a feeling of absolute emptiness, absolute loss, and pure devastation. The feelings cannot be put into words. Nobody tells you about the rollercoaster ride that mourning is; there is never really an ending to it. We may experience moments when we think the storm is over for a while and yet the littlest thing can send you right back into the gut wrenching pit of anguish only to begin slowly pulling yourself out of it again.

Nobody can explain how much worse things hurt without your mom or how angry you are that you've lost her. Everything is escalated. Everything seems worse. Everything has become so unfair. Nobody can explain what it feels like the first time you go to call your mom and every time after. Nobody can prepare you for how different you feel as a person with her gone.

For the first time in your life maybe you are different. You've gone through something so many people around you haven't. You feel different everywhere you go. You feel different in conversations. Your life is no longer the same and there is nothing you can do about it.

Both of these monumental life shifts have taught me that when we are confronted with situations we cannot control, we are challenged to change ourselves and that is one of the hardest lessons for me. For many of us, change is hard. It's unnatural. We like our routines and our way of life as we know it. But it's in the swirling circle of change where we learn to hold on to our faith in Christ as it is unchangeable and the only constant.

Many times since Mom has passed away, I feel like God is saying to me, "Rest in Me. You have journeyed up a steep and rugged path. The way ahead is shrouded in uncertainty. Don't look behind you or ahead of you. Stay focused on Me in the here and now. Trust me that I will equip you with the tools you need for your journey ahead. Remember I am with you, watching over you wherever you go." There have been many times when I wanted to give up and have felt like I don't have the inner strength to keep going without her. But I am my mother's daughter and a child of God and giving up is not an option. She would tell me, "Rise up, Kimberly. You can do this." I am learning to trust God to bring me out on the other side, stronger and with a deeper and abiding faith.

As I continue on this journey called life and get ready each morning for the day ahead, I read a passage on a beautiful plaque Mom gave me three years ago and I realize how profound a message it really is: "Faith: Sorrow looks back. Worry looks around. Faith looks up."

I promise you Mom, I will look up and rise up each day even when it seems insurmountable, determined to live for Jesus, continuing to let God have his way in my life, and honoring you and the legacy you left behind and within me. It won't always be easy but I know He will keep molding and shifting me into the direction I am supposed to go. "For we live by faith, not by sight" (2 Corinthians 5:7). These are my marching orders with every breathe I take. *Shift 5: Serenity.*

LEAP AND THE NET WILL APPEAR

BY VALETA SUTTON

"Use me God, show me how to take who I am, who I want to be and use it for a purpose greater than myself."
                                                    –Martin L. King, Jr.

Have you ever sat still long enough to ask God, "What is my purpose?" I must admit, I didn't do this until later in life. I received this quote by Dr. Martin L. King, Jr. after attending Oprah Winfrey's conference in 2005. Its meaning moved me to print it out, memorize it, and say it every day. Each day it strengthened my soul and pushed away the fear of what I was about to embark upon. I had been preparing for the day when I could leave Corporate America and pursue a career in acting. My journey had its challenges, but I live each day with no regrets.

I had been performing all my life in some capacity. Whether it was singing, ballet recitals, and a variety of talents shows, performing brought me joy. After returning home from college, I learned that Tim Reid opened New Millennium Studios in Petersburg, Virginia. I was already commuting to Petersburg while getting my Master's degree in 1997.

A black-owned business in the movie industry in my own back yard! They were filming the hit comedy series "Linc's Bar and Grill", which ran for two seasons on Showtime. "Linc's" resembled a black "Cheers". The stars included Steven Williams, George Stanford Brown, and the infamous Pam Grier. The show needed background actors and I ran to this opportunity.

It was such an amazing experience and pivotal time in my life. One major thing that touched me was being able to take a picture with Pam Grier. This was huge because the background actors were advised not to approach Mrs. Grier or ask for pictures. Basically, we needed be seen and not heard. One day, Mrs. Grier and I were positioned to walk through a door together on the set of the bar. As repetition led, we had to do several takes and we were alone. I admit I was star stuck and in awe of being in her presence. I also snuck my camera in my pocket for these exact moments. I respectfully asked if she would mind taking a picture with me. She not only did that, she held the camera to get the best picture and took several shots.

This made my day, my year, and gave me the realization that actors are regular human beings just like me. She was not untouchable, and not just the sexy "Foxy Brown" that I had heard my father and the world speak about. She also was very professional and kind. By now, I had caught the acting bug, so I set out to find acting classes. I began to study with Ernie McClintock and learned what he called Jazz Acting. This was my humbled beginning and I met several extraordinary actors.

While taping the show "Linc's", I also met Debbie Allen and Bill Dike who directed several episodes. I learned how the industry is not all about being in front of the camera but also life behind the camera. I also met and was in scenes with the late Gregory Hines. I watched his genius first hand. I would also go on to work and study with Mr. Duke again in his Actor's Boot Camp at the American Black Film Festival.

His foundation of acting and life lessons about the industry resonate with me today. Attending his boot camp allowed me to reconnect with him again in 2006. He was then directing the documentary, "Prince Among Slaves" and allowed me and a fellow actor to shadow him. We drove over two hours to Hollywood,

Maryland to be on set with him daily. He allowed us to be up close and personal, watching and explaining his film direction, as well as attending business meetings with film executives in his trailer. He is one of the most phenomenal men I have ever met who continues to educate aspiring actors. He is a giant in his own right. To this day, I still return to the American Black Film Festival to attend his workshops.

This experience pushed me to want more than what Richmond, Virginia could offer. So I left in 2000 and headed to Washington, D.C. I jumped into a sales career and I met some amazing people that became family to me, their purpose to later be discovered. Everyone has a reason and a season. I'm sure you, too, can attest to this.

One of these amazing people was MJB, my best friend. She bought me a magnet and it read: "LEAP and the NET WILL APPEAR." This little three by five magnet has resonated with me since then and I didn't even know it. I read it often, and the quote pushes me every morning to leap out on faith each and every day, to have faith that GOD has already made a way out of no way... and HE has.

I soon was living the life of a young professional in a new city, but I missed acting and acting training. Thus, I set up to find acting classes in Washington, D.C. I began studying with Professor Vera Katz who trained many artist that came out of Duke Ellington School of the Arts and Howard University. I also began studying Screen Acting with Martin Blank, of Martin Blank Studios. Both of these coaches taught me the skills that prepared me for stage and screen. I still train with Martin today. You see, I was slowly climbing this mountain to get to the other side. Even though I didn't know where I was going yet, I would soon have to LEAP!

God places unexpected people in your life that have the power to change your path. This person for me was my instructor for a "Seven Habits of Highly Effective People" seminar given by my current sales company. The words that flowed out of my mouth when I was called on about my future career plans had absolutely nothing to do with my sales career. I scribed about creative arts, acting, being in a play, and managing out my five year plan to study my craft and to act full-time. My story was vastly different from the other stories in the room of climbing up the corporate ladder. It made me acknowledge what my true goals and passions were at the time.

Then I was given an additional gift, words of wisdom from my instructor at the end of the seminar. He shared his story of his own path to Harvard University, which was then thwarted due to life changes. He also shared how he ended up a lead instructor for Steven Covey. As he shared his story it was like he and I were the only people in the room. He took a LEAP of faith and followed his passion. He told the class how he loves acting and how he took a few years off to perform in theater productions. Then he met a wonderful woman, fell in love, and wanted to start a family. I was filled. I quickly wiped away tears before anyone in the room could see them. He ended by saying that he now produces plays and runs a community theater company. I waited to speak with him after class and shared how his words sang in my ears. I asked if I could stay in contact with him and perhaps audition for his next play.

Quite some time passed, then one day I received an email with the flyer to audition for roles in the play "Annie". I was super excited! I called MJB, shared my excitement of how I planned to make the two hour commute to audition in a few weeks. I also asked her if she could ride with me because she lived in an area half way to the audition location.

The audition day came and I stopped at her house. Fear settled in. I was nervous; I knew that I wanted the role of Grace Farrell, but questioned if I could sing in the soprano bravado that was required for the part. I was also scared to drive further to the audition. I second guessed everything. Then I had a Forrest Gump moment along with some coaxing from MJB. The quote ringing through my head: "If I have come this far, then I might as well go a little farther." So we got in the car and made it to the audition.

The audition went very well. The prepared audition song I had to sing went well and was in key. I was then asked if I would be willing, better yet committed, to take the role of Grace Farrell and drive two hours to come to rehearsals weekly and on the weekends. Of course I would, if given the chance! I was the only minority in the cast that auditioned and I questioned myself. So I drove home and waited for the callback. I got it! I got the role of Grace Farrell in Annie. This was the start of my adventure…each new step prepared me for my LEAP.

Next up was being able to walk out on faith…well, for me God pushed me… literally. The year was 2007, I had a sales manager from hell with a huge Napoleon complex. I can say it now, he was a complete jerk. He harassed me every time that we had a field ride together. He knew I acted, which my last two managers supported and even came out to support my plays. They believed in a constructive work-life balance.

Mr. Napoleon began to say that I looked like I did not want to "be here." Maybe deep down I did not, but what the heck does that look like anyway? No matter whether it was a good or bad day that he observed me with my customers, he ended it questioning my work ethic. I felt miserable. I started to keep a log of all of his comments. *Who can I tell?* I needed my job. I'm a single female just trying to get by. Day after day of having to have a ride-a-long with him, I came home and cried.

Several months later, after downsizing and other challenges… no more sales job. I know now that if I had never been through that experience, if I was not let go, then I would not have taken the LEAP. I was scared and had no idea how I was going to make it. I was afraid to no longer have a consistent income, free car, and 401k. The question is, "What to do now"? Apply for the next sales job…or LEAP out on faith and pursue my acting career? This was my opportunity, if not now, then maybe never. I was prepared to make that next move. I had built my acting resume enough with my work and experiences to go a step further.

Audition after audition, traveling back and forth to New York took its toll. I could not afford the train, so I began to take the Chinese Bus. It was filled with loud noises, languages that I did not understand, as well as food scents that I was not accustomed to. I remember standing alone in unsavory pick up areas where all types of people were constantly walking past. All the while, I'm praying not to get robbed or hurt.

Then, after arriving in New York City, I had to take the A train to Brooklyn or Harlem. Many times getting up there in the early AM hours, it would only be me and a homeless person on the train sleeping or trying to stay warm. I am not sure if you ever get used to the pee stench in some of the staircases or the rats running below that are as large as cats. One cannot forget the train performers seeking your attention for their act, good or bad, and then your money.

The one thing I am thankful for are my NYC friends, who opened their homes to me while I was acting in New York. I appreciate being able to sleep on their couch or futon to pursue my journey, my belongings in a small suitcase and backpack in tow. I also had PJ there to guide me through the NYC acting circuit. This was my life and I loved it!

This was no glorified experience. I was away from all of my friends in Washington, D.C. I was away from my past social life. I was also watching every dollar as I had taken out my 401K to live off until it ran out and/or I started to make more money from my acting gigs. As my life and goals changed, so did my surroundings. There was also still one thing that was missing...LOVE.

I was lacking companionship. A few men came and went; most did not stay around because of my lack of availability. Each promising to be my foundation, to help me financially...to save me. I realized that I was not afraid of scavenging through the gritty streets of New York and of rejection from not getting callbacks from my auditions. Yet, I was still a single women trying to maintain on her own. Life still met me at my doorstep when I came back to D.C. on the weekends. The bills were piling up, the loneliness and instability were setting in. This led me into some tumultuous relationships and poor decision making. Yet one stood out, because it became an evolving door.

Early in the season of my transition to New York City, in the summer of 2008, I met a guy at a networking social in D. C. Let's call him "The Eight Year Professor." I was stopped by this tall, handsome gentleman in, of all places, the bathroom line. Have you ever had that instant connection with someone? When we reconvened on the dance floor, he asked me to dance. Anyone who knows me knows that is my most favorite thing. We were inseparable for months. He even kept my dog, Jazz, as I traveled back and forth to New York. I was falling for him. Then I shared with him that my work was growing and that I was now moving to New York full-time.

One day when we talked, he shared a story of a young lady that he dated that had also moved to New York. Okay, I am now asking myself, *Where was this going?* Then the kicker came in; he does not do long distance relationships. I was devastated because this connection just seemed to work. It took me eight years of rejection, disappointment, and tears to walk away from the thought of him. We would see each other through the years and reconnect, magnetically, attracted to each other every time we crossed paths at a social function.

We both made our mistakes mostly due to lack of communication. Nonetheless, he had always been honest and shown me who he was. I was not ready to receive it. I even took a chance in 2014 to share with him how I felt and that I was willing to "give this a try if he was." I had hoped that he would take a LEAP. Unfortunately, he didn't; he actually did nothing. No communication, no dates….nothing. I then realized that he was not going to choose me. I cried, I prayed, and released the vision of "us" and now years later, that is okay with my soul. The lesson I learned here is that I had to LEAP out of what I thought was my "Dream Relationship" and into the reality that had been shown to me over the years.

Being ostracized during this journey did not stop with men. I also learned that you can't share your dreams with your friends. People will try to talk you out of your dream if you let them. Mostly because they let fear guide them. They will walk out of your life because you are now doing something different and they can't relate to you. Sadly, this happened to me. I slowly was pushed out of, what I then thought, was my inner circle of girlfriends. I imagine, they could no longer relate to my decisions and my journey.

I could now only eat salad and have water, instead of dropping eighty dollars on a group dinner for someone's birthday. This sucked, but I was living my dream and pursuing my passion. The interesting thing is that one of my friends in particular asked for me to help her pursue acting. I did all that I could to help. I helped her with her first head shot, shared auditioning websites, and even came back from New York to see her in her first play. She had helped me with money for groceries when my money was low. I was beyond grateful. Yet, in the months and years went on, the calls stopped coming. I was no longer invited to social events. The friendship had eventually dissolved. The thing I can say proudly is that I was living my dream, even though it was a lonely place.

After long hours of background work and several auditions later, something unexpected happened. The agents from two major soap operas called me back: "All My Children" and "Guiding Light". My background work lead to an upgrade to U5 (Under Five Lines). This bump in pay allowed me to be able to pay some bills and not rely on my savings. I became a regular of "Guiding Light" as the Cedar Hospital nurse and I was being called in regularly.

Some of my favorite moments were walking to Balducci's to get a small salad with tuna for lunch every day. This was all I could afford as I was watching my weight. I sat along the Hudson River outside of ABC studios where "All My Children" was located, basking in my experience. I lost a lot of weight during this time, becoming a size 4. The average size of many of the female actors, including Susan Lucci, was a size zero.

One day in particular changed my perspective of this industry. I had been on the set of "All My Children" all day without being used in any scene. I had asked the casting director if I could be released to make an audition. She came back over and said that she had some good and bad news. She stated that I couldn't leave which surprised me because she had just eluded that leaving would probably be okay.

The look of confusion on my face sparked her to hurry up and share the good news. Mr. Peebles, that's Mario Van Peebles, had asked that I be his assistant District Attorney in the court case with Erica Kane (Susan Lucci). I was immediately his right hand man. I read lines with him and discussed the scenes. He was not only acting in the scenes, but also directing the current episodes. This led to weeks of extended work that I would not have had. The next day I gave him a thank you card.

He said that I did not have to do that. I replied, "Yes, I did!" He showed me that humility and fame still go hand in hand. He is an icon, yet he wasn't untouchable. He was different; he brought his family with him to set weekly, as well as greeted all of the background actors every morning when he came in to get his coffee in the background holding area. Most importantly he left a blueprint of what an accomplished yet humble actor looks like.

I was now sending out email blast to family members on when my segments on the soaps would be aired. I had joined the American Federation of Television and Radio Artist union and I wanted all my friends and family to know. What I learned was that naysayers would come crashing in. This includes family, yes I said it... family. My parents did not approve of me leaving a corporate job to pursue a dream in my early thirties. So, I stopped sharing my struggles with them. I only sent them updates of when I would be aired on television.

My mom never understood what I was doing. She was present for most of my plays, yet I never got the response that I would have loved to hear: "Valeta, you did an amazing job!" I was always seeking her approval. My mother had her vision of what was best for me, like all mothers do. Today she is fighting dementia. Sadly now, she will not know the excitement that I have of sharing my story with you.

I am blessed that my father was able to say, "Never in my wildest dreams did I think I would see my daughter on network television!" I'm overjoyed that we experienced that moment together since he is no longer with us. I also realize now that the only person that can now stop me from my goals would be myself and fear to succeed.

Reflecting on being open to adapt to change brought me back to Washington, D.C. The soaps went off the air or moved to Los Angeles, California. The work slowed and then stopped. The paychecks stopped, too. I still had my home and mortgage payments. I had lived off my 401k through the years while I was working in New York City.

The fear of not being able to pay my bills set in. I prayed, I cried, I did not know where to turn. I had depleted all of my reserved funds. I had to humble myself and apply for a sales job again. I thought to myself that I was a failure, back where I started. I also realized that I was being too hard on myself, because no one can take back the experiences that I had. My parents were older and I did not want to move to Los Angeles, CA to be far away from them. I knew that I had a skill set to fall back on and only enough money to pay one more mortgage bill.

God stepped in one more time; I got a job back in sales and was able to act whenever I could. He also allowed me to become a union member of the Screen Actors Guild by booking a local commercial spot for the Washington Capitals, D.C.'s hockey team. This was wonderful! I accomplished my goal of becoming a union actor. This meant more pay for my acting work. Although I missed New York, I was thankful to have met some amazing people along the way, as well as being close to home when my father got sick and I had to go on leave to care for him until he passed.

When my father passed, a piece of me also died that day. I have his blood running through me, his voice saying how proud he was of me. His jokes, even the not so clean ones, making me laugh. He left me with these words, "Valeta, I believe that you can do anything that you set your mind to." I can say that when I stay focused, I have achieved this with his guidance and God's favor. You see, he loved acting too, which I did not learn until the last few years of his life. I now have a picture of him performing Hamlet that is a reminder that acting is in my blood.

What I want to leave you with is that it's never too late. Don't wait for the time to be right for change. Don't wait for the approval of your friends and family. Start now on building a foundation of your passion. Your story is already written, all you have to do is fill in the gaps. Take the classes, see lots of plays, write your story, network with people...and watch it all come together. Take the good with the bad. Also, see your vision, feel it...own it! On my vision board it reads..."I am an actor."

Be open that your vision will constantly change and evolve. Pray for guidance and be able to adapt. Even though I am no longer in New York City full-time, I maintain consistent work in Industrial Films and Commercials. Today, I am still taking acting classes and developing my own content. Never stop working and believing in your dream. The tables may have turned in my life, but I can't imagine it any other way. I challenge you to take that first step of faith or even better, just LEAP!

COUNT THE MIRACLES ALONG THE WAY

BY NICOLE JOHNSON

"With man this is impossible, but with God all things are possible."

Matthew 19:26

On March 24, 2014, my life forever changed. Some might say for the good and some for the worst. I'd always heard, "Life is full of swift transitions." That day gave the statement a whole new meaning for me because my mother became ill. Her health began to fail in unimaginable ways. When I received the call she was ill, I packed only four outfits and drove to Savannah, Georgia. I was thinking I would go see her, confirm she would be well, and return to my home in Atlanta. I expected to be there for 2-4 days. However, I didn't step foot back into my house until 21 days later. Yes, my life transitioned in just a moment. My mother had shaped, guided, counseled me, and was the epitome of strength in my eyes. The woman I loved most was seriously ill. It was simply devastating.

I was a registered nurse so I knew Mom was very ill immediately upon seeing her. It was the first time that I literally saw my mother on her back. I prayed earnestly that she would get well. Friends and associates from all over the world prayed with me. As the days moved on, I thought she would get better. My family and

387

I witnessed ups and downs in her health but were still hopeful God would heal her completely.

We all know there will come a time we will have to deal with losing a loved one. We pray God will strengthen and prepare us for those moments. I believed God prepared me spiritually but I was not quite as prepared mentally for this occurrence. In fact, one of my greatest strengths is planning and preparing for things ahead of time. I usually have plan A, B, C, and D. I had all kinds of plans and alternative plans for my career and personal life. However, I had not prepared for caring for an ill parent and becoming a full-time caregiver this soon in my life. Within a week, I went from being a full-time employee to, unexpectedly, taking a leave of absence from my job.

As I mentioned, my planned stay of four days would become an extended one. I slept on a hospital cot for 21 days, never leaving my mother's bedside. Diagnosed with end-stage kidney and liver disease, she would experience victories and setbacks as she battled for her life. The doctors informed me, my father, and two older brothers that she, possibly, had a few weeks to live. We were devastated by the news. In my quiet time, I prayed, cried, and begged God to save my mother's life. My family, friends, and even those who didn't know us well were praying that the terminal diagnosis would be reversed, we would receive a miracle, and Mom would be healed. Instead of hearing miraculous news she would be going home completely healed, we prepared ourselves for palliative care and/or hospice. Palliative care is provided by a team of specialists and care providers and is aimed at controlling suffering, improving the patient's quality of life, increasing function, and assisting with decision-making. Hospice care provides medical services, emotional support, and spiritual resources for people who are in the last stages of a serious illness. Hospice care also helps family members manage the practical details and emotional challenges of caring for a dying loved one. The goal is to keep a person comfortable and improve his/her quality of life. It is painful to see a loved one told, "You have a very short time to live and there is nothing we can do to save you." On the outside, I tried to hold it all together with my immediate family members. On the inside, I felt like everything in my world was falling apart.

My mom represented so much in my life. Not only was I concerned about how I would deal with losing her, I was even more concerned about how she was taking the news of her diagnosis. I remember after praying one day asking my mom, "Mom, how does it feel for someone to tell you that you have a terminal illness and that you won't have very long to live?"

My mother, in her infinite wisdom and displaying such strength, simply looked at me and said, "You know, if I live it will be wonderful because I would have more time with you all, but if I die that's okay, too, because I'll go to heaven to be with the Lord!"

This would be the first time I would have even imagined or would think of my mom actually being in a win-win situation. She actually gave me comfort in what I thought was her time of need by helping me to view life on earth and eternal life in a very different way. A valuable lesson learned here was when one knows who you are and whose you are, one doesn't have to be afraid of that which is inevitable, which is death.

As we prepared to leave the hospital, there were many meetings that had to occur. Things like social work help, the decision to go with palliative care versus hospice, the signing of an advanced directive and living will, all which can be extremely challenging to do in the midst of knowing you're likely losing a loved one. I remember some of the greatest advice that I received one day while having to make these tough decisions. It came from a childhood/grade school teacher named Sister Donna Marie. She saw I was completely devastated by the news regarding my mom and I was not ready to let her go. As I was praying in the chapel at the hospital, Sister Donna Marie came in to provide me with some words of comfort. She held my hand and said she had gone through a similar situation. Her father was diagnosed with a terminal illness and transitioned six months after the diagnosis. Of course, I was thinking, *What does that have to do with me?* It certainly was not the message of inspiration or encouragement I wanted to hear. Then she looked at me and said, "There were many miracles along the way before my father transitioned. I want you to do one thing as you travel this road with your mother."

I said, "What's that, Sister Donna Marie?"

She simply said, "I want you to count the miracles along the way."

At the time that statement didn't have a great deal of meaning for me. I understood what she meant by using the word miracles. However, I didn't see how she wanted me to connect her story to counting miracles along the way. After all, her father ended up dying. How could there have possibly been any miracles along the way? Shucks, we were told that my mother was dying. The only miracles I wanted to hear were that my mom was cured, her health was restored, and we would be telling everyone of that miracle. Well, little did I know, a valuable lesson would be taught to me over the next ten months about miracles.

On the day of discharge, my mom and I got in the car to go home. While on the way, she requested that we stop at the nursing home to visit her aunt whom she loved dearly. When we walked in the door of my "Auntie's" room, Auntie looked in amazement and with excitement saying, "You're the last person I expected to see!" You see, Mom was told she would not make it through this time because of her illnesses. My mother was moving around with a condition that absolutely defied existence. Though weak in her body, Mom's will and mind were strong. My mom came in and sat down on the bed. We began to converse and enjoy our time together. Even though my mom should not have come home from the hospital, it was a miracle to be sitting in the midst of three generations of strong women again. *Count the miracles along the way!*

From there, we went to my parents' house. My brother and father helped as much as they could; however, I led and managed the majority of the healthcare planning and efforts for my mom. Over the next two weeks, decisions had to be made, such as if my mother would stay in Savannah or move to Atlanta with me. If she moved to Atlanta, that meant the dynamics would drastically change in my life. I would go from being a carefree, well-accomplished professional to a part-time caregiver. I would have to take an Intermittent Leave of Absence; meaning if I woke up and needed to take care of my mom, I could call in and take the day off. It would also mean the dynamics in Savannah would change for so many people, including my father, my aunts who were like mothers to my mom, my extended family, and all of my mother's friends.

Within the next week after Mom's discharge, we went from palliative care to my mom being readmitted back into the hospital to finally having to accept that we would have to place her in home hospice.

It was an overwhelming time for me, yet I gained my strength from God as well as the amazing wisdom and bravery of my courageous mother, Gail Clarke Johnson. We prayed about what we were going to do next. As I watched hospice come in and out of the house to speak with my mom, it was both an unbelievable and heartbreaking experience. I knew if all things were perfect, Mom wouldn't want to be sick. I also wouldn't want to see her sick and we certainly wouldn't be preparing for her to transition to another life in heaven with God. But that was our reality at that moment. So after much prayer and consideration, my mother decided to move. I was grateful that God had given me the ability and capacity to move my mother, father, and brother back to Atlanta with me. It was always my desire, with the help of God, to be able to have a place my parents could come whenever they got too old to live alone and/or too sick to take care of themselves. However, that time arrived unexpectedly. So we packed up the majority of their belongings and off we went to a new life in Atlanta.

As I drove, I kept glancing over at my mom as we were having great conversations and laughter along the way. In my mind, I kept thinking, *This is an absolute miracle.* I had been a nurse for over 16 years and I had never seen anyone with her diagnosis be able to take a ride for four hours in a car, without having any additional medical intervention. Indeed, this was a miracle. *Count the miracles along the way!*

God blessed us to get to Atlanta and everything was prepared for my mom—her room, the refrigerator in the room, and a customized shower was installed. Everything had been amended to accommodate her. I had friends who worked to quickly get my home prepared for her arrival while I was still in Savannah. It was, indeed, a blessing. Her official transition to hospice would begin the next day.

Over the next eight months there would be many ups, downs, and miracles along the way. My mom would be temporarily moved from hospice and admitted to the hospital after a visit to the emergency room. Instead of giving us a dire diagnosis as we had gotten in Savannah, we had a glimmer of hope. The doctors in Atlanta set my mom up for a transplant evaluation and from there we moved onto the road of possibility...a possible chance for a transplant. *Count the miracles along the way!*

We knew what we were about to embark upon would not be an easy journey, but it certainly gave us a glimmer of hope and was worth a try. While in the hospital, Mom was placed on dialysis and shortly thereafter experienced a brain bleed. It could not be resolved surgically. Mom could no longer move nor communicate with us. The doctors gave up hope at this point. However, we never did. We believed the Lord would not have brought us this far to leave us. We prayed, earnestly, for her healing. Mom's brain bleed resolved itself over the next several weeks. She miraculously awakened on a Sunday morning and the doctors were amazed. With that, the doctors ordered occupational, speech, and physical therapy for her. Over the next six weeks, Mom would begin to speak and become mobile again. Despite all odds, she was able to be flown to Minnesota to one of the best hospitals in the USA—the Mayo Clinic—to be evaluated for transplant. Her trip to Minnesota was nothing short of a miracle. *Count the miracles along the way!*

In Minnesota, we found out that she was not a candidate for a transplant. We were saddened by the news after all of the miracles that we witnessed to get us to this point. However, God still gave us rest in our spirits. You see, God allowed us to take my mother as far as we could to get her the best medical care. That was a complete blessing and nothing short of a miracle. We flew Mom back to Atlanta, and God gave us one more glimmer of hope. Just as the Mayo Clinic in Minnesota denied her, we arrived back in Atlanta to receive notification that the Mayo Clinic in Jacksonville, Florida had selected my mother as a candidate for a transplant evaluation. Hallelujah! To God be the glory for the miracles that He had shown us!

By now, I had realized what Sister Donna Marie was saying about *counting the miracles along the way*. Oh yes, I was counting them. Each time I witnessed a miracle, my faith grew stronger. Each time I witnessed a miracle, I found myself being in a better place about what was occurring with my mother. I found myself resting more in the will of God.

One day after arriving back home in Atlanta, my mom was resting in her bed before she stated, "Take me back to the hospital...I don't feel well." We took her back to the emergency room and they ended up admitting her. This was mid-September 2014. Though we had a glimmer of hope, we were clearly concerned that the end could be nearing. Over the next few months, my mother resided in the hospital. Many of the doctors who had cared for her in past hospitalizations came by to express how blessed they were by Mom's warm spirit and faith as well as the strength she exhibited during the time of her illness. Some of her caregivers were Christians and some were not. A few became curious about Christianity as a result of watching some of the medical miracles that occurred with her. The majority blessed us by saying they believed in a higher power because of the miracles that had occurred with Mom during her hospitalization.

By November 2014, my mother continued to grow weaker and less communicative. I was visiting with her one particular day and I could see that look of tiredness in her eyes. She had fought a good fight. I knew that much of that fight was due to her undying love for her family. She knew how much we loved her and how hard it would be for us to let go. In the past, when I asked her if she was tired, she would say, "No, keep going!" However, this particular morning, her answer was not the same. So as we sat quietly in the room, I grabbed her hand and said a prayer with her. After saying that prayer, I asked Mom if she was tired. Without a mumbling word, she nodded her head indicating yes. I was surprised by my emotions. I had a rest in my spirit. I was okay with her answer. One of the greatest blessings and miracle for me was God loved me so much that he allowed me, as a nurse, along with my family to exhaust everything we could humanly do to aid in my mom's recovery. There was now nothing left to do but accept His will and let Mom rest in peace.

Some family members, Mom's pastor from Savannah, as well as local priest, and lay ministered had frequently visited her in Atlanta. My mom did have one last request. That request was to go back home to Savannah. Savannah was where all of her family and friends were. However, her specific request was to see her Auntie that we had visited in the Nursing Home when she was discharged from the hospital in Savannah. The only issue with the request was it would cost us thousands of dollars to get her home. Mom was no longer in any condition to take a four-hour car ride and time was of the essence. Mom had opted to stop all aggressive medical efforts and allow Hospice Care to be provided until her transition. I wanted to honor her last request but I just didn't know how my family nor I could make that happen. But how many of you know that we serve a God who makes the impossible possible? Because the staff and social workers had watched how we cared for and supported Mom with such love for months, the hospital gifted us a trip back to Savannah by ambulance to the Hospice of Savannah. *Count the miracles along the way!* God is sho nuff in the blessing business!

So off we went by ambulance to Savannah; Mom, two paramedics for transport, and myself. I was grateful that not only was I able to be a daughter but I was able to be her nurse one last time when she was in need. Quite frankly, I needed to be able to care for my mother once more as I knew her end was nearing. So we journeyed to Savannah and we arrived at hospice. The hospice nurses got my mom settled in comfortably. My brother arrived with my auntie so that she could see my mom. It was a gentle, beautiful connection with the very last person that she wanted to see and communicate with. I could tell once my auntie held Mom's hand and caressed her head, my mom was at peace and ready to be at rest. What a blessing!

Over the next few days, I was able to experience some blessed moments with my mom. Things like being able to get in the bed with her, wrapping my arms around her, and letting her put her head on my shoulder. I was able to experience having one more conversation about how wonderful of a mom she was too me, and she had told me how great a daughter I was to her. I thanked her for all she had done for me and for making me the woman that I am. And she thanked me for being a wonderful daughter and taking care of her. During our last conversation, as difficult as it was, I was able to convince her that I loved her, would miss her, but I would be okay. I reminded her that I was her daughter and made out of the same fabric she was. Until that moment, as tough as it was, God had been preparing me along the journey to be able to get through this very moment. I promised her I would do my very best to carry on the mantle of helping to oversee our family with prayers, love, and support. Lastly, I told her to rest peacefully and I loved her very much. She replied, "I love you, too!" For the next couple of days, my mom rested in peace until she went home to be with the Lord.

After my mom's transition, there was an indescribable pain and void.

I found this to be the greatest loss I had ever experienced. I had to learn to live without one of my greatest supporters, my mother. However, the grace, courage, bravery, wisdom, and love Mom exhibited during her entire illness gave me the strength to move beyond my grief and find complete closure in losing her. I decided to move beyond my circumstances and live life to the fullest.

I would like to encourage those who have experienced loss in any form. There is life after loss. Several other major losses came on the heels of losing my mother. I had to let go of things I could not change nor control and refocus on my purpose. I was able to gain victory over my losses with a great support system, faith and finding causes that were bigger than me. My prayer is for you to find peace and healing. As you reflect on your journey, look for the miracles experienced along the way. I hope my story serves as a catalyst to move you beyond current circumstances. Pursue your purpose and live life to the fullest. The best is yet to come.